BLIND READING

or

Reading Material for the Hunting Blind

AUTHOR

JAMES L. (SONNY) BOYER

Helpful Hints and Information Told in Story Form and Taken From a Lifetime of Experiences in the Outdoors

BLIND READING

ISBN--0978-0-9849099-4

First printing

Georgia Mountain Writers Club Publishing has allowed this work to remain exactly as the author intended, verbatim, without editorial input.

Georgia Mountain Writers Club Publishing
Printed By Create Space- an Amazon Company
Available on Kindle

Dedication

I wish to dedicate these writings to all that I have mentioned herein. Most have gone on to be with our Lord, with a few like me hanging on. I have made fun of some but it is all in jest, for I have truly treasured the life experiences that we have shared.

To my wife, Laurie and my mother, Bate, who had great understanding as they put up with my escapades in the outdoors. To my two sons, Stephen and Jaime, who learned to love nature along with me; To Ron, my cousin, and Ding, (Gene) my nephew, as they observed the wonders of nature with me in their younger lives. I feel that I have lived through the greatest time in history and my goal with my writings is to share in some of my experiences.

To have you, the reader, understand some of the the people that are part of this book I have placed my conception about them, along with photos, at the very end of the manuscript. I suggest that you read those first so you will understand my stories better.

As we started to get really old, my wife and I removed most of our mirrors so we would still think of ourselves as we used to look. That's the way I like to remember the people in this book.

Acknowledgements

The very first one that allowed me to enjoy my life, I attribute to my Savior Jesus for He has been my guiding light. I stumbled often but He brought me back in line. Many individuals helped me with my story telling without ever realizing it.

George Volker, my mentor, was a master story teller of hunting experiences and used a lot of exaggeration. In the end the story was very entertaining; so who cared? To my uncle Jack who opened my eyes to the adventures found in the ocean and to my boyhood friends- Bruce, Thomas, TJ, and George, as we explored life. To my adult partners: Art, Charlie, Bill, and Gill, as they shared in my hunting and fishing experiences. The boys in my scout troop 210, who taught me patience, as I tried to teach them the wonders of nature at their young ages.

I was surely a problem for most of my teachers, but a few got through to me without me even realizing it. Miss Barbara Garfunkle gets the credit for teaching me school can be interesting. Mrs. Spach who helped me with my art ambitions; and Mr. Malone taught me mechanical and architectural drawing. These are considered minor subjects but are the ones that helped me the most in my life work. Mrs. Harding was able to channel my love of animals into studying biology and enjoying it. My mom and dad who were poor and didn't show it, but knew how to use what they could to feed and entertain my sister and I. They made our young lives an adventure.

My Outlook on life

I thought I would start off by saying "In the beginning" but a better author than I was way ahead of me with that one. I'll just tell my views.

I will admit, I was a poor student. I let too many things distract me when I was supposed to be paying attention. For me, windows in a classroom were very dangerous. I loved to daydream and an open window was an invitation to the universe. I was constantly told that I was lazy, but looking back, I don't think that was the case.

At twelve, I found a sunken, rotten kayak, and enough scrap wood from nearby construction sites to copy the pieces of the framework. I cut out each piece with a coping saw, and by duplicating the rotten parts, I made my own boat.

I always found a lot of interesting things to occupy my mind. I don't blame my parents or my teachers for my poor study habits; it was strictly my fault. I actually developed a hatred for school. I picked up the basics fairly easy and could see no reason for all the repetition.

My attitude was, "*If I pass, Mom and Dad won't come down too hard on me, so why bother?*"

That's just what I did most of the way through school. I misjudged and had to repeat once; that really hit me hard for being so stupid.

"Now I have to waste all this time to sit through all this nonsense again."

The tests were not my problem, for I was always good at tests. Even later in life in the military service, civil service exams, and my state building contractors' license, I always scored high. My problem was homework. That was my time, so I turned in very few assignments. It was embarrassing for me not to have it ready, but unless it meant passing or failing, I suffered the consequences.

I discovered around the time I was in junior high that I had a talent for art, and actually enjoyed being in a class. I enjoyed the science classes to the point of learning about the habits of critters, and I especially loved pulling something over on a teacher. I gained quite a reputation of being the boy with the animals. I remember that the class was assigned to bring in an example of nature that related to science and our environment. You know "show and tell." Well the class brought in butterflies, frogs, fish, and the usual. I brought a knitting box, laid it on the teacher's desk and took my seat. I thought I had brought in the most unique specimen of the class. Mrs. Phossey was not too amused when she lifted the lid. My alligator jumped out of the box and started running around the room.

In High school my biology teacher gave a lecture about the different kinds of shrimp and crustaceans in the south Florida waters. When she finished describing them, I asked her why she didn't mention the large ten to twelve inch ones that grew here. She told me there were no such critters in Florida and kind of embarrassed me. That night after I spent several hours, I caught a rather large one. I came to school the next day early and dropped it in her fresh water aquarium in our class.

When she saw it she said, "Well I don't have to guess where this came from."

As a class, we discovered that it was a Prawn and very few people knew that they lived in south Florida.

Later when she was talking about eels being only found in the adult stage and it was thought they had their young in the Sargasso Sea.

My hand went up and she gave me an inquisitive look and asked, "Do you have something to add to that Mr. Boyer?"

I answered, "Yes ma'am. I happen to have several about two inches long in my aquarium that I caught in the canal."

She never got upset with me, in fact we became good friends.

I was fascinated with mechanical and architectural drawing and made good grades, but I disliked math and thought English was a waste of time. The only good grade I got in English was by combining my art ability with an English assignment. We were studying Shakespeare and we had to do a newspaper using the plays as a theme. I hand printed it all in old English with a speed ball pen and the teacher put it on display in the front office.

Ironically having to return to school for a year actually changed my whole outlook on life. As a fluke I took a Journalism class under Miss Barbara Garfunkle and I finally understood why I needed to understand the structure of a sentence. I was invited to join the staff of the high school newspaper and thoroughly enjoyed my extra time in school. Everything I liked to do, I used in my attempts at writing. I even wrote an article published in the Florida Wildlife Magazine. My art teacher wanted a live subject from the wild for the class to draw so I suggested an owl. I said I could catch one without harming it and I would return it to the wild when we were finished. I brought the owl in and we all drew it. Miss Garfunkel heard about the owl and suggested I write a story for our paper featuring the owl. I wrote the story from the owl's point of view (from capture to release) and tried to make it comical. Unknown to me, she submitted my drawing and story, and the Florida Wildlife Magazine published it.

I have earned all of my spending money since I was seven, but I left school with an inferior attitude of my abilities. I didn't see myself as being very smart. I found that the military had a cross section of life that I had not experienced. I met people with high educations that couldn't do the things that I could. I discovered that I had a talent for accomplishing difficult tasks and have utilized that ability throughout my life. I now have a philosophy that you learn from birth, and it is how you use that knowledge that makes the difference. The military is the best example of people doing jobs that they are not qualified to do. By seeing that fault in society, the military prepared me for adulthood before I had to face the outside world. An old kayak and the difficulty of duplicating it, gave me the confidence to build and do things that most people are afraid to attempt.

I came to realize that we all are talented in some way, even ditch diggers and menial jobholders. So I have developed a respect for any good job. I look at all mankind as equal and respect accomplishment. I don't feel that anyone is more important than I, nor is anyone beneath me. I hate corruption and the misuse of power and have stayed in controversy in my later years, because I try to expose what I find. That's my right as a citizen of this great country we live in. I consider it my right and duty to try and correct corruption, no matter what is said or done to try and stop me.

My three AKA's

"Sonny," Was given to me by my mother when I was a small child. It stuck. Most address me this way.

"Uncle Turkey," Was tacked on to me by my nieces and nephews because of my turkey hunting.

"Misfit," A handle given to me by our Union County Sole Commissioner, because I questioned shady government manipulations.

Sonny Picking a Turkey at Brier Creek Hunting Camp

Introduction

This is the beginning of, what I hope will be, an informative text that combines a little humor, a little knowledge, and multiple experiences I have had while spending a lifetime hunting and fishing both in South Florida, the Everglades, and in Georgia. As I am composing this, I am eighty two years old and more than likely will be several years older before I finish. I begin this with a little more confidence than I had when my oldest son suggested I do this some ten years ago. My first novel, "The Pot" was recently published. It was a result of attending a creative writing class, so I could write a book about turkey hunting, as my son suggested. The instructor advised I do a novel for the purpose of the class, because she didn't know anything about turkey hunting. I got started on a book about Calusa Indians in the class. With all the research and effort it took to prepare a manuscript for publishing, I find myself over a decade later picking back up on the turkey idea.

Thinking back over my life, I find I can't limit my tales to only turkey, so I will probably tell more turkey stories in this "reminiscing manual" as I call it. I never was a golfer or tennis player, my love is for the outdoors and nature. Believe me, I have had outdoor experiences. I was one of those kids that endured school and daydreamed about Friday at three o'clock, when I could begin the weekend and the outdoors. I was lucky enough to have a mother and a wife that allowed me to have these experiences. I believe these stories and information will help you in your quest for whatever game you are seeking, and if not, I sincerely hope you find them entertaining. I will try to keep the "lying" down to a minimum. I am writing it with multipurpose goals. One to keep you from making the same dumb mistakes that I made have through the years, another, hopefully to be amused by some of the odd things that have happened in my life, and lastly, something to read as you sit in a blind or tree stand for those long hours. Hence the name.......

"Blind Reading"

I have to confess turkey hunting is my favorite hunting sport. If I had a situation where I could have my choice of harvesting a ten point buck or a gobbler with a ten inch beard, I would choose the gobbler. I have been lucky and have had the opportunity to hunt most of the game found in the southeastern United States. I love the outdoors and have a big respect for Mother Nature.

Although I was not a good conservationist as a child, as an adult I have made it my practice to try and follow the game laws regardless of whether I thought they were good laws or not. I never felt that I had the right to criticize lifelong bad habits of other people that I encountered. I went about enjoying the outdoors and I wasn't perfect. However, there have been several laws that I obeyed that I fought tooth and nail to get changed.

Fishing and hunting consumed my childhood spare time and much of my adulthood as I have rambled through my life.

My father built a house on the outskirts of Miami and there wasn't much west of us, other than a

Seminole Indian Village and open Everglades. About three hundred yards to the north of us was the Tamiami Canal which runs from the east coast to the west coast of Florida. My dad set several boundaries for my roaming and was rather strict about me following them. He would take me to the canal to fish, but I was not allowed on my own until I could learn to swim to his satisfaction. I got a double barrel BB gun for my ninth birthday, from my grandfather, and it came with rules.

"A BB gun is not for killing anything. It is only for target shooting**. Don't aim it at anyone**. Be careful, it can put out someone's eye," he said with a sternness that needed no interpretation.

I even hunted professionally at an early age by collecting live mice and tree frogs for a man who sold snakes.

Coon hunting was not popular in south Florida because of the overabundance of raccoons. Grey Fox hunting was the thing in early Miami. It was a Saturday night adventure I started in my teens. After the fox areas started being developed, we switched to using the hounds for wildcat hunting. I don't ever remember killing a fox with the dogs because if they were a Gray fox they always went to tree. The few red foxes in south Florida would either outsmart the dogs or hole up in their dens. We just pulled the dogs off and ran them again the next week.

I made an attempt to commercial fish for spiney lobster and did fairly well until I started developing skin cancer. Luckily, all of my family enjoys the outdoors and I never had any trouble getting them to join me on an adventure. Even my mother waded through the Everglades to see one of my hunting camps when she was sixty eight at the time. I have led a great life, my way, and I believe my Savior will accept me without too much reprimand.....

Introduction to Guns and Hunting

There are a lot of different thoughts about what type of gun is best for turkey hunting. During my early years in Florida when I hunted in the Everglades, I started off with a single shot, full choke, 12 gauge shot gun, with a thirty inch barrel. The main reason was because I couldn't afford anything better. I grew up in an age where, due to the war, shells were very hard to come by. My father, in his wisdom, gave to me a single-shot 22 rifle for my first real gun.

I wasn't allowed to use it during the week, except in the summer; so I couldn't wait for the weekends. The first Saturday after my birthday, I went to my father for some shells. Much to my surprise, he handed me one shell and told me the rules:

I was to start with one shell on Saturday morning. If I killed **something to eat** and brought it home, he would give me another shell.

I was to hunt by myself and always tell him where I was going.

I was to maintain my grades at school, or lose the privilege of using the gun until my grades came back up.

I didn't argue with him because I knew he meant what he said.

Now you have to understand, I was eleven years old and I had started my safety training much earlier. I was given a double barreled Daisy BB gun on my 9th birthday, by my grandfather, and had been guided along a course of safety as I used it. I had been on many excursions with my father where guns were involved and had been tutored, to his satisfaction, that I could handle a gun safely.

I went out that first morning, with my real gun, and stalked a robin in a near-by strawberry field. I fired my single shell and made my first kill. I returned home triumphant, and was surprised at my dad's reaction. My dad meant exactly what he said, “Something to eat."

With his supervision I cleaned the robin, cooked it, and ate it. I didn't think those rules were very fair at the time, but I later realized that he taught me several good lessons. I never, to this day, shoot anything that I can't eat. One shot-at-a-time kept me from wasting ammunition. Shells were very hard to get, and it kept me from shooting irresponsibly. You can bet when I pulled the trigger, I usually hit what I was aiming at. I didn't want to spend a Saturday without any shells.

I later realized that my father only had a small hoard of shells and he had no idea how long he would have to wait before he could purchase more. My early childhood was during the Second World War.

This training made it easy to accept a single shot, shotgun as my hunting gun for my teen years.

My boyhood friend, Bruce DeVay, and I attained jobs as trap boys at, "Peck a Way" gun club, while we were in high school. We loaded the clay pigeons and scored the hits and misses. By this time the war was over, but we still had military personnel that used the club, and we were able to obtain shells so we could go dove and marsh hen hunting. The owner of the club gave us each a handful of number 4 bird shot. He let us hunt on his ranch in Indian Town while we were on a work trip for him. These shells were the old paper kind and I carried some of them for years. I carried them so long that the number identifying the size came off. When the paper started to rub off I had to re-mark them. I'll say one thing for them, I have never had a factory loaded shell misfire, the only ones I ever had trouble with were the shells that were hand loaded.

My buddy Bruce's 80 year old grandfather made us each a box turkey call that I still have. The calls made somewhat of a decent turkey sound. We hacked away on those boxes until they darn near wore out, and I still haven't killed a turkey with mine.

The trouble was there was no one around to tell us what mistakes we were making. Turkey hunting in the Everglades, at that time, was almost a lost art. There were only a few people around that could call a turkey. We didn't have the privilege of knowing any turkey hunters other than Mr. Manry, Bruce's grandfather. He had become old, but he was still active and a great story teller. He was the only one we knew that could call a turkey.

Mr. Manry was quite a character and he was my idol. I thought he knew everything. He worked at Peck-a-Way-Gun Club, and also at the White Belt Dairy where the gun club was. Our life was guided by Mr. Manry's fox hunting on Saturday night. He had a pack of Walker hounds and spent every Saturday night hunting fox and occasionally a wildcat. Our parents never wondered where we were on Saturday night, for they knew that when Mr. Manry pulled away from the dairy at 12.00 Bruce and I would be there for the hunt.

Guns for Turkey

Modern shot guns are made in .410, 28, 20, 16, 12, and 10 gauges. There are larger gauges, but they are not made anymore. They were used for market hunting ducks and thank goodness that was outlawed years ago. The gauge was originally determined by the number of lead balls made in the same diameter as the inside dimension of the barrel that it would take to make one pound of lead. In other words, it will take 10 lead balls that would fit in the barrel of a 10 gauge to make one pound of lead. A 20 gauge is half the size of a 10 gauge, so it would take 20 balls of lead to make one pound. In reality the .410 is not a gauge at all, but is a bore size even though it is commonly referred to as a gauge size. The actual gauge size is 67 gauge. I think that the best gauge for turkey hunting is the 12, for a lot of reasons. The 410 is way too small, the 28 was made for specialty trap and skeet shooting. It would be almost impossible to find shot size for turkey hunting unless you loaded them yourself. In the late 1800's the 10 gauge originally was the most popular, but as the manufactures perfected both the guns and powder, the 12 gauge has taken over as the most popular. The original 12 gauge shell was loaded with one ounce of lead shot or pellets. In the early 1950's the powders were being improved, which allowed heavier shot loads and lead to higher velocity shells, The 12 gauge 3 inch magnum carries 1 & 7/8 ounces of shot and the 12 gauge 3 & ½ inch magnum shell carries a full 2 ounces of shot. A standard 12 gauge field and target, 2 ¾ inch shell is loaded with 1 1/8 ounces of shot. The smaller 20 gauge, shooting magnum loads is now almost as efficient as the older 12 gauges. I have hunted with friends that only wanted to use the 410 and told me they wanted to give the turkey a fairer chance. I don't agree with that line of thinking for I want to make a clean kill when I shoot and there is too much danger of wounded birds with a small gun.

Mr. Volker, the man that took me quail hunting, bought his sons double-barrel guns, when they were old enough to hunt. One of the guns he bought was a Ansley Fox double-barrel. I was still hunting with my single shot 12 gauge and I admit I was coveting those guns. I made up my mind right then, I wanted a gun like that. I soon discovered that they were rare guns and it would be no easy task to find one. As it was, I didn't find one until I was released from the service after the Korean War. The gun proved to be an excellent gun for the Osceola strain of turkey found in the Everglades. You had to use high velocity shells for turkey loads. The gun was light, and both barrels were choked very well. I found the south Florida birds didn't have the heavy plumage that the birds have in the northern climates, and the shot penetrates easier. The smaller size of the Osceola also makes it an easier kill. When I moved to the mountains of North Georgia, it took me one turkey season to discover that my short double barrel would not cut the mustard. I found that spring in Florida was a lot different than spring in the mountains. In Florida the birds have a pretty good supply of food all year long, and when the gobblers build up their storage of fat for mating season and they are fat all over. By comparison, the mountain turkey has a poor diet all winter. By the time spring comes, he has lost most if not all of his mating fat. What I am talking about here, is the fact that a male turkey will build up a layer of fat on his chest just before spring and mating season. Most of the time they will not eat during the mating season, which can last over a month. During this time their body survives off of this layer of fat.

The Eastern Turkey has evolved into a much larger bird than the Osceola, for he needs the larger body mass to survive the cold temperatures. They also have much more dense feathers. The eastern birds are big and are much lankier than the domestic bronze, which is similar in appearance but compared to the Osceola, they look fat. When you see an Osceola gobbler and he is not in strut, they look almost fragile. They always look taller in the wild and can run like the wind. They amaze me how they can disappear in a field with very little cover.

The largest bird that I ever shot in Florida was 19 1/2 pounds; the largest mountain bird was 23 1/2 pounds. This really doesn't seem like too much of a difference until you consider that the Florida bird was as fat as a butterball, and the mountain bird did not have an ounce of fat on it anywhere. I would guess that if the mountain bird was as fat as the Florida bird, he would have weighed at least thirty pounds.

I was always afraid to shoot magnum shells in my Ansley Fox, for fear of injury to the gun. For a standard older 12 gauge, there are three loads that you can purchase that will fit in the breach of a 2 3⁄4 gun. The first is the low brass, used for quail or dove and clay pigeons. The second is the high brass or high velocity that was designed for ducks and larger birds. They packed more punch, with more powder and shot. The third is the more modern magnum loads and are dangerous to use in some of the older thin barrel shot guns.

I decided to shop for a new gun. I didn't want to lose another gobbler because I didn't have the proper equipment.

You can get by, using the older standard gun by purchasing 2 3⁄4 inch magnum loaded shells.

Remember these older guns were not designed for more powerful loads and I always felt like I was pushing-my-luck to use them. In a shot-gun, a magnum shell means the manufacturer has increased the number of shot in each shell and in doing so, they have had to use a more powerful type of powder. Originally this was not supposed to increase the punch or power, yet in reality they have more punch. If you really want to tailor a gun to suit your needs, there are a few things that you can do to make sure that you have the right gun for you. If you are going to purchase a gun especially for turkey hunting, you might as well go for one that shoots the magnum three inch, or the newer three and one half inch shells. The fault with the three and one half inch shell is they are not carried by all supply places, plus not all manufactures produce a gun that shoots that size.

You will shoot your gun so seldom at a turkey; you surely don't want to buy something that won't do a proper job. I will not try to influence you on what brand name to buy. I believe sometimes you can pay several hundred dollars more for just, "A name."

There are two schools of thought about the length of the barrel. Originally the shell manufactures claimed that you-needed at least a thirty inch barrel and a thirty two inch would be ideal to get maximum burn-out of the powder in a magnum shell. Anything less meant you couldn't get maximum efficiency from your shell. Turkey hunters found these long barreled guns very awkward to shoot in some of the places and positions you can find yourself. In trying to get off a shot at a very quick adversary, a shorter barrel is easier to swing. The gun manufactures decided a shorter gun would sell better for this reason. They re-developed the powder where it burns faster and they produced shorter barreled guns. The long barrels were choked by narrowing the opening in the barrel itself. Duck hunters still favor the long guns.

With the short barrels, and even some of the long guns, most are choked by metal inserts that are screwed into the end of the barrel or tube. This allows you to change the patterns that you can shoot, without changing guns. Several manufactures are producing guns, especially made for turkey hunting. They have parkerized finishes on the exposed metal, and dull finished stocks, and now some even use composite or plastic for stocks. Some guns are even painted with camouflaged patterns. There are even tape kits that do a good job of concealing the gun. I had good success painting guns with camouflage patterns with an air brush. I always reasoned that you can remove it if you tire of it.

One of the advantages, to me, of a smaller gun, is the lighter weight. You can walk long distances when trying to locate birds. A few pounds lighter gun over a day's hunting will sure make it more comfortable for you. Don't forget though, any time you cut the weight and increase the power, you end up with a gun that kicks harder. I rationalize it this way. I only shoot my gun three or four times during a season and I walk many miles, so I take the lighter weight. I never remember the kick when I have just shot at a gobbler!

If you don't understand what I mean by, "choke," I will explain.

What you are shooting in a shotgun at birds, are small heavy pellets that are loaded in a shot shell in the front end. They are separated, from the powder, by paper or plastic, called wadding. The powder (which sits in contact with the primer) is in the base of the shell. This primer requires a sharp blow to ignite it, and when you pull the trigger, the hammer or firing pin snaps down on that primer. This ignites the powder and pushes the wadding, shot or pellets, out of the barrel and towards what you are aiming at. These pellets in bird shot range from the very small number 9 (about the size of a period) to the BB size that most people are familiar with. The BB size is the same as the BB that you used for bullets in your first BB gun that most boys get as a child. The larger pellets are called buck shot and they are used for game animals. The most common range is in size from number one buck to the common oo and ooo buck. The object of a full choke gun is to keep the shot or small lead pellet's grouped together for as long a distance as possible. Shot, or pellets, can scatter to the point that you will have holes in the pattern that will not allow your target to be covered.

Pattern is the grouping of shot, or pellets as they arrive at the distance you have chosen. A bad pattern is one that scatters the pellets too wide and may leave holes where the pellets do not strike what you have shot at.

For quail hunting you need the smaller shot to

scatter more, so you would need something like an improved cylinder or a modified barrel, which allows the shot to scatter more. A rule of thumb about choosing shot size is:

"The smaller the bird the bigger the number."

"This rule of thumb scale is not written in stone. Some people like to use the smaller #7 ½ and #6 for turkey.

Some Thoughts about the Barrel of the Gun

You can purchase a gun with or without ribs. Solid ribs or ventilated ribs are placed on the barrel to give you a better sight plane. If you go into a gun shop you will see people picking up guns and pulling them to their shoulder, like they are getting ready to shoot them. What they are doing is snapping them to their shoulder and sighting down the barrel to see if they can see the sights properly, without having to adjust their body or head. You have a natural shooting position when you bring a gun to your shoulder, the sights should line up with whatever you are looking at, without adjusting anything. If you have to compensate at all, up, down or sideways, the gun doesn't fit you properly.

I developed two bad habits shooting my old double barreled BB gun and it has affected the way I shoot ever since. I lost the bead sight off the end of the barrels soon after I got it and I developed a habit of sighting down the shiny side of the barrel. The stock was very short, so I didn't have to move my head forward to sight. If I have time, like when a turkey is moving my way slowly, I can force myself to move my head forward and properly sight down the sight plane and use both beads. However if I only have a millisecond to sight, I can still catch myself using the side of the barrel.

When I discovered that my old standard fox double barrel wasn't good enough against the larger eastern turkey, I searched and found what I thought would be the perfect gun for me. I found a twelve gauge, three inch magnum pump shot gun. It only held three shells, so I didn't have to worry about having to plug the magazine. Some shot guns will hold from three to seven shells, however most states limit you to three shells while turkey hunting. To compensate for this law you are required to install a plug, (like a fake shell) replacing the space in the magazine that the extra shells would have occupied. You can purchase these plugs at most gun stores or if you are handy, you can make one easily.

Magazine -- *where the shells are held in reserve in a gun.*

Chamber--*where the shell is locked in place waiting to be fired.*

The new gun had a 30 inch ribbed barrel and the stock was a little long for me. I had decided to shorten the stock, so I thought I had better put on a cushioned butt plate while I was at it. After I had this done the gun almost fit me perfectly. The only problem now was the bright finish. It was a fairly new gun, and I didn't have a whole lot of money invested, so I decided this would be a good candidate for a camouflage paint job. I had saved an article from one of the sports magazine on how to do a professional looking job. I ended up substituting my air brush, rather than a paint brush and it came out nice.

I took the gun to a local gun club and was able to break a reasonable amount of clay pigeons. Now I felt confident that I wouldn't leave any cripple birds. The gun came through for me on my first two chances for birds. Only one problem; I only had to fire one time on each hunt. On the third hunt, I got the end of the barrel tangled in a small vine and completely missed on the first shot. I got the barrel out from under the vine, and by this time the bird was in the air, rapidly getting out of range! I swung slightly ahead of the turkey, lined my sights up properly, and squeezed the trigger. Nothing happened! Now I really did squeeze, still nothing happened; too late! The bird was long gone! What happened? After thirty five years of hunting with a gun that all you had to do was pull the trigger, I had forgotten to pump a new shell into the chamber. I could work the mechanism fine, shooting clay pigeons or, just practicing, but in the excitement of the hunt, I would forget to pump altogether, or I would pump too lightly, and get the expended shell hung up in the mechanism. After this happened to me several times I decided maybe I had better start looking for a different gun. If you are used to a pump type shotgun and it is your first gun, they are excellent.

I have watched Fred Etchen challenge anyone to a speed shooting contest with a pump gun against an automatic, and he always won; so I knew that pump guns in the right hands can be fired rapidly.

Fred was a world champion skeet and trap shooter that owned a gun club in early Miami. He also restocked guns with beautiful pistol grip custom stocks that were sought by shooters worldwide.

I soon settled on an automatic that has the parkerized (dull finish) with all the features that I needed, a ribbed barrel, three inch magnum shells, a 30 inch barrel and it fit well. It was even called, "A Turkey Special!" This gun is rather heavy, but with the gas operated ejection system, it has a very light kick. I have used this gun several times under hunting conditions. It has only failed once and that was due to an old shell, so I can't blame the gun. It didn't upset me too much, because I was dove hunting. It really was hard to maneuver this long barrel in a blind. It was about this time that the manufactures of shells decided to convert the magnum shells to where they were efficient in shorter barrels. When I heard about this I was wishing that I had waited. Although I can't find anything wrong

Two Guns I Painted

with the operation of this gun I still half way expect it to fail me every time I pull the trigger. This is probably due to the fact that (all my life) I have heard other hunters complaining about their automatic's jamming on them at crucial times. Also I am probably flinching, because it feels like my pump gun. At the time I bought the automatic, I had never heard of a good double barreled gun that shot magnum shells. Low and behold about a year after I purchased the automatic, I was in a store with my wife that had a gun display. In this display was a short barreled twelve gauge 3 inch magnum, "Turkey special" that was made in Spain. After looking it over closely I made an offhand remark to my wife that this is the gun that I wish I knew existed before I purchased my automatic. Six months later, guess what I found under the Christmas tree? This is a well-made gun almost a copy in looks to my Ansley Fox, except much heavier. It's parkerized and has the screw in choke tubes, short barrels and even has a carrying sling. The only thing I don't like about the gun is that it kicks like a mule. Every time I shoot a magnum shell at game, I end up with a bruise on the second finger that lies outside the trigger cover. When shooting targets or clay pigeons, I have no trouble holding the gun properly and tight to my shoulder; but under the excitement of a kill situation, I am not thinking about holding it properly. All my concentration is on the game and I have a tendency to hold the gun in a relaxed position. It doesn't hurt my shoulder, but later I notice the hickey on my finger.

First Gobbler with My New Spanish Double-Barrel

I guess the only style gun that I haven't talked about is the over and under. To me this is only a side by side double turned sideways. I have always loved to shoot them, but they have always been out of my price range. I have always thought of them as a gun to shoot skeet or trap. I guess that idea comes from the fact that I was always secretly envious of people who owned them, and I made excuses that they weren't as good as my old double barrel. It's all up to your personal choice and pocketbook; and if you like it, then it's the gun you should shoot. I started off with a 30 inch single shot H&R with a hammer and no shell ejection, and it was my old standby for years. I still have it and every time I pick it up it brings back a lot of good memories. I did a lot of quail hunting as a kid and this old gun was all I had.

The afore mentioned Mr. Volker and his two boys were all excellent shots. When walking up on a covey rise we all had a set pattern that we followed. It wasn't written down, it just developed that way. Mr. Volker controlled the dogs with his voice and they all obeyed.

He walked in close behind the lead pointing dog as he softly spoke, "Easy Trix, steady now, hold it steady."

His two boys were younger than me and they covered both his left and his right, and were behind him about a step back and seven or eight yards to the side. Depending on the terrain, I moved in to the left or right and also about a step back. On the covey rise there was some rapid shooting for a few seconds. I got in the habit of counting the shots. Mr. Volker shot a Browning

Trixie, George, Sweet 16, Ann- 1946

sweet sixteen which held three shots and both boys had

double barrels and those seven shots didn't take them very long to fire. All their guns were shorter barrels and designed for quail hunting while my old long tom was a general purpose gun and it really had a tight choke. It was great for dove, duck or turkey shooting, but using it for quail wasn't the best idea. I soon found that if I shot quickly, I usually missed, and if I was lucky enough to hit one in close there wasn't enough left to bother cleaning them. They would explode like a clay pigeon with a puff of feathers. I got a lot more birds waiting for them to unload and then pick one that was getting out of range for them and I would use the long range ability of my gun.

A shiny gun when it flashes from the sun light will spook a turkey and you won't even know it. My guns will never pass any beauty contest for I look on them as a tool rather than something to show off with. They have scratches and dents in them but they all operate well. When I am challenging a wise old bird I am not above crawling on the ground to get myself in a better position for a shot. My mind is on what that old bird is doing and not on worrying about my stock getting scratched. I don't ever plan on selling any of them. I have even engraved my name on some of them, for protection against theft.

I remember one cold morning just after the Second World War, we, George Volker, Dub Woolsey and I were camped out on Fish Eating Creek waiting for daylight and the opening of hunting season.

George got up from the log he was sitting on and made the remark, “I have to do something before we get started.”

He went to his jeep, took out the box that had his brand new, never been fired, 16 gauge sweet sixteen. He opened the box took out the gun, walked over to the creek and threw it in the shallow water.

He leaned over and retrieved the gun shaking the water out and muttered to himself, “Now I don’t have to worry about scratching this SOB anymore.”

That was vintage George Volker.

As one my hunting partners used to say "What a man needs is a double barrel automatic pump."

Choosing a Rifle

The process of shooting a shotgun is a whole different effort because you only have to be close. The pattern in most cases is wide enough to compensate for slight sighting errors. When I started experimenting with a rifle, hunting for deer, I ran into several problems. I was a pretty good shot with iron sights and was well satisfied but I started to have problems. The first thing that happens as you age is that your eyesight starts going. What made me panic was that I got to where, when I tried to sight my rifle, I couldn't focus in on all three objects anymore. (The rear sight, the front sight, and whatever I was aiming at.) Reading the newspaper didn't bother me that much, for my arms were still long enough, but not being able to sight my gun sent me straight away to the eye doctor. Glasses helped but I was still having major problems aiming my gun.

An old friend of mine suggested that I put a scope on my rifle.

He said by doing this I would lose one of the three points of sighting. "When you use a scope all you have is the object and the crosshairs to line up."

He was right, but this didn't solve my problem because of my bad aiming problems. I explained that I had looked through scopes on other rifles and I always had a problem of seeing a clear field in the scope. He had me pick up his gun with a scope and he watched me bring it to my shoulder. He asked me several questions about my posture and like a good doctor he prescribed a cure for me. He knew that I shot a Winchester 94, for deer hunting. The only way a scope can be mounted is on the side because of the empty shells ejecting from the top. He suggested that I side mount a scope and this would solve the habit of sighting down the side of the barrel. He said the way I kept my head back on the stock could be solved by bringing the scope back as far as I could. This brought the eye relief into a place that was natural for me. He suggested that I practice, over and over; bringing the gun to my shoulder so that when I did it for real it would be natural.

Eye relief --- the 2 inches or so of space that you can move your head back and forth on the stock and can still see clearly through a scope.

My black powder muzzle loading 50 caliber Hawken gave me another problem. Florida will not allow a scope on a black powder gun because it

My Favored Rifle-Winchester 94-25-35

then ceases to be a primitive weapon. I solved this problem by having a peep sight installed in the rear and even with bad eyes it was easy to learn to be very accurate again.

When I get excited I have always had a problem overshooting my target. When you shoot a gun with a ribbed barrel, that fits, it seems to make it easier to line up everything when you are excited. Excitement can make you do strange things.

As I said, my favorite big game gun is a little strange for most hunters. I started off deer hunting with a sporterized military carbine. Early on in my life I was under the misconception that throwing out a lot of lead in a hurry was the way to go. In my early days of hunting I walked constantly and this gun claimed a lot of deer for me because I was a fairly good shot. I always shot deer that I had jumped and at the close range the small carbine would do the trick. It had one major problem though; it would jamb because of the soft nosed bullets that you had to use while hunting. Several times I have hit a deer with my first shot and have had my gun jamb, leaving the wounded deer to run away while I am franticly trying to un-jamb the gun. This happened several times and I decided that I needed a more powerful gun that was designed for hunting. Quite by accident a friend of mine was in financial trouble and offered me his Winchester model ninety four and eight boxes of shells for only sixty dollars.

It was 1955!

I was well educated in shotguns from my previous experiences but my knowledge about rifles was limited. I was started off with a 22 rim fire and had shot the standard military guns but this was new to me. After I bought the gun I learned that the caliber of this gun was not the most common caliber in the model 94. What I had been sold was a 25-35 caliber. Several people told me I would be sorry because everyone didn't carry 25 35 shells.

I thought to myself, *"Man! How many times do they think I am going to shoot this gun I do have eight boxes of shells. That's 160 shots! Little did they know how I had been trained*?"

It turned out to be made for me and I got to where I could drive tacks with it because it was so accurate. My younger son took up hunting and borrowed it from me about 15 years ago and someone stole it from him before he returned it. I found the gun in a police station where they had taken it away from a criminal but because I had never written down the serial number they refused to give it back. I bet you know what I did? I went home and wrote down all the serial numbers of all the guns I own and I keep the list in a safety deposit box.

I have an excellent 300 Savage lever action and I just don't feel comfortable with it. When I decided to stop walking and reverted to tree stand or still hunting, I discovered that one well-placed shot was a lot more effective way of killing deer.

Over the last ten years I drug out the gun that I broke in my boys with. I bought a H&R Topper single shot that has a 20 gauge barrel and interchanges with a 30 30 barrel. I had a scope mounted on it and that's what I hunt deer with now. I even killed a seven point buck holding it like a pistol. I was on a tripod type stand and I stood out like a sore thumb. There were does all around me and I couldn't swing my body around without them spooking, so I brought my one hand up very slowly and managed to nail him. I almost dropped the gun though because it being so light, it kicks like a mule.

If you are familiar with your gun and it is sighted in properly, I am a believer that a well-placed shot is more important than the caliber you are using. Of course different conditions require different guns. I have no idea how many different shells and calibers of guns that are made today, but it has to be in the thousands. If you belong to a hunting lease or club you will more than likely gravitate to a certain type of gun. I have only killed two deer at long range, but most have been in the fifty to hundred yard range.

The club I joined in Georgia was in South Georgia and dogs were used. During the dog hunting it was all shotguns and it was really enjoyable. You had to have really good reflexes. To stand in a small logging road about 12 feet wide and be able to bring your gun up and hit a deer that is running flat out is no easy task. The only warning you have is the dogs running and there is no way to tell how far the deer is out in front of the dogs; nor can you always tell which way the dogs are going. I loved this type of hunting because it was the way I had been raised. First fox hunting with Mr. Manry and with George's bird dogs and then I joined with a group that had black and tans and we hunted wildcats in the very lower part of Florida. Here in the mountains they hunt raccoons and rabbits with the dogs and in North Carolina they go after bear.

When we moved to Georgia I brought three Walker-Redbone cross and the mother a full blooded redbone hound. I had used them for deer hunting in the lease I joined where we had 5600 acres. I knew that I couldn't use them for deer hunting in the mountains but I just could not leave them in Florida and I couldn't find a hunting home for them. Hunting with dogs has a special meaning to someone who has done it. There is nothing like the sound of dogs on a slow trail, it's a mournful sound like a train whistle way off in the distance. When the dogs jump, whatever they have been tracking, and that brand new excited sound comes from them your own heart begins to race in anticipation. Most of the times the dogs take the quarry away from you, but you are on full alert hoping they will bring the chase back to you. Just the sounds of the hunt are enough to bring you back to hunt time after time. It's a shame but the do gooders are slowly regulating dog hunting away from being done at all. To that bunch in South Georgia, dog hunting was a way of life and to have stopped it was like killing off a breed of human being, and they are now becoming extinct.

Patterning your Shotgun and Sighting your Rifle

Number four bird shot is the size that is accepted as the standard for turkey and will do a fine job. But it may not be the best shot size for your gun. You can purchase targets at the gun shop that simulate a turkey's head. They have a large 36 inch circle drawn around the edge with a turkeys head drawn in the center. Take this target and place it forty yards from where you will shoot. Make sure that it has a safe background. Don't forget, even bird shot can hurt you out beyond a hundred yards. Line up the front and back sight beads on the head in the target and make sure your sight plane is level! Hold your gun steady and fire.

Don't ever make a misjudgment and shoot at a turkey's body. 99% of the time a body shot means a lost and injured bird. That's why they have the head highlighted on the target. Look at the target and count the number of shot inside the circle. Each size shot has a different number of shot in the shell and you need to establish what percentage of shot hit within the circle. The range of shot sizes that you can use for turkey hunting is controlled by your individual state. They range somewhere between bb size on the larger end and seven and one half chilled shot on the small size. There are copper coated steel and lead versions of most of these sizes. Check your state law. Most states furnish you with basic hunting regulations when you purchase your hunting license.

I try the range of shells to see which size gets the best coverage and doesn't leave any spaces where the head or neck would not be hit by some shot. After I arrive at the shot size that has the best coverage, I then test the different brand names to see the ones that have the best penetration. You can take a large big city phone book or if some are not available, you can substitute several magazines taped together. I soak the books when I do this for it seems to work better. Stand the books, flat side toward you, at that same forty yards. Fire one of the shells you have chosen and then see how many pages the shot penetrated into the book. Next take a shell, different brand, same shot size and do the same thing to the back side of the phone book. You will be surprised at the difference in penetration. This method has worked well for me over the years, and doesn't seem to have anything to do with the brand of shells, but more with the particular gun. It may seem like an unnecessary step but if you want to be sure that you are shooting the best shell for your gun this is an excellent way to find out. When I tested my guns I had to buy a box of 25 to do the testing, but now you can buy them five at a time until you arrive at what brand

and size fits your gun the best. My old Ansley Fox Double, shot a number 4 bird shot in the left barrel which had the better choke and the right barrel, which I shot first, handled the number 6 bird shot the best. My newer Spanish Magnum Double shoots the number 4 size shot in either barrel with the same efficiency.

I realize I need to side track here and explain why sometimes I am telling you such basic facts. You are probably saying to yourself "I know that."

Well, I know several times in my life I wished that someone had given me a basic manual, so I wouldn't appear so dumb when I made some simple error that (everyone thought) I should have known. Sometimes I would not ask what something meant, hoping that I could figure it out later, so I didn't appear dumb. I have a very old cook book that explains all of the terms used in cooking. It is one of my most prized possessions and makes cooking so much easier. That old book goes into the "why" you are doing something a certain way. For example – In making a pie crust it will come closer to being flakey if you use everything cold. The reason is warm flour, utensils, lard milk etc. melt the lard-flour droplets causing them to melt together rather than layering and making the desired flaky crust.

3 (A) Sighting Rifles

Iron sighted rifles are more inclined to shoot like the man holding the gun. I know that my old single shot 22, shot a little to the left and a little low. When my buddy shot it, it didn't shoot that way for him. I guess it was in the difference in the way we held the gun. I have adjusted front sights where they were bumped and the front sight was obviously moved in the track it sits in. Most guns with iron sights are factory set and very seldom move during the life of the gun. I just compensated in my aiming to make any allowances I found.

Sighting in a scope is another thing. I have seen hunters shoot a whole box of shells and still not get their sights where they want them. I consider myself a pretty good shot and didn't even realize it until I went into the service and basic training. I had never shot high powered rifles, only 22's and my drill sergeant had me scared of them with his cautions about how the gun kicked. Now he was training us in the use of the M1 Carbine. I don't remember how many shots we had to make, but I was so indoctrinated by the time I took my first shot I flinched and missed the bull's eye.

I lost a lot of respect for him but I guess he had to try and get us to do it the army way for safety reasons. I know I shot the rest of the required shots and came in one point under the range record for the carbine and broke the record the next time I shot.

I was in the motor pool and sometimes drove the bus down to the range when a group had to qualify. That range sergeant and I had a good racket going for a while. He would suggest that they have a pool for the best score of the day and winner take all of a pot where everyone contributes a buck each.

He would say, "You don't mind if the bus driver gets in on this?"

To sight a rifle, I first make sure that my scope is mounted securely and there are no loose screws.

I built a stand, or contraption that set on our picnic table that we had just outside our cook shack in the camp I belonged to. It was near the Big Cypress Indian reservation. Anyone could sit in the bench and rest his gun in this equipment and squeeze off a round. It would be as accurate as the individual person could shoot, because you are comfortable.

The front was a U shaped padded holder that was adjustable with a bolt that moved up or down so it would fit any rifle. It would also adjust left or right. The back end was V shaped and also padded and when you attempted a perfect shot with your rifle, nothing was fastened down. **Very important! Don't fasten your gun down and fire it!** You tried to adjust everything to where it was just resting in this cradle. You still had to hold on to the gun because it would jump out of the gadget otherwise when you fired off a round.

We had a dry pond out in front of the cook shack so you could place a target at any distance you preferred to sight it in at. One of the members had a good spotting scope so it made the next step easier. I always drew a cross on the target to sight my gun for it was easier to line up the cross hairs. This first shot is the most important, for if you were confident that you had taken your best shot, then that was the only shot you would have to take to sight your gun in. I bet I have some eyebrows raised here? Sometimes I would ask the person sighting in to fire off three shots in this method, more to see if they could shoot well.

Of course the one or three shot grouping would be off the cross in the center of the target, but at this point it didn't matter. After it was established where the gun was shooting, (before any adjustment) you can place the gun back in this cradle and this time you are not going to shoot. This stand had clamps that you now use to fasten your rifle down securely. You don't want it to move at all during the next steps. Use only the adjustable bolts to move the gun to where the crosshairs are back on the target as accurate as you can get them.

Without moving the gun, sight through the scope, move the crosshairs with the adjusting screws on the scope to where they align with the single hole you shot in the target. If you shot three times for a group, then center the hairs on that grouping. Don't move or bump the gun while you are moving those crosshairs, because if you do, you might as well start over. This method is very accurate and it is a good idea to test your sighting before hunting season. I only use two shots one for effect, and the second to test after I have gone through the routine. I have seen some guys spend a couple of boxes of shells and run their legs off trying to adjust a scope by moving the crosshairs one click at a time. I prefer this method. There are now similar devises on the market that will allow you to zero in your gun with this method.

(B) Aiming your Gun Properly

When I first purchased my Ansley Fox double barrel I took it to a place where I could fire it safely. The first way I fired it, was to have my wife throw up a can for me to shoot at. In the first two shots I missed the can completely and my heart sank. I just knew that I had bought a defective gun. I set up a target to see how far off my pattern was in relation to a piece of newspaper set out at about forty yards. I lay the gun across the hood of the car, took dead aim and fired. I walked down to the target and discovered that the gun was on target perfectly, and also had a real good tight pattern. This tight pattern was what was causing me to miss. The gun I had been shooting did not have as tight a choke and I had gotten careless with my aiming. I tried the cans again and discovered that if I was dead on with my shot I could not only hit them but was able to knock them several yards farther out.

(C) Shooting Over your Target

This story will illustrate how you can shoot over your target without even realizing it.

Mr. Volker, his boys and I started joining up with another neighbor (Mr. Horton) who also had pretty good bird dogs and was very woods wise. Everything went fine until all of us started to notice that on a covey rise he was claiming birds that one of the others were sure that they had shot. Mr. Volker, after listening to our complaints in private, advised us to overlook it.

He said, "We are taking home plenty of birds and he is an old man. There is no real way to tell who really shot the birds, so quit complaining and enjoy the hunt."

It was hard but we all endured and kept our mouths shut. The only trouble was it got worse and worse. We went on a hunt shortly after Christmas and Mr. Horton also went along. On this trip Mr. Volker's brother-in-law joined us with his new 16 millimeter movie camera. He came along just to film the dogs in action and was not hunting. He would stand off to the side and film the dogs as they were working the birds, and sometimes he stood on the hard top of the jeep, and would film the whole sequence. He would start the camera when we released the dogs, when they first located the smell of quail, when they were working a covey. Then he followed them until they came down into a point and filmed the covey rise and gun action.

It was several weeks later and the season was over when I was invited over to the Volker house to see the film Mr. Woolsey had taken. He hung a bed sheet on the wall and Mr. Woolsey, Mr. Volker, the Volker boys and I settled in to watch the film. As I remember, it was pretty good film work and we were enjoying the memories.

All of a sudden Mr. Volker jumps up spouting a few expletives and said, “Back that thing up, I just saw something I can’t believe!”

When Mr. Woolsey backed up the film and showed it again, Mr. Volker pointed to Mr. Horton, and there he was on the covey rise shooting his gun in the air. I mean his gun was at a 45 degree angle in the air.

Bobby shouted, “I told you daddy, he was claiming my birds!”

Throughout the rest of the film, when there was a clear shot of Mr. Horton on the covey rise, he was doing the same thing.

We boys were really upset and Mr. Volker in his wisdom calmed us down and brought us back into reality.

"Mr. Horton has no idea that he is doing that and I guess it is because of his age. We can't go to him and accuse him of this, even though we have the proof. He is a good hearted old man and has done us all favors with his machinist skills; and he is the one who brings the ice cream that everyone enjoys so much. This season is over now and we don't have to let it bother us until next season. Before any accusations, maybe we can avoid hunting with him next year; not because he is claiming the birds. What he is doing is a dangerous habit and we can't take the chance of him hitting one of us."

As it turned out Mr. Horton was injured during the summer and was not able to hunt the following year.

> What was done right?
>
> Mr. Volker solved the problem without hurting the old man's feeling.

(D) Searching for Wounded Game

Next to safety, I believe this is probably the most important section of this manual. I have a lot of compassion for game in the woods and when I believe that I have wounded something, I will make an all-out effort to locate it. If you wound an animal you should consider the hunt over for the day; now the true test of your sportsmanship comes into play. Sometimes finding wounded game takes as much skill as the effort it took to get close enough to shoot at it.

Hunting really is a weird game that man loves to play, and I suppose it satisfies some craving that is left over from our primitive days. It is not hard for me to switch from that primitive mode at the end of a hunting season, back to where I just love to observe the woods. I have several different strains of turkey that I raise and I love to observe their antics. I also have two Piney Woods Rooters in my pasture that I have had as pets for ten years.

"Piney Woods Rooter" is the name given to feral hogs in the Everglades.

Nothing insults me or my wife more, than for someone to stop and ask us if we will sell one of our domestic turkeys for their Thanksgiving dinner. We just don't look at them as something to eat, and when one dies we both actually grieve for them.

No one has fought harder than I to see the wild turkey population increase, and I watch out for them all year long. This is probably hard to understand, for some of the do gooders that are trying to ban hunting everywhere. I know that the increase in the turkey population was brought about mainly by the money spent by hunters for licensing fees. I love to see a large flock of turkeys, or deer, on the off season and I have no desire to kill them out of season.

I might make a comment to myself or my wife, “Now why don't I see that in the regular season?"

I try real hard to get my allotted turkeys each year, and when I wound one, I put my every effort into finding it. After all he put his life on the line for you and the least you can do is make a gallant effort to locate him.

(E) Finding a Lost Deer

I want to tell this story about a deer hunt to show the type of effort that I had to put into finding a wounded deer.

My favorite way of hunting deer in the Everglades was with my old beagle Tiny. He was so old that he couldn’t waste much effort. He didn't run unless he was chasing a deer, and he always did his own thing. All I had to do was amble along through the woods and Tiny would go his own way, always checking in with me every so often; coming up behind me, wagging his tail and looking for a pat on the head. He didn't like to follow a cold trail anymore, unless he just happened to be going that way, and would not join another dog that was running a deer. The best habit that he developed in his later years was his ability to tell a doe from a buck. If he jumped a doe, he would run her for five or ten minutes and then give up. If he jumped a buck he would stay with it until someone shot it or someone caught him and pulled him away from the trail. We very seldom had a doe day in Florida and I suppose he decided nobody was going to shoot them, so why bother chasing them.

Whenever he would jump a deer I would listen to see which way he was headed. Then I would strike out in a ninety degree angle away from that direction, and travel about two hundred yards, and look for a clearing that I could watch. The deer in the Everglades, on flat ground, when they jump, will run hard for several hundred yards. They will then circle and turn back a couple of hundred yards over and return in the opposite direction. I got to where I could guess from the terrain which side they would come back; at least I had a fifty-fifty chance.

This one particular morning, Tiny jumped a deer and I made my move. Only when I got over to about to the right distance, there were only tall palmettos and I didn't think I was going to get a shot. I heard Tiny coming back towards me, and I turned around looking for some kind of a path that the deer might use. Naturally I heard (before any adjustment) the deer slap a palmetto behind me. I wheeled around just as this huge buck was jumping over a large palmetto clump. I had my rifle up and fired, making probably the best shot of my life. The buck crashed down right in the center of the palmetto clump and started flopping around. I never go directly to a deer because I have chased several away from where they would have died, if I had not been so impatient. My problem was that Tiny was still coming; and if he jumped the deer and smelled the blood, he would not open his mouth again. This is exactly what happened. I couldn't catch him because of the tall palmettos, and he ran the deer out of the clump that he was in.

This all happened about eight thirty in the morning on the last day of hunting season, and I knew I had my work cut out for me. I went into the clump of palmettos where I had last heard the deer and found a large pile of foamy blood along with several bone fragments. I knew then that he was going to die and it was up to me to find him. It seems like first blood trails are easy to follow and the farther you go the less you find. One of the men at camp had heard me shoot. When I didn't return for lunch, he came looking for me. He crossed my trail of toilet paper that I was dropping everywhere that I found a spot of blood. He followed the paper to where I was and brought me some lunch and something to drink. By now Tiny had returned with a full belly and blood all over him, so I knew that the deer was down and dead.

Tom, the fellow from camp stayed with me until late in the afternoon. We were now over a mile from where I had shot at the deer. I told him that I was going to stay an extra day and burn off the area in the morning when the wind was not so strong. He told me he would call my wife for me, but he thought that I had looked long enough. I returned to that spot the next day and was lucky that the wind was blowing toward the swamp, and the fire would soon burn itself out. We periodically burnt the whole lease, with the consent of the owners and the blessing of the game commission; so I set the fire.

About seventy five yards farther than I had looked I found my deer, a nine point that is still the largest that I ever shot. I brought the meat home for dog food, and my wife claimed the horns for her biology class because the ninth horn was growing out of the center of its head.

What did I do wrong?

> I shouldn't have tried to make a shot like that; nine times out of ten I would have never hit it.

What did I do right?

> I didn't give up looking as long as I still had a chance, no one would have blamed me for giving up, except myself.

This was carrying the search a little to the extreme and it was my longest search ever, but I couldn't stop as long as I continued to find blood.

(F) Story with Extensive Search

The largest bird that I ever killed in the mountains I almost gave up on before I found him.

A thirteen mile road goes through the national forest and begins about 200 yards from where my property ends. I love to travel this road at daylight and listen for gobblers sounding off. I use this road on rainy mornings, or when sleeping seems better than turkey hunting. I know that I can sleep until the last minute, just before daylight, and in just a few minutes still be where I could listen. If it is raining, I can stay in my truck and listen. By moving about 2 or 3 hundred yards at a time, I can cover the whole length of the road during this early morning gobbling time. The road pretty much follows the ridge of the mountain range. I travel the road so that the driver's side of the truck is on the downhill side of the mountain. I open the door at my first stop and then leave the door propped open with my foot, as I move from spot to spot.

I find that turkey will let a quiet, running vehicle pass fairly close to where they are, without spooking. You had better not stop if they can see the vehicle! This will most always send them on their way, even if you do not get out to look. I have driven up on birds feeding right along the edge of the road, and as long as I don't change the speed of the motor, or attempt to stop, they don't seem to pay much attention. I have been trying to call a gobbler in the woods and hear someone stop a vehicle, and then close their door. When they hear the vehicle noises they will stretch their neck and listen, only to relax at the moment that the noise passes or stops. When they hear the door close, or slam, they drop their head and move out of the area. Sometimes I use a call, (owl or crow) to get them to give away their location, but mostly I just listen, as there are a

23 ½ pounds

lot of owls. Sometimes, on a clear still morning, way off on the distant ridges I can hear several birds sounding off. On these kinds of days within my hearing, as many as ten birds will announce their area, so I know that the turkey are hearing many more than I am.

On this particular morning I was driving the road, stopping every so often, and I passed an extra-long lead that ran at right angles to the road. I had almost gone too far, but I could hear a gobbler sound off on one of the sub leads, that ran from the main lead. I was far enough past his position and I was able to leave my truck where it was without making any noise. I didn't want to warn him of my presence. I assembled my gear, eased my door shut and started down the mountain to where I thought he might be. He was quite a distance, and I stopped several times to listen to how close I was getting to him. He continued to gobble, and I was able to work in fairly close, before I set up my blind. There was only one small valley between where I set up, and where he was strutting, so I didn't dare try to get any closer. I would have had to go across the valley floor, and I was sure he would see me if I did. It only took me a couple of minutes to set up and relax enough to start calling.

I called one series of mating calls and he answered me immediately! I could tell that he had dropped over the edge of the ridge and had started to the next ridge, but I felt confident that I was close enough to turn him back toward me. I waited several minutes and attempted another series of calls. He answered again! Only he wasn't coming my way, he was already across the next valley and had started up the next ridge. I attempted to call again, only to have him move even farther away and farther up the ridge. I knew now that I had to move from where I was, and that I had to attempt to move even closer on my next try. I threw my gear into my pack, hustled down the ridge, across the valley and up almost to the top of the next ridge. As I approached the ridge I slowed down, and started to peer over the edge to see if I could visually locate him. I saw him climbing the next ridge and froze where I was until he reached the top. When I couldn't see him any more I looked around and could see that the ridge that I was on was flat for about seventy five yards. Just where it dropped off, was a large old chestnut log, lying just right for me to use as a natural blind. I could see that the angle was alright for me to crawl from where I was, and the turkey would not see me from where he was. I shed my pack, and bota bag, dropped down, and crawled as fast as I could until I reached the protection of that log. When I finally got there, I pulled my net down over my face, and eased my head up until I could see the next ridge. At first I couldn't see him, so I made a soft call and he answered right behind my call. I saw him come out from behind a tree and go into a strut. He was using the flat crest of the ridge as a strutting area.

I thought to myself, *"I can ease back down behind this log and call him across the valley and back up the hill. I will be able to hear him walking up the hill, because of all of the dry leaves. He will probably gobble as he comes, because he has been sounding off all morning."*

I slipped back down and made another seductive call, and he gave another gobble. I waited about ten minutes and didn't hear a sound. I let out another soft call and nothing! Not a sound. I waited another few minutes and decided to look up over the log to see if I could still see him on the ridge.

As I raised my head to look over the log, I found myself peering face to face with a horney looking gobbler! I don't know which of us was the most startled, me or the gobbler? I do know which one of us reacted the fastest. No contest, he was gone before I could shoulder my gun.

He had jumped up to land on the log just as I started to peer over the log. His reaction was like that of a gymnast vaulting over a pummel horse, his feet touched the top of that log, just a second, and he went straight up in the air. I know that he didn't even attempt to open his wings until he was five or six feet into the air! By the time I got my gun up and swung around, he was already about thirty yards away and gaining speed. I was so rattled that my first shot was so far off that I probably wasn't in the same county with him. Now I forced myself to calm down.

I swung the gun up with just the right lead and now

the darn thing wouldn't fire again. My mind and heart were both racing!

"What's wrong now!" I thought, then I remembered; *"This is a pump gun!"*

I ejected the shell and slammed in a new one, but by now he was headed to the valley below. I fired in desperation, for he was at least seventy five yards away and seemed like he was traveling at least that many miles an hour. I didn't cut a feather with either shot. I stood there in disbelief as he sailed down the mountain and behind some big trees that were blocking my view of the valley floor. I was making up my mind right then that I had too many years shooting a gun that you didn't have to pump, to learn how to do it automatically. I was kicking my butt, mentally, for doing two dumb things and letting that bird out do me.

It was one of those still clear mornings and the shots had made all of the woods noises cease temporarily. As I was standing there going over everything that I had done wrong, I hear a flopping noise way down on the valley floor.

I thought to myself, *"Can that be the turkey flopping as he's dying?"*

I listened real close and heard it again; now I was almost sure I was hearing him way down the mountain.

I knew that it had to be at least a half a mile away and I needed to plan my search before I moved a step.

The first thing that I did was to line up a tree; from where I was standing that would put the noise, the tree, and me in a direct line. I knew the last time that I had seen the turkey he was over the top of the ridge, in front of me, and he was sailing down the mountain using the crest of that ridge as a guide. I planned that if I went in a direct line toward the last place that I heard the noise, and went until I intersected the base of that ridge, I should be somewhere near where the turkey was lying. I knew that once they get into their glide they most always go in a straight line. I marked where I was standing with my empty shotgun shell, looked again at the tree that I was going to sight with, leaned my shotgun against the log and went back for my poncho and bota bag. I decided to strip most of the gear out of my pack and leave it there, for I knew that I would have to come back up to get to my truck. I decided to even leave my gun.

I took everything that I didn't need in my search and wrapped it up in my raincoat and hid it in the end of the log. I took my almost empty pack, my bota bag a partial roll of toilet paper and my compass. I took a sighting on the tree (that I had marked in my mind) and found the correct degree setting by rotating the face of my compass. About every ten or fifteen yards I tied a small piece of toilet paper to a branch about shoulder high. When I got to the base of the tree that I had originally used for sighting, I aimed my compass with that same setting and picked out another object to continue the same line down the mountain. This took several minutes more than just trying to walk straight to it. It was a little farther than I had thought and I was beginning to wonder if this was a waste of time. When I reached the intersection of the ridge with my toilet paper trail, I tied a small piece of fluorescent orange material to a branch at that intersection. I carry a small amount in my pack and I use it to put around a turkey when I am carrying it. I tied it head high so I could use this as a reference point. I have found that if you don't establish an accurate point to begin your search, you will very quickly lose your area and will find yourself far away from where you should be looking. I then started to circle, still using the toilet paper to form my circles. I was looking under logs and in bushes as I slowly formed wider and wider circles. I knew that when wounded, an animal will conceal themselves in small places. I had been doing this for about an hour when I walked out into a clearing about a hundred yards farther down the valley. Lying right out in the open, feet sticking straight up in the air, lay my turkey. He had probably sighted in on that clearing as a place to land and when he hit the ground he died. When I cleaned him, all I found was one pellet in his neck. He weighed twenty three and a half pounds and had an eleven inch beard with one inch spurs. The largest I ever killed!

What did I do wrong?

I should have been more familiar with my gun. Throwing the safety off, pumping the gun, sighting, and selecting triggers should all be done automatically. Shooting clay pigeons is not only fun but it gives you a chance to become automatic with your handling of your gun.

I should not have taken that first wild shot. Normally I am pretty good about taking my time to aim. I think being startled, looking right in the turkey's eye, caused me to react that way. Sometimes I even wait too long to shoot, this comes from my father only giving me one shell when I was a child.

What did I do right?

My plan of attack was correct. After I shot I stayed alert to what was happening.

I planned out my search rather than charging down the mountain.

I took my time and stuck with the search.

(G) Buck Fever

I built a lightweight swamp buggy out of a jeep chassis that had large tractor tires for buoyancy and traction. It had a 9 horse Onan engine, was chain driven, and used a centrifugal clutch. It was surefooted, but slow. A friend of mine, that was not much of a hunter, decided to join me on one of my trips on a wet prairie in south Florida. I had turned my beagles loose and they were working in and out of the small patches of brush scattered everywhere. The method of hunting was to try and jump a deer out of one of these patches. The seat on the buggy sat up high and there was no structure in front of the steering wheel.

All of a sudden two bucks jump out of a clump with two of my beagles screaming at the top of their lungs. The one that broke my way to the left was a spike and I concentrated in on him and left the other for my friend. I shot three times before I hit him with a stopping shot. He ran a little father but I could tell he was mortally wounded and kept my eye on him to see where he dropped.

After I spotted him down, I turned to my friend and asked him, "Why didn't you shoot?"

He answered, "I did shoot, and I ran out of shells. I guess I just missed him because he is still going."

I didn't argue with him I just climbed out of the

buggy and started picking up all seven of his shells that he had ejected out of his Winchester 94 without firing a single one. He was embarrassed, but I made up my mind not to tell on him. He was a good sport and told the story on himself.

What was done wrong?

There is no reason or explanation. Buck fever happens in many forms. You just have to be careful with firearms.

Lost? What Do You Do Now?

A few simple preparations would make a problem like this a lot easier. I have learned the hard way and I always carry a compass. I am not paranoid about it, but I don't know how many times I would have been in real trouble if it had not been in my pocket.

I bought a Timex watch once that had a very small compass imbedded into the watchband. Even after the watch wore out I removed that small dime size compass and carried it in my wallet for years. I did a lot of service work and I found that the little compass helped to re-orient me several times when I got turned around searching for an address.

To get in a place where you have to dig out a compass and look at it, is a rather helpless feeling if you got out of your car in the dark, in a strange place, and didn't orient yourself to start with. It only takes a second to pull out your compass and see in what general direction the road lies. If the road lies east and west and you are going to hunt on the south side, if you get turned around and need to find the road, you know that you have to go in a north direction to at least cross the road.

I wounded a turkey once and went home to get my dog to see if he could find where the turkey had finally died. When I got back I made the mistake of leaving my pack in the car.

I thought, *"I won't need that, I was close to the road and the dog will either smell where the turkey went or not. I won't be gone long enough to worry with it."*

The dog got real excited when we reached the spot where I had shot at the bird and started slow trailing it off through the woods. I was thinking that any minute we were going to flush the bird or find it dead. This went on for about an hour before my dog sat down and turned around giving me one of those, "What do I do now looks."

Only then did I look around and realize that nothing looked familiar. It was one of those bright days and I thought it would be easy to find my way out. About an hour later I lost my confidence and decided to sit down, and take a rest, and find out which way was which.

I chose the stick method to point me on my way. I found a clear spot where the sun was shining and a straight stick about two feet long. I stuck the stick in the ground and pointed the top toward the sun, so that the stick did not cast a shadow. While I was taking that break I could see a shadow forming on one side of the stick. I waited until the shadow was about 6 inches long. It was long enough to establish a shadow line away from the stick. I knew because of the approximate time of the day (12 noon,) that the line would be from east to west. I knew that the road was in the same east to west direction, and that I was on the south side of the road. Where the stick was shoved into the ground was the west end of the line, so that told me which way north was. This works well enough to get a general direction most of the day, but works best close to noon.

I grinned and thought to myself, *"The good old Boy Scouts come through again."*

Finding the direction doesn't end the problem, for you still have to keep in a straight line as you try to find a familiar mark or area to find your way out.

To walk a straight line is not easy, but you need to do it right to keep from going in a circle. From where you shoved the stick in the ground you know the direction you need to go, so you need to start off as accurate as you can. Ideally, find an object close to the stick that you can see from a good distance as you travel in your chosen direction. You need to be able to see the object you have chosen, a distant object, and one that is in between the two. When you reach the middle object you must find a way to line up the most distant object and a new object. Using this method you can leap frog, object to object, until you find your way out.

If you are separated from another person or group and have no idea where anything is, **STAY PUT**! It is easier for them to find you. The universal lost or distressed signal is three shouts, gun shots, whistle blasts in quick succession. The answer that you have been heard, is two noises in succession.

We, being members of the small camp in the Everglades and having the habit of walking good distances away from camp to roost turkeys, often found ourselves turned around. I carried three bird shot loads for my shotgun to use for just that. We went a little father with our signaling. When we were in camp and heard the telltale three shots, we would answer with one shot, wait ten minutes and fire again. We would repeat this interval until the" bewildered" one showed up back at camp.

It is not a good idea to try and find your way in the night for everything changes after dark. If you are hopelessly lost and darkness is approaching, you need to prepare for spending the night. If you have matches and are in a place where you can build a fire, build 3 fires separated six feet apart. Three fires are also a distress signal. Drag up some fallen limbs and make a crude shelter. Pine branches leaning against a tree that has been bent over, will shed a lot of water from dew or even rain if applied thickly. Rake up a pile of dry leaves. They make a good insulation against the cold, both under you and as a covering.

Map Compass made by Silva

Now to the Compass

and

How to Use It

The compass is divided basically into four parts starting at the North (0 degrees or 360 degrees) and traveling clockwise around the face, east is 90 degrees, south 180 degrees, west 270 degrees. A compass needle points north all the time no matter which way you hold the base. The needle has a colored end (usually red) on the north pointing end. The type I like to carry has a base plate that has a permanent arrow pointing to one end of a plastic rectangle plate about the size of a pack of cigarettes. Mounted on this plate is the actual circular compass container. Inside this clear fluid filled container is the needle balanced on a pinnacle. This compass container also has an arrow drawn on the base and it has the degrees etched into the outer edge. It is made so that you can rotate the compass container and it is held in place by friction.

On a ship the compass is set on gimbals to compensate for the wave action and the list of the ship. Compasses are set or calibrated to each ship so that north on the compass is the exact way the ship is pointed. Consequently, with the deferent degree settings etched into the face of the compass, all the helmsman does is turn the ship until the needle points to the degree he wants it to go.

When I was a scoutmaster I used to take the boys to a stadium or a marked off football field and set up a course for the boys to practice their compass skills. It took some work with the senior boys, but it was fun exercise and we always awarded the most accurate with a prize.

Everyone's stride is different when you are walking normally. If I remember right mine is 28 inches. That is the measurement from heal to heal or toe to toe as you are walking. It is easy to measure your stride while walking in sand or mud, because you leave a track.

We would go to the center of the field and place a numbered marker every ten yards from one end to the other. Then starting from the side line at a particular ten yard marker, we would lay out a different course for each boy. We had them draw from a hat for the one they would follow. The paper they would draw gave instructions in feet and degree. The paper would read:

Go from the 20 yard line on a 20 degree line 57 feet, change to an angle of 120 degrees for 40 yards and then to an angle of 300 degrees for 80 feet. Then write down which yard line you exit off the field.

As the boys got more efficient we would add more directions. I always had the boys follow a plotted course that I set up when camping in the Everglades. These exercises were good for them because it made them use their heads. As a youngster, my uncle Jack would give me real life exercises on his yawl sailboat. He would give me a chart of the area; have me estimate how many knots we were traveling, what degree to set our course on the compass, and tell him what time we would arrive at the next channel marker or buoy. What he did after I got fairly efficient at these exercises, was to do the same thing after dark.

He would always say, "Tell me when arrival time at the buoy is ten minutes away, because when I turn on the spotlight, I had better be able to see it!" This training saved our lives when my wife and I got caught in a hurricane outside Biscayne Bay. We made it home when I could not see the buoy.

I was always critical of school because most teachers taught math, but there was seldom a practical use that makes the exercise sink home.

I now live on the edge of the national forest in the mountains of N.E. Georgia and it is really wild country. I leave my property and follow a degree setting of 60 degrees and I maintain this until I top the ridge about a mile away. I hunt in this area for turkey. I leave before daylight, so I use my compass. I know that this setting will bring me out on a field where I like to call. When I am ready to go back, I reverse the direction. To do this, I point the base arrow on the base plate on my compass toward the direction I want to go. I rotate the wheel with the degree settings around until the needle is pointing directly north. This places the arrow (on the base plate and 60 degrees) in line. I will walk for a good distance and when I stop I pull my compass out; and all I have to do is line up the needle on north, and the base plate is pointing the way for me to walk. Coming back I just set my compass on 240 degrees and it brings me right back to my property.

You can use an analog watch to find direction in the day time by holding your wrist level and pointing the hour hand as accurately as you can toward the sun. Take a tooth pick or match stick or even a blade of grass and lay it across the face of the watch. Then line it up half way between the hour hand and the 12 on the face. The end of the toothpick that is closer to the sun end will be pointing in a southerly direction.

You can also look at a stump and tell generally which way is north by the thickness of the growth rings. The ones on the north side of the stump will be closer together than the ones on the south face.

Some old timers say that more moss will grow on the north bark of a tree than the south. I would be desperate to trust this method.

At night the North Star (In the northern hemisphere) is always true north, and all you have to do is draw a straight line to the horizon and (knowing the compass points) you are on your way. I used this method to walk out of the Everglades when our buggy broke down just after dark and we had about 10 miles to get out. I was glad that I could identify it. To find the star, look for the little dipper and look at the last star in the handle. To make sure you have the right one, the two last stars in the cup of the big dipper also are in line with the North Star.

Look at the moon, if it is not full and if it has risen before the sun has set the light side is facing west. If it rises after midnight (standard time) then the light side is facing east. These are only rough directions but it will help you get started in the right direction. There are a lot of better made complex compasses on the market but the one I have is fine for my uses and I only gave ten or twelve dollars for it. If you want to be really safe, you can purchase a GPS that will identify your position within inches. It does require learning how to use it, and it is just something else to carry. I love one for the boat, because it will carry you back to that good fishing spot with little effort, but I have just enough ego to do it the old fashion way in the woods.

Unpleasant Critter Section

I will start with the smallest Critters and work my way up to the largest

(a) Red Bugs (Chiggers)

Early Experience

I guess the most bothersome thing that attacks the new hunter right away is the lowly chigger or red bug.

You never even think about them when you go into the woods and it's the next day, or so, when you begin to suffer.

I was on a fishing trip with a neighbor on Lake Okeechobee when I was 15 and I got my first bad case. We were fishing for shell crackers on the bed and had really good luck. My neighbor took me along and he knew what he was doing. He found a mussel bed in about four foot of water, and had us stomp around in it until the water was good and cloudy. We had traveled out onto the lake along a dredged canal. We left the boat on the spoil bank of the canal and waded several hundred yards before we found a mussel bed. We were using cane poles and worms, and had a large galvanized wash tub (that was fitted inside of a truck inner tube) that carried our gear. The fish we were catching all were huge and it was an experience that I never forgot.

Mr. Alderman said that I could fish for bass later on that afternoon, but he wanted to get as many shell crackers as he could before we left to go back.

When we had enough for his liking he said, "Let's

go over to the spoil bank, get something to eat, and take a short nap."

I remember devouring whatever it was we brought for lunch. We laid down on grass in the shade of some brush that was growing there. I had trouble going to sleep because I could feel something crawling all over me. At first I couldn't see anything, I could just feel it. With my young eyes looking real close, I could see tiny little red colored bugs moving all over my clothes and body.

I asked if I could wade and try for some bass, and he said, "Go ahead; I will call you when I'm ready to go."

I took my home made casting rod, a plug that I had made, and a fish chain and started casting. There was a limit on bass at that time, and I think it was 8." Whatever it was, I very shortly had the limit, but I couldn't be satisfied. I would catch another, measure it to the smallest one on the string, add the new one and release the smaller. It was like a paradise!

Two things happen in that short time that made me really nervous. Where we were fishing the water looked black, there were patches of wire grass, but it was mostly open. I was casting and noticed a snake swimming toward me. I stopped and watched; when I realized it was a moccasin and he was headed straight toward me. My rod was homemade and rather stiff, about six feet long. It was made out a female Calcutta cane and I had used coat hangers to make the guides. I knew it was strong but I didn't want to break it. I think the snake was looking for some place to get out of the water. I waved my arms around trying to discourage him from coming any closer, but it didn't work, he kept coming. I tried to lift him out of the way with the tip of the rod, or at least change his direction, but he kept coming. All of this time I was backing up as fast as I could, not wanting to smack him with my rod and take a chance of breaking it. It came to the point where I had to frail him or get bit, so I whacked him a good one. It worked; he was stunned and turned over on his back. I put some distance between me and him before he woke up.

Needless to say I was now rather nervous and a little too cautious to concentrate on my casting. I figured I would amble back to where Mr. Aldermen and the others were napping. I was about fifty yards from reaching the bank when my fish chain hung up on something. I turned, grabbed it about four fish down, and pulled it towards me. As the fish cleared the water I realized the last fish was about half way down a gator's throat. I know it scared me, but it must have startled him too, for he turned loose and I departed the area. I made so much noise coming ashore that I woke the nappers.

We stopped at an ice house somewhere on the lake and covered the gutted fish with crushed ice. Mr. Alderman (as well as my father) used an ice bag made out of canvas with a metal bottom as a container to keep things cold. Very few had the means to buy a manufactured ice chest that we use today.

I tried to sleep on that trip back to Miami in the back seat of that model A, but I was conscious of something crawling on me. Little did I know what was in store for me!

Over the next couple of days, I looked like I had a bad case of the chicken pox. My mom knew what I had and thought it was funny. Her method of treating redbugs was to wash me down with baking soda and water. It didn't work and it didn't keep me from attending school. My teachers questioned what was wrong but were satisfied with my answer, as they smiled and went on with the class.

I eventually recovered and I never was attacked, severe, like that, again.

Both of my sons, when they were young, came down with hundreds of bites once in their lives; but they too never had it happen again. The three of us are occasionally bothered with bites around the belt line, but never extreme like the first time. Most agree that after you have been bitten, you are going to have to suffer through the cycle. I used to think you became immune to them after getting a bad case, but they say it has to do with the thickness of the skin.

Larva-Nymph-Adult of Harvest Mite

Commonly known as --

(Red Bug)

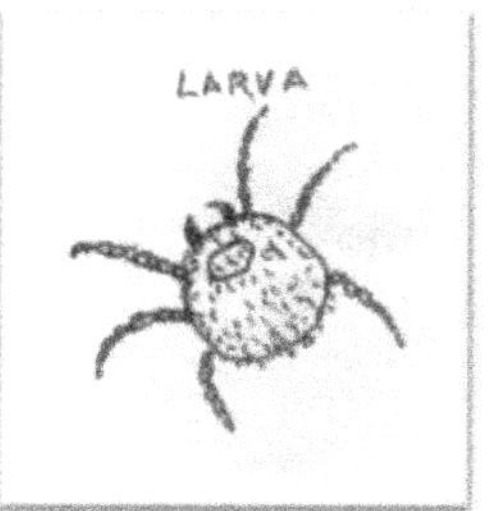

Red bugs or chiggers are the larvae stage of a Harvest Mite. They are actually red or bright orange in color. They are almost invisible to the human eye and are actually 0.5 millimeter in size. Under a microscope they are round, hairy and six legged. They bore a hole in your skin, and their saliva actually dissolves the cells under the skin surface. They feed on these dissolved cells. They bite you where the skin is the thinnest, feed on the liquid and drop off. The Larva stage has to have this dissolved skin to transform into the Nymph stage. It will develop two more legs and become larger, eventually becoming the Adult Harvest Mite. Both the Nymph and the Adult Harvest Mite only feed on vegetable material.

After the initial bite, it is from eight to forty-eight hours later when you discover what has happened; and you find these small red welts on your body. This delay in time will lead some to think they have an infestation around their home.

They pick spots on the body, to bite, around ankles, belt line or any place the skin is thin. The welts are the effect of the saliva injection under the skin. Some think the red spot, on top of the welt, where they bore this hole is actually the chigger; and try to remove it. It is long gone; you are wasting your time. The red welts will drive you crazy with the itching. Scratching will sometimes cause a sore to develop and they can even become infected. **Don't scratch**! It only makes it worse.

A trick that I use that will stop the itching is to use a hemorrhoid cream that has a Novocain base. Just a touch will deaden the skin and stop the itching. Covering your clothing with insect spray before entering the woods goes a long way toward protecting you from chiggers and ticks. Take a shower after returning from the woods. Any remaining Larva that hasn't bitten you will easily wash off.

I know a lot of people will find this explanation of the life cycle of the "harvest mite," hard to believe as I believed otherwise for years. It was hard for me to accept. All my teachers (my mother, grandmother, most old-timers) had been teaching me different all my life, but ***they were mistaken***.

(b) Sand Fly or No-See-Ums

I made this drawing from a photograph I found On-Line. I never knew what sand flies actually looked like.

After all, they can climb through a standard screen and it is 16 squares to the inch.

If you happen to choose a spot to seek some type of game or fish where these guys are in abundance you are more stable mentally, than I am. They are so small they can go through the standard screen wire and are vicious. I have no idea how people can exist on the shore where they are prevalent. Smudge candles, aerosol sprays, and good breeze will help, but early mornings and late evenings are when they are the fiercest. When camping. I spray the screen on the tent with an insect spray right after I put it up. I repeat the spraying before I go in for the night, which is when they are out. As you can tell I don't like these little rascals. When I am sitting in a blind and they start biting, I take a squeeze bottle of insecticide that I carry in my back pack and squeeze a small amount around the brim of my hat. I also have a small bag (that I used to use as camouflage when turkey hunting) that I slip over my head and tuck down into my shirt. The mesh is very fine (like a piece of sheer curtain material) so it keeps them from penetrating. I even put some of the repellant on that material. Some people put the repellant right on their skin, but personally that makes me awfully uncomfortable for the rest of the day.

In the early fifties, (before development) Marco Island Beach was a favorite spot for fishing and picnicking for my family and friends. You could drive up and down the beach; and with finger mullet being plentiful; we could always catch a good mess of fish.

My buddy George and I had decided to go over for a weekend of fishing. It was a last minute decision so we grabbed my cast net and gear and away we went. It was late to start across the Tamiami trail. Our normal routine was to leave before daylight and catch the early morning fishing. This time we decided to fish late in the evening, cook on the beach and if we wanted we could catch a nap in the car.

Everything worked out until just before sunset when the sand flies started in. We had no escape from them, other than getting in George's old straight eight Pontiac and roll up the windows. They were fierce! They were crawling in my ears, in my eyebrows and anywhere there was bare skin. I know it was the most miserable night that I have ever spent. It was a hot night. Both of us were wrapped up in one of those army surplus wool blankets and both of us were too stubborn to give up and go home. Did I mention it was also the longest night I have ever spent? The flies didn't quit all night! Finally as the sun started breaking, we looked at the glass on the windows and windshield and we couldn't believe what we saw. The moisture that collects on the inside of the glass when you are trying to romance your honey or spend the night as we two fools had done, was completely black. There had been so many on the inside of the car that they had drowned in the moisture and stuck there. They impaired our vision looking out of the glass. We packed it in and went home.

They are not as bad as they used to be, I guess from the encroachment of civilization. They are found the thickest around the shoreline, but occasionally I have found them inland in spots. Smudge pots or punk candles just don't seem to work as well with them as they do with mosquitoes.

I recently met a lady that was raised on old Marco Island and she told me they painted their screens with repellant every evening in order to survive.

(c) Mosquitoes

Florida, especially south Florida, has always been noted for their mosquito population. When, I was young, in the 1930, 40, 50's mosquitoes were thick. Anywhere around salt water, in those years, was murder at night, or at sunrise, or sunset. Literally hundreds of mosquitoes would light on your arms, and not only after dark. If you waded through a grass patch you stirred them up, as I remember doing near Jewfish Creek; you were going to be attacked even in the daytime. I learned to live with them and we kids developed ways to protect ourselves from them. We always camped on the breezy side of the islands and away from the underbrush. Smothering a fire with green leaves, causing more smoke, and sleeping downwind helped a lot. The government (state and county) has developed vigorous programs to eliminate the habitat that allows huge populations of mosquitoes and sand flies to multiply.

At one time the limit on lobster was counted, so many per boat and not by the person. My buddy Bruce and I loved to bully net them in shallow water, so we would both take a boat and catch enough for the limit. We would anchor the bigger boat with that limit aboard and then take the other boat and catch the limit for that boat. My young son begged me once to go along and he said he would stay out of the way. I relented and told him he could stay with the anchored boat and fish for snapper while we tried to fill our limit for the second boat. He jumped at the idea. We left him with plenty of candy, a radio, a can of mosquito spray and we anchored the boat well away from the shore, so the mosquitoes would not be so bad. We weren't that far away and could plainly see the running light on the boat he was in. It was a perfect night for bully netting. The water was still, and it was crystal clear. We netted several crawfish but they all but one measured under the 3 inches required by law, so with great reluctance, we released them back into the water. We ignored the mosquitoes that were following us because we were enjoying the adventure. We started just north of Jewfish creek and we were working the shoreline on the eastern side of Card Sound going north toward Steam Boat Creek. It must have taken us several hours to pole the entire shore line. We were about ready give up and crank the little three horse Eska motor and go back to where my son was fishing. We hadn't seen any lobster at all for quite a while and daylight would be breaking soon.

All of a sudden these bright lights came on as a huge engine roared to life, and big boat erupted out of the mouth of Steam Boat Creek. It headed right at us and we were only fifty yards away from them.

Scared the do do out of Bruce and I!

The boat ran aground throwing three men overboard and they landed just a few feet from where Bruce and I were polling our 11 foot boat. The backwash almost turned us over. What was going on was, the boat was the marine patrol and their plan was to charge up on us and catch us with illegal lobsters.

Two men were planning to jump into the water with full diving gear on so, in case we threw illegal lobster overboard, they could retrieve the evidence. They had misjudged the depth and promptly stuck their boat in the mud, for the water was only about 12 inches deep. The big cigarette type boat had run aground throwing the two divers overboard, as well as a fully clothed officer that hadn't planned on swimming that night.

At first I thought, "*That was a close call. We almost got run over by those fools.*"

Then I noticed the print on the side of their boat and it dawned on me what had happened. I started laughing and it pissed off the guy that was in charge.

He barked, "What's so damn funny?"

I answered, " I can just picture you guys laying up in the mouth of that creek, watching us for hours as we polled along the shore line, "*Thinking we are going to nail these guys with a boat load of illegal lobster, while the mosquitoes were eating you alive.*

"Search our ice box and you will find two cokes, two peanut butter sandwiches and one legal lobster by 1/4 inch."

By this time Bruce was laughing and it was contagious as several of the men on the boat started chuckling. Before they left we were all joking about it and Bruce and I even got out and helped push them out of the mud.

When we finally returned to my son and the other boat, we found him a raving maniac. To this day he tells me that was the worst time he ever spent in his life. The mosquitoes couldn't have been any worse than they were biting us, but all he had to think about was the mosquitoes.

The Florida Keys today are nothing like they were when I was young. If you want to experience how it used to be, take a trip down to Flamingo and try to stay out at night. They are so noted for mosquitoes that in the gift shop they sell a T-shirt that has a big mosquito drawn on it and underneath it says the "Flamingo National Bird."

When I first moved to the mountains I didn't see any mosquitoes at all; but gradually I am seeing more and more. I can still camp out, uncovered, and there are not enough to keep me from sleeping. The locals complain though and blame it on the "Floridiots" as they call us. They could be right, for I brought a lot of gear with me; and who knows I could have brought some larvae in and old tire or something.

When I first moved to the mountains there wasn't any turkey season; they were still trying to repopulate the area. The deer were scarce because they had all been killed off for food. Although there is a lot of forest service land and plenty of feed, the old habits of killing deer and turkey any time of the year were hard to break. Only recently have they allowed doe days.

I decided to join a hunting group that was in Screven County, Georgia, for two reasons. (1) They had plenty of deer and (2) they were allowed to hunt with dogs. After I had hunted there several years the state decided the turkey population was large enough open up a spring gobbler season, so I went down. I soon discovered that anywhere around the Savanna River (in the spring) they also had a humongous mosquito population; and when the river was just right they would almost carry you away. The actual mosquito there is much larger than the small ones I had been used to around south Florida. When they were out, they were fierce, day and night. We had to protect ourselves (like a bee keeper) when we were outside the tent.

There are all kinds of miracle products on the market that are supposed to do wonders to protect you, but I only find most of them mildly protective. Smudge pots and smoke rings are somewhat effective around a campsite; and things that work for you may not work for others. God put them on this earth for a reason and when He thinks they have served whatever purpose they are here for, He will allow man to figure out a way to eliminate them.

Insects That Can Hurt You

I include in this group bees, wasps, hornets, yellow jackets, ants, scorpions and even some caterpillars. I need to briefly tell about the different kind of insects that you may find in your hunting excursion. There are not any more dangerous in the woods than they are around your home. Unlike the other stinging insects that I have talked about, these guys hurt and can be dangerous to some people.

(d) Bees

Honey bees sting and inject their poison and leave their stinger in your skin. You need to remove it as soon as possible, because even though it is pulled out of the body of the bee, it is still pumping away. Most of the other type-of-bees live on to sting again. Bees have short compact bodies that are hairy and they even have hairy legs. They're not very aggressive, unless you are near their hive. They feed on nectar and pollen and serve a great benefit to nature, by carrying the pollen around from plant to plant, allowing the plants to reproduce. This is called "Pollinating."

(e) Wasps, Hornets, & Yellow Jackets

These critters have more streamlined bodies with a very narrow waist (or separation between their thorax and abdomen) and are not hairy. They are capable of stinging you, removing the stinger, and stinging you again. Your desire is to kill them, but the best thing to do is to **get away** from them. If they are attacking you; more than likely you disturbed their nests in some way. Once they are aroused, they don't give up easy.

These types feed as predators on other insects; they are scavengers and some even like sweets. The worst bite I ever had was from a yellow jacket who had climbed into a cold drink can I was drinking from. It bit me on the tongue and not only was it painful, but my tongue swelled so much I could not talk for several hours.

Some solitary wasps (dirt daubers as example) build nests from clay and deposit an egg along with an insect or spider that the larvae use for food as it grows. The community type of wasp build a paper nest, some open and some closed. Most will be under some type of cover from the rain. On the open kind, the whole nest is open on one end; the individual cells will be formed together and the exit end will be facing down, to ward off the water. In the case of the yellow jacket the nest is most always underground. The more familiar is the hornet nest one will find hanging in brush or trees. It will generally be in a football shape with a small opening at the bottom.

(f) Ants

There are many species but the one that can really get your attention is what is commonly called the Fire ant. There were not many colonies around south Florida when I moved to North Georgia in 1978. They had not found the mountains yet, so I was oblivious to the danger.

Fire ants, not native, were accidentally introduced in 1918 in the city of Mobile, Alabama; and they have been spreading steadily from state to state. When I joined a hunting camp in South Georgia, I got my initiation. It was during turkey season and I went before daylight to a spot I thought might be a good turkey roost. I picked a stump that was just the right size to be comfortable, while I waited for daylight and a possible turkey gobble. What I didn't notice was a mound of sand that was built up against the stump. I had been settled in about ten minutes when I started to sting all over. It was like they all got on me and counted, "one, two, three, bite."

I tried to brush them off at first, but I wasn't getting anywhere. I ran to where my pickup was parked, turned on the headlights, and stripped to get them off. Luckily I have never been allergic to any bite (but a caterpillar) but I sure check good now, before I sit down.

These ants build a large soil nest above ground and in open pastures. It is easy to see how they spread by the line of nests.

In the Everglades the biggest danger was from wasps. Several times while walking in at night, I would brush one of their paper nest and the wasps would fall on my clothing or down the back of my neck. I have found that if you want to eliminate a nest, you need to do it at night, for they all gang up on the nest and very seldom will fly. That is a good time to use that wasp spray.

The remedy I use for the Yellow Jackets is to locate the entrance in daylight, return after dark, and pour about two cups of gasoline into the entrance hole. **Be careful,** gasoline is dangerous!

(g) Scorpions

There are around 1700 different types of scorpions in the world and only 25 of these are deadly to humans. I have seen small ones in North Georgia, but have never been stung by one since I moved to the mountains. In Florida they come in a small size, and I have seen them several inches long. I have been bitten twice. The first time I put on a pair of lace up, knee high boots and went dove hunting several miles away. When I got out of the car and started walking, one started stinging me on my big toe. The sting affected me about like a wasp. The other time I had one in my suit pocket. It stung my hand when I went to retrieve an object from my pocket. My advice is to check bedding or clothing before donning them, and especially dump your boots or shoes out before you put them on.

Saddleback Caterpillar

(h) Caterpillars

You may think it odd that I include a caterpillar to this list, but there is one that grows in Florida that gave me one of the most painful experiences of my life. It's called a "Saddle Back Caterpillar." They are not very big, an inch or so long, with double horns on each end and a spot in the middle of its back that resembles a target. All you have to do is brush up against one with exposed skin and you will suffer.

I was about twelve and I climbed up in a tree in front of my house. I was barefooted and in shorts, I didn't see it until it stung, but I had brushed up against it on my thigh. The pain was immediate and it intensified as I ran for home. I remember it was in the morning when it happened and the pain increased all day. The lymph node in my groin swelled up to the size of my testicle and I could hardly walk. I didn't sleep at all that night and it was the next day before the pain and swelling started to subside. I don't know if there is any antidote, for I can only remember a few times in my childhood when I was taken to a doctor.

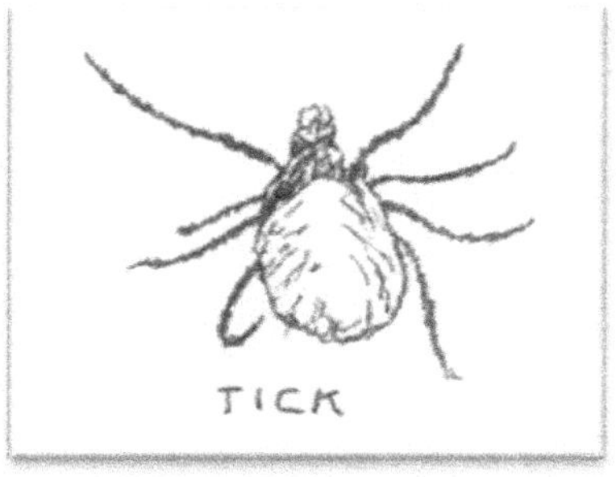

(i) Ticks

This is a critter that doesn't bother me that bad. I guess I have been lucky. In Florida they were a problem to keep off our animals, and sometimes they would come in the house. I don't ever remember actually having one bite me in the woods while I was in Florida. Here in the mountains I will occasionally have one bite me, and it will leave a sore place for several days. I do find them crawling on me several times a week in the spring and summer. A lot of the people, I hunt with, that live in the city, always, before they start in the woods spray their pants legs and sleeves with a repellant to keep them off. They don't bother my dogs because I put tick collars on their necks to provide protection. If they get bad on me I guess I could try to wear a collar around my neck.

I shouldn't be factious for **Lyme disease is a terrible illness** and protecting yourself from ticks is a good idea. A friend of mine was bitten in 1987 and she has gone through hell ever since. First of all it is a very hard disease to diagnose, for it has symptoms that mimic many infections. The symptoms range from a mild rash right up the chain to heart problems. One symptom that can develop is what is called "Bulls eye rash." It will appear around the bite several days after being bitten and expand with time. It looks like a bulls-eye target. Not everyone that gets Lyme disease will get this rash, but if it appears, it is an early warning that you may have Lymes disease and you **need to get medical help**.

There are many sub species of ticks but the main carriers of Lyme disease in the United States are commonly called the western black legged tick found in California and the eastern Black Legged Tick found along the eastern part of the United States. They are also known as deer ticks because they are found on deer, but can be found on many birds and mammals. The common dog tick is not a carrier of Lyme disease, although it can carry Rocky Mountain spotted fever.

Trying to find something to compare the size of a common dog tick, I would say legs and body would be near the size of the circumference of a pencil eraser when looking at it from the top. Keep in mind the Deer Tick is less than half that size, and not much larger than a pin head.

The safest way to remove a tick once he has attached itself to your body is to grasp it with small tip tweezers as close to where it has attached to your skin as possible. Don't squeeze its body, but tug on it trying to get it to release on its own. After removal you will more than likely have a small red spot that can itch and be sore for several days, but it is not an indication you have Lyme disease. If you are a person that frequents the outdoors and starts to have problems with swollen joints, muscle soreness, headaches etc. and your doctor is having trouble pinning down your problem; it might be good ideas to have your doctor give you a blood test looking specifically for Lyme disease. If you have been bitten by a suspicious deer tick and you are worried that you may have contacted Lyme disease, be sure and save the tick you removed. You can place the tick, or ticks in a plastic bag or small glass jar, label it and keep it in your freezer. If you come down with symptoms the tick remains will make it easier for the experts to make an accurate diagnosis.

(j) Deer Flies and Horse Flies

These kinds of biting flies can be really aggravating and they hurt when they bite. The only time that they really bothered me was a couple of times that I found a reason to be out in the glades in the summer. Thank goodness that they don't usually come in huge droves like mosquitoes or sand fly's. When they bite me they actually hurt, but they don't produce the sting like the mosquito. Everybody reacts to insects differently, but these nasty things don't even leave a welt on me. Don't get me wrong, when they start in on me I find another way to entertain myself rather quickly. They seem to like heat, or at least they will follow a heat source like a guided missile. In order to keep our hunting lease north of Alligator Alley, we were required to install a barbed wire fence all the way round the 5600 acres; and all the members worked through the summer to accomplish it. I noticed that when we were riding on our buggies, the horse flies would be swarming along with us, and they would really attack us. As soon as we would arrive at our work site for the day and kill off the few that followed us there, only an occasional fly would bother us. I became aware that they were using the heat exhaust of the buggies to home in on us. The other time that they were bad on us was when we were building our cabin inside the area known as the Loop Road. It runs south from highway

41 at the Munroe Station, out through the Glades and returns back to highway 41 some 35 miles later. The road was made by using oolite rock, (coral rock) dug from several quarries along its length).

I was surprised to learn recently that the Loop Road was actually built before the Tamiami trail and went from west to east. In some places they dug trenches and used the rock from them to form the road. At one time the road was a haven for rednecks, where men and women could act out their fantasies. All kinds of shacks and dwellings were spaced along its 35 mile length.

About half way through the Loop is Pine Crest, a small beer joint, or store that sold beer, that was the focal point on the weekends. I guess the most famous resident of the Loop road was Al Capone. The ruins of his house still stand. Everyone surmises why he was there and built a home and hunting camp during prohibition. It really is out of the beaten path and would have taken only two guards to watch the road.

The most famous fellah I ran into one weekend was (Ervin T. Rouse) that wrote, "The Orange Blossom Special." If you happened to stop there and there were a few picking, you could hear some pretty good music. I was really surprised once when I was looking for Mr. Volker and found him there playing a harmonica in an impromptu group that had Mr. Rouse on the fiddle.

George Volker, the man that I attribute teaching me to love the outdoors, moved away from Miami and bought land alongside one of those abandoned quarries, lived out the rest of his life and made his living hunting frogs, making frog gigs and repairing air boats. Irene, his wife (was well known for being feisty) and she had her own airboat. The last time I visited them I was waiting at the dock for one of them to come in from the Glades and I see Irene coming across the Glades. She was turning 360's with the boat just for the fun of it. She was probably sixty five years old at the time. It was an unusual community and to fit in and be accepted, you had to hate the city and not complain about the strange things your neighbors were doing.

(k) National Park Service

I write about the Park service in this part of this book because I have about the same regard for them as I have for snakes and mosquitoes.

Just like most things in my life, the US government, in the form of the National Park Service, came along and screwed everything up. Because the land, where, "Fools Paradise" was, (close to the Everglades National Park), they, (with the help of congress) took over supervision of the land and **proceeded to ruin everything**. This was land that had been used by the public since the beginning of Florida and if anything, (now that the National Park service husbands the area), has done nothing but deteriorate from what it used to be when I was a young man. The National Park service held hearings where they promised everything would remain the same and then, after they were granted control of the land, they broke every promise that was made at those hearings.

All the ones they could bluff, they bought their land and burnt their houses. All the hundreds of hunting camps that were scattered throughout that area (and some had been there for 50 years) they burnt. They stopped all the buggy traffic and only allowed walk in traffic, and then they treated everyone like they were drug dealers, conducting strip searches, etc. They stopped all the dog hunting and that was a way of life for a whole lot of people. To me the worst thing they did was stop the burning of the underbrush. The game wardens were good shepherds of the land and realized the importance of burning off the underbrush. Once a year in the fall, if the water was high, they would ask us to start fires in the late evening to burn off the prairies.

After I had been away from Florida for 15 years living in the mountains, I developed trouble with my heart. I decided that before I got too bad to travel that foot trail, I would go one more time and spend a week at the old campsite. I went during turkey season in the spring, because the Everglades are the most beautiful during that time of the year. I was by myself and I didn't tell anyone, other than my wife, where I was going. I really wanted the quiet time by myself. The news about my heart had depressed me and it was hard for me to accept because I had been so active in my life so far. I enjoyed loading my pack and digging out my old Seva stove and pot kit. I was well trained at carrying the bare essentials to have a successful trip for several days. Being scoutmaster of troop 210 for years and my experience of walking in and out the trails to "Fool's Paradise" gave me confidence on what to take. I knew that someone had stolen the pump and the building was burnt down but the Zoysa grass should still be on the ground. I had my military poncho to substitute for the building and to ward off mosquitoes I had this neat contraption that unfolded like an umbrella, made out of netting that covered the whole front of your sleeping bag. I was planning to stay for a week, but water was going to be my problem. With a gallon of water, sleeping bag, rubber mat, stove kit, food, clothing, and all the as sundry items I needed for hunting and staying a week, my pack weighed in at 40 pounds. When walking I had to add on the weight of my gun and another quart of water in my Boda bag.

My wife said, "You're crazy, you know you are 66 years old."

I got to the trail about 10 PM and walked in to the first dry island. I saw my nephews boat turned upside down, just off the foot trail. I decided to use it as a bed off the ground, to spend the night there and go the rest of the way in the morning. The first part of the trail was just the same as I had remembered from some 15 years before. The next morning when I walked through the branch off Robert's Strand, I knew I was within 100 yards of the old camp; I stood in shock. The little myrtle bushes that used to be only knee high, were now huge bushes; they obstructed the view of everything. I knew right away that this was the result of the new policy of no burning of the park service. I would not fully realize until later that day what a changes had occurred.

I spent the rest of the day and struggled my way across land (that I had memorized) where I could walk in the dark. It was now like a strange planet. Gone were the small palmetto patches and open fields. The area had been replaced by gigantic bushes and it was completely foreign looking. The next day I located the open prairie I was looking for. I was just in time to hear the gobblers sounding off in the area. It was a still, spring morning and I was full of hope and anticipation to play the game that I had played for years before. I would hit my gobbler call or my crow call and then listen as the gobblers responded. From where I was standing I had been able to hear gobblers responding in all directions. The trick was to determine which one gave me the best opportunity to move in on. I know that you could hear them gobble for at least 2 miles away.

I hit my call at just the right time and craned my ears to listen. Nothing! Not the first sound! I called and called and called. No answer anywhere. I was starting to get worried. I spent the rest of the morning going from place to place where the turkey normally feed. I found no tracks. This area is easy to find tracks for it has a lot of silky mud that keeps the tracks fresh looking for weeks. I went back to where I had camped and ate a good meal, and then I did some more exploring in a different direction. It was really dry and I went up in a gator pond that was just behind our old camp. There was still plenty of water and mud around the edge. Plenty of water bird tracks and plenty of small animal tracks, but no turkey sign at all. I went back out to the prairie that evening to listen for the late evening territorial gobbles that we were always able to hear and nothing again.

I spent the next day in much the same way, except I went a greater distance from the camp. I covered the area as thoroughly as a person could and I came to the eventual conclusion that all the birds were gone. I decided that I would try again, once more in the morning and if I didn't hear or see any sign in the morning, I would pack up and try something else.

I heard nothing that morning, so I repacked my pack and headed back to the Tamiami Trail and to my pickup. It was warm that afternoon. By the time I got to the truck I was ready for an iced down Pepsi and a fresh ham sandwich. I decided to go to Monroe Station and have supper there and then go a short ways down the Loop Road and camp out. Then I planned to get up at daylight and do like I had been doing in the mountains. Drive a little way, give a call, listen, and if I heard nothing, I would drive a little farther and call again.

I had finished my sandwich and drink, had packed my gun and gear away, kicked both doors open and lay down in the seat to catch a nap in the shade of the tree my truck was in. I hadn't been there long when I hear a vehicle pass me and apply it's brakes. I could tell it turned around and came back to where I was trying to nap. This guy gets out of an unmarked car and approaches my pickup.

He said, "What are you doing."

I had set up by now and I replied, "Trying to take a nap. Why do you want to know?"

He said, "I'm going to have to see your hunting license."

I said, "You don't look like any game warden I ever saw."

He spouted off in anger, "Oh you're going to be a smart ass I see."

I replied, "You're the one that comes up here in an unmarked car with no uniform on, no visible gun or badge, and wants to see my hunting license when I'm not hunting, I'm just sleeping in my truck. I think you are the one who should show some ID."

He was red faced by now and he wheeled and went to his car. He returned in a few minutes with his ID and now had a pistol on his side.

He flashed his ID in my face and started to put it back in his pocket and I said, “Wait a minute that didn’t say Fish and Wildlife.”

He said, “No I am an officer with the National Park Service and I have the same arrest powers as the game and fish officers, in fact even more.

Now again, let me see your license.”

I reached in my pocket, pulled out my wallet and laid it on the hood of my truck as I slowly took out the many cards and papers that I had managed to accumulate. I knew exactly where the item I was looking for was, but he was mad and I was pushing it. I finally came up with my Georgia Honorary Hunting and Fish license and handed it to him.

He said, “This isn’t a Florida hunting license.”

I answered, “No kidding.”

He made me turn around and cuffed me rather roughly; then he made me sit down next to the highway. He proceeded to rip everything out of my truck while he searched every nook and cranny. Finding nothing he took my shotgun and put it in the trunk of his car and me in the back seat.

Every time I opened my mouth to say something after that he told me to shut my mouth or he would shut it for me. What he didn't know (and I was fully aware of) was that Georgia honorary license holders could hunt in Florida and the Florida honorary holders could do the same in Georgia. I knew that the danger here was that this jerk might get cute and try to manhandle me, so I should cool it with my smart answers. I had double checked both with Florida and Georgia before I left, so I knew I was in the right. He took me to the ranger station (near where that airplane used to hang out over the road) and pulled me into the building.

A uniformed officer looked up from his desk and asked, "What have you got here?"

He started telling him what a bad character I was and how I had tried to pull one over on him by showing him a permit from Georgia.

The uniformed officer was obviously his boss. He listened patiently and calmly told the officer to un-cuff me.

When he looked at his superior with a quizzical look; the uniformed man said, "Did you hear what I said? Do it now! I think you had better shut your mouth."

He still wanted to argue, but by then the uniformed officer had searched through some papers. He handed one to the one in the street clothes. “If you had read this when it came in you wouldn’t have gotten us in another mess like this. This man has every right to hunt there and if you weren’t always trying to act like a hot shot, you wouldn’t make dumb mistakes like this. What the hell are you doing asking for someone’s license in your personal car on your day off anyway? I wouldn’t have shown you anything dressed like that and in your personal car.”

He paused for a minute and again spoke “Get your sorry ass in your car and get out of here before I really get mad.” I was taking this all in, but I spoke up and asked if I could have my shotgun back first.

After he left the officer apologized and explained that he was trying to get him transferred. He had tried to get him fired, but once you were hired and served out your probation, it was almost impossible. I told him that I planned to eat supper at Monroe Station and he glanced at his watch and said I don’t think you have enough time to go back to your truck and get there before they close. Instead he closed a little early and took me to the Munroe Station; where we both had supper before he took me to my truck. He even paid for my dinner. I enjoyed my evening with him and we got a rather long conversation about how the Park Service had changed the flora and fauna of the Loop. He said he knew that stopping the burning had a big effect on the density of the underbrush, but he didn’t believe that it had any effect on the turkey population. He argued that the increase in the swine population was what was destroying the turkeys. I told him I thought he was wrong, because I had been hunting inside the Loop for fifty years. I had scouted a huge area over the past couple of days and I had seen a whole lot less hog sign that I used to see. Twenty years ago and there were plenty of turkey. I told him if they ever got a real dry spell and a fire happened to start, all that extra kindling would kill a lot of trees instead of just scorching the bark like it used to do. I think he realized they were making some bad errors but he explained that Washington set the policy and he could only follow it.

Their authority was just to assist the game commission, but they have taken over like gang busters. My nephew and his 12 year old son were awakened in the middle of the night by battle uniformed NPS agents and strip searched in their camp area. They never were given a reason why or what they were looking for. They had landed a helicopter close by to make the raid with M16's, with the safeties in the **off** position. **This kind of activity was un-called for and an infringement on constitutional rights**.

(Note) I have learned that the NPS now owns the Munroe Station and is contemplating leveling it. That would be a shame. It was made into a historical landmark. Why not restore it?

Munroe Station (1930's)

The Way I Remember It (1970?)

Munroe Station (2014)

Eastern Diamond Back Rattler

(l) Snakes

Moccasin (cotton mouth)

(1) Childhood Experience with a Moccasin

Living in South Florida all young boys that liked the outdoors had their experiences with snakes at an early age. My dad showed me the difference between poisonous and nonpoisonous snakes. He told me you can catch and have nonpoisonous snakes, but he forbade me messing with poisonous specimens.

When I was twelve I had a paper route and on this route I had a customer that had a collection of hundreds of snakes. I don't know what he did with them; I guess he sold them. He asked me one day if I would be interested in catching mice and frogs for him.

He paid me fifteen cents for a mouse and a nickel apiece for each tree frog. He instructed me on how to build a trap out of a tin can and a regular mouse trap, using a small piece of hardware cloth to close off the can when the extended trigger was sprung. He took me on a walk through the woods and showed me where I could find little tree frogs. He also paid me fifteen cents a foot for snakes and fifty cents a foot for poisonous ones.

I furnished him with so many mice and frogs he had to put a hold on my hunting. Eventually he would stop me on my paper route and tell me when he needed more. The snakes though, he would always take what I brought him. As I got older I became more daring; despite what my dad had told me, and started catching small moccasins. I caught a small one, (about 15 inches) and had it gripped in my right hand. For some reason I tried to shift it to my left hand and one of his fangs pricked the forefinger of my hand. It started burning like fire and I grabbed it, scared to death. I knew my dad was going to kill me.

I went to the Indian village that was on the path back to my house and told my friend Billy what had happened. He brought his dad over and he told me he knew how to take care of it. He went over to some weeds and came up with a stink bug. He squeezed the bug until it produced a drop of fluid that fell on the place the fang had stuck me. He told me my biggest problem now was how to get my ring off my finger.

During World War II, when my dad was in Trinidad, he made me a monel steel ring. By now my hand had swollen to where I couldn't get it off. My wrist and hand had swollen until the time Billy's father put the bug juice on it. By the time I got home the swelling had stopped creeping up my arm.

My dad took one look and told me to get in the car. He took me to a machine shop where they put my finger in a vice under a drill press and proceeded to drill holes into the ring to get it off my finger. It took forever to get it off and all the while my finger was purple. When it finally came off the finger actually hurt more.

On the way home my dad asked. "Why did your hand swell up like that?"

I lied and said, "I got stuck by a catfish."

I never told him what really happened, but I never messed with poisonous snakes after that.

(2) Turner River Rattler

I consider the Eastern Diamond Back Rattler the most dangerous thing in the woods. If they bite you, you are in big trouble. I am deathly afraid of them and if I see one in the wild, I might as well pack it in for the day and go home. I cannot hunt any more. All my senses are enhanced to looking for rattlers, and I can't pay attention to hunting. I might as well go home.

I can't even bring myself to eat rattlesnake meat. When I try, I can smell the musky smell that they omit. I know that it's my imagination, but I just can't help it. I have always been cautious of where I walk. I usually clear a path with my eyes; walk to that spot, stop, and then look around for game. It's when you are not cautious; then it becomes dangerous.

I had been hunting near Turner River in the afternoon, when I met back up with my partner for the day. We had a mile to walk to return to our camp, and were walking across an open field. The grass was like it had just been mowed. We had our guns slung backwards over our shoulders, walking casually, jawing over the mornings happening; when I spotted a rattler coiled and sleeping in the sun. I was mid-stride; my foot was already coming down to where I was going to step right in the middle of that coil. I don't think my foot was over four inches from making contact. There was no way I could avoid stepping on him; I was off balance and committed to the step. Somehow I managed to jerk my foot back up with such force that I popped myself in the chin with my knee, so hard I chipped one of my front teeth. Lurching sideways, I knocked the rifle off my friends shoulder. He hadn't seen the snake yet.

(3) Ding and Rattlesnake

When we decided to build a permanent solid wood cabin on our wood floor, we asked George Foot (a neighbor of mine), if he wanted to join in with us. He had a couple of young boys he wanted to teach about the woods, and he eagerly accepted our offer. That gave us quite a good work crew to help drag all of the materials into the camp. Mostly we made long day trips out of our building excursions, because of a lack of sleeping supplies. Everyone knew what we wanted to do. I had drawn plans and numbered the pieces so any of us could continue from where we had stopped. One thing I hadn't planned on was the hardness of the wood. I salvaged the 2x4's out of an old house in Coconut Grove and they were made out of Dade County Pine. Fifty year old Dade County Pine is as hard and dense as steel. We couldn't drive a nail, not even a concrete nail, without bending it. We ended up bringing one of those old twist drills,(the ones that look like an old egg beater), and pre drilling all the holes. It worked; it just took a long time to assemble.

Our goal was to have it ready for hunting season and we barely made it. Ding (my nephew was about twelve), George Foot and his oldest boy, and Art Pryor were out that weekend to christen it. George wanted to have his boy with him as he wasn't used to the woods, Art went his own way and I took Ding with me. I placed him in a tree stand that was right along the edge of

Roberts Strand. He knew the rules I had laid out for him and had always done as I told him.

I went on to my spot and had just gotten settled when I hear him shoot. It really ticked me off, because I knew he only had one shell. When he started hollering for me, I knew something was wrong.

I thought, *"There goes our first day, there won't be any game around the rest of the day."*

I rushed over as fast as I could, and when I got close I could see he was still in the tree.

"That's odd I thought, why would he be in the tree with no shells?

When Ding saw me he said "Don't come any closer, Uncle Sonny, there's a huge rattlesnake under the tree.

I had been wading in a straight line toward him, but now I picked my path very carefully. Sure enough when I got to the base of the tree, there it was. I decapitated him with my 25/35 and drug him out in the open. We took him back to the camp where we had a ruler and scales. He was 7'4" and 27 pounds. George came in later and you could see it visibly affected him. He came over to my house sometime during the following week and told me to give his share of the camp to someone else. He had no idea there were snakes that large out there and he would never go back.

(4) 1947 Hurricane

Nineteen forty seven was the year for snakes in south Florida. We had a hurricane that dumped so much water that things stayed flooded for several months.

Everything was stranded on the roads, which were barely above water. Snakes rabbits, possums, wildcats, skunks, coons, all the animals were sharing the dry spots. I know my dad killed a lot of snakes that time and I am sure others did the same. My friends and I were on one of these roads one night catching leopard frogs. My mom had promised to fry them up the next night and invite all the neighbors. Some kind of a back yard cookout was almost a weekly thing at our house. The neighbors all knew to save their bacon grease for my dad's big fryer. Anyway, we were finding plenty of frogs and that the road was also overrun with snakes. How we managed to keep from being bit I don't know. We didn't see any rattlers but moccasins were everywhere.

We saw one snake that night that is still a mystery to me. It was a smoky gray in color, with a nonpoisonous shaped head and it was huge. It had the body shape and look of an indigo snake, only it was a light gray color. The length was around twelve feet or longer and its mid-body was as big as a football. We didn't hurt it as we watched it slither away through the underbrush. I have seen all kinds of exotic snakes from around the world, but I have never seen anything like that in any book or zoo. I know that the Everglades are overrun now with huge exotic snakes that have been turned loose because they got too big for the owners.

Billy's father the, Seminole, told me that he had heard tales about a huge snake that was in the Everglades. Who knows, maybe we saw the last of a species.

(5) Bill Haas and Tom

Tom Knowles, a friend of mine, was a Dade County Sheriff deputy and we were into quail hunting. I had just bought a pretty little setter and we were taking her to a place to see if she would work any birds. We were south of Miami in what they call the Redlands. Tom had seen a couple of coveys in that area when he was patrolling. We put the dog out and she hadn't gone very far when she started working birds. Tom took his army 45 and started following her. He wanted to see if she was gun shy and he was going to shoot in the air if she flushed a covey. He hadn't gone very far when he hollered and jumped in the air and started shooting. By then I knew what he was shooting at, for I could hear the rattler singing.

He stopped shooting and called to me and said, “Come here, I have shot all but one of my shells and haven’t hit this thing yet. It scared me so bad I can’t aim the gun.”

He told me where to walk and I came up to him. The snake was lying under a log that was about six inches off the ground. What Tom had done was step over the log right on the snakes back near its tail. The snake reacted by rolling back towards Tom to bite him. The only thing that kept Tom from being bitten was the log would not let him strike far enough. When I got there the snake was coiled and mad.

Tom handed me the 45 and said, “Make a good shot. It’s my last shell.”

I rested my hands on a branch (that was protruding away from the log), took careful aim and squeezed of that last round. I hit him dead between the eyes.

Usually when you kill a snake they will move for a long time afterward, but this one did not move again. I don’t remember how many rattles he had but we did measure him and he was 7’-4” long.

Tom and I drug him out to the road (after we calmed down) and Tom said, “Let’s take him over and show him to Bill.”

Tom was good friends with Bill Haas, the world

famous snake handler and his Serpentarium exhibit was on the way home. Although I had never met the senior Mr. Haas, I had gone to school with his son Bill Jr. He told Tom that the snake was really a big one and that large ones were becoming scarce.

During our discussion about the snake Tom asked Mr. Haas, "Bill if I got bitten by that snake what would you suggest that I do?"

Mr. Haas stooped down where he could feel the snake and he turned it over and opened its mouth.

He looked at Tom and asked, "Tom do you smoke?"

Tom answered, "Matter of fact I do."

Bill spoke again and said, "Well he hasn't eaten for quite a while and his poison sacks look like they are full, so I would suggest that you sit down and smoke a cigarette, because its gona be your last."

The hair stood up on the back of my neck and I never forgot that statement.

(6) Clewiston Doctor and Snakes

Later on in my life I was a member of a hunting camp that was north of Alligator Alley and quite remote from civilization. One of our members was a doctor from Clewiston, Florida. Clewiston is right in the heart of the sugar cane farms in south central Florida. The doctor at one of our yearly meetings brought up the subject of snakes and made a suggestion.

He asked, "How many of you have snake bite kits?"

Several of us raised our hands, but not all.

He then said, "Get them and put them on the table."

We were at the camp, so we all went to our cabin or buggy and returned with an assortment of kits.

He looked at them and shook his head from side to side; then he started to speak again, "All of you know that I practice in Clewiston and I probably treat more snakebite cases than anybody in the country. The cane cutters get careless. Rattlers and moccasins exist in the cane fields because of rabbit's, rats, and frogs that live there. I see that Sonny is the only one that has an antivenin kit."

He asked, "Where did you get yours?"

I told him, "I met Bill Hass and he advised me to have one, so I bought it."

"The suction cups and razor blades your snake kits contain should be outlawed and I'll tell you why. When a rattler or moccasin bites you one of the things that starts immediately is your flesh starts to deteriorate.

The smaller the person is, the more rapidly the poison spreads. Statically the part of the body that a rattler bites, even with proper care; 35 percent will lose that part of their body. The infection is terrible and it is horrible to even look at. These kits here with the suction cups don't help, they only make things worse. Most instruct you to put a tourniquet above the fang mark, cut over the fang marks with a razor blade and place the suction cup over them to draw the venom out. The only thing in that kit you can use is the suction cup if it makes you feel better. The only good it does is calm you down while you are trying to suck this poison out of the wound. It doesn't work. The cuts you make only increase the chance of a greater infection. The tourniquet confines the poison to one area and only makes it more likely that you will eventually lose that arm or leg where you are bitten. This kit that Sonny has is the same as I use in the hospital. This little bottle will give you more time to get to a hospital. It won't cure you, just give you more time to get to a place where they can administer more antivenin. What the antivenin does is dilute the venom and slow down the distribution of the poison as it circulates through the body. A small person that has been bitten will require many more vials of anti-venom to stabilize them, than a heavy set man. The snake actually injects its poison into its quarry to eventually kill it, and the venom starts the digestion process by breaking down the tissue.

'The anti-venom is in a dry form in this bottle and the fluid in the other bottle is sterile water. You don't have to mix the two until after someone has been bitten, so the shelf life is quite long. It has extensive instructions in the kit about giving yourself a test to see if you are allergic to the anti-venom. I always ask the cane workers if the snake that bit them made a noise, trying to determine if it was a rattler or a moccasin. If I can determine that the snake was a moccasin then I will give the test to see if they are allergic. If I am sure that it was a rattler, I don't bother with the test. Because in a hospital setting I can deal with the allergy easier than I can afford to delay treating the victim with anti-venom. A rattler's venom is much more dangerous than a moccasin.'

'Administering the test is not a bad idea because of what it forces you to do. Anybody that is bitten becomes deathly afraid and their heart rate increases tremendously. This is bad because it causes the poison to circulate faster than normal. **Remaining calm is very important**. Running for help, or laboring, will increase your heart rate. Sit down and read the instructions; this will have the effect of calming you down and that is a good thing."

After our instructions from the doc we all decided to purchase an anti-venom kit and keep them in the camp refrigerator. Thank God none of us were ever bitten.

(7) Rabbit and Snake

I was sitting against a tree one morning, on an open prairie, watching a strand of cypress and listening to see if any turkey had used it for a roost the previous night. There was a clump of palmettos to my left and fifty feet in front of me was another small low clump of palmettos. I saw a rabbit emerge from the clump on my left and head for the clump in front of me. There was obviously something wrong with the rabbit for he was staggering like he had been on a drunk. I sat there for another twenty minutes pondering what was wrong with that rabbit, when I saw a rather large rattler immerge from the same spot the rabbit had. It was following the same path the rabbit used to get to the other clump of palmettos.

Now I knew why that rabbit was staggering. The clump they entered was small and I could see from where I was that they were still in there. I waited for some time before I tried to find them. I wanted to make sure that snake had the rabbit halfway swallowed before I started pulling back those fronds. A snake with an animal half swallowed is a lot safer to approach than one that can bite you.

(8) Snake Bite Under Water

I worked in and around Hollywood, Florida on construction sites, where I became acquainted with two brothers that did soffit work. One of the brothers was a big man and the other was much smaller.

One day when I went to work, the bigger brother wasn't there, so I asked the smaller one, "Where is your brother?"

He answered, "He got snake bit this week end."

I asked, "Is he OK?"

This opened him up, and he started telling me what had happened to them. This was the time that they were building highway 84, better known as Alligator Alley, across the glades. The two brothers were avid fishermen and they found the fishing was excellent where the drag lines were working, some ten miles out on the alley. They would take a seine with them, catch a bucket full of minnows in some shallow water, and use them for bait. Then they were able to load up with specks when they went.

The brother said, "We hadn't been out there very long. We both took off our shoes, rolled our pants up, and were pulling the seine back and forth through the grass. We caught a bunch, when Bobby hollered ouch and grabbed at his foot."

“Something bit me” he said.

“Bobby and I waded back to the shore; and sure enough, there were two fang marks right next to his ankle. By now he was jumping around telling me it was stinging like hell. We threw our gear in the car and started hauling butt to town. About half way back there was a highway patrol car. He saw us coming and flashed his lights for us to stop. When he saw why we were in such a hurry, he told us to get in his car and he would take us to the hospital in Hollywood. He almost tore up that car getting us there. He was talking on his radio, calling ahead telling them what had happened. We arrived at the hospital shortly.

‘Well when we got there, they took us right in to the emergency room. They cut Bobby’s pants leg of, washed the mud off his leg, and started asking dumb questions about the snake. How much did it weigh? They gave me a bunch of papers to fill out and sign. They weren’t doing anything to help Bobby’s foot, and it was swelling something awful. He was really hurting and his foot was getting bigger and bigger. I had pulled up a chair and they had pulled curtains around us so no one could see in. I guess we had been there about an hour and Bobby started getting really ticked”

He kept asking me, “When are they going to do something?”

‘After a while a male nurse or doctor stuck his head in the room I guess to take Bobby’s temperature or something.

Bobby grabbed him by the front of his shirt and pulled his face right up to the docs face and said, “Somebody better start doing something pretty damn quick or I’m going to start kicking some ass. I ain’t got a thing to lose.”

‘It really scared the man because anybody could tell Bobby was serious.’

‘He got all apologetic and started to explain, “I thought someone told you, we don’t have any antivenin and we had to send for some. Bill Hass at the Serpentarium is bringing it personally by helicopter; and they should be here any time now.”

‘Mr. Hass looked at the wound and said it must have been a small one, because apparently it didn’t inject much venom. He said he thought Bobby would be OK in a couple of weeks.”

(9) Mounted Snake

Once going home from Crooked Pine camp I almost got bit by a good size rattler. The camp next to us had a house trailer beside our border fence, and sometime during the week, it caught fire and burnt to the ground. We stopped to look it over and to see if anything was left. I spotted an old scissor type jack lying in the rubble, reached down to pick it up. As I reached down, a snake drew back, poised to strike. I was concentrating on what I could find. I had not seen him and he was lying right in plain sight. His having to draw back before striking, gave me that split second to get my hand out of the way; he missed! I didn't have anything to kill him with, so I told my son to watch him, and I went back to the buggy. When I returned, the snake had gone back in a hole he was using for a home. The scary part about this was that the hole was under the two metal steps that had been the entrance to the trailer. The guys that had hunted out of that trailer had been stepping over that rattler for years, and they didn't have any idea he was there.

My wife, a biology teacher, had collected specimens for her class for years. She begged me for years to mount a rattlesnake for her classroom. I decided this would make her a good mount. I poured about a cup full of gasoline down the hole to drive him back to the surface. Within seconds he came out. I pinned him down with a good heavy stick and took an ice pick and stuck it through his brain to kill him. As I stuck him, he rolled his head up in the air, opened his mouth wide, and sprayed out his venom. It went all over the front of my son; and to this day he thinks I planned it so he would get sprayed.

A friend mounted the snake for me, in the shape of a raised coiled snake poised to strike. I could never get used to it. In the summer when school was out, she would bring it home, and put it on a small table that was at the end of the hall. Every time I came down that hall, as I would round the corner into the living room, I would react, or jump away. It was just my instincts. I let Winslow King borrow it for display in his gun shop, and he gave it back because his customers were also having bad reactions. It was something some people never can get used to.

(10) Live Snake

Here in the mountains my friend Winslow told me of an incident that happened between his brother, Thee and him. One of the favorite dishes of truly mountain families is a big pan of squirrels and gravy. Consequently a lot of time was spent hunting these small critters. One afternoon the two brothers found a cove where there was evidence of squirrel's cutting hickory nuts and acorns. Their method was to pick a spot where they knew there were squirrels, find a comfortable spot, sit down and be still. After a time when the woods quieted down the squirrels would start moving through the woods.

This particular day Winslow was about a hundred yards higher up on the mountain and had chosen a fallen log to sit beside. Both had pretty good luck and met back where Thee was, so they could get back to their house before dark.

As Winslow got back to his brother he told Thee about the rattler he had shot while he was waiting in the cove.

Thee asked, "How big was it? Did you cut the rattles off?"

Winslow answered, "He was about four feet, and I never even thought about the rattles."

Thee said, "Damn Winslow, you know I have been collecting rattles for years. Where is he? I'll go back up and cut them off and you wait here for me."

Winslow told him, "The snake is beside that old chestnut log I was sitting by."

Thee scrambled back up to retrieve them. When Thee got to the log, Winslow heard him holler and then shoot his shotgun.

When Thee got back to Winslow, he held two rattles out for him to see.

He said, "When I got up there I could see the snake's tail sticking out from the log; so I leaned my gun against it and reached for its tail. Just as I did the damn thing starts rattling and I realized it was a live snake. I was a cussing you, as I stumbled backwards and fell flat on my butt. Only then, when I got up, did I see the snake you had shot laying at the other end of the log."

I tell this story because several times in my life, I have found more than one rattler in the near vicinity. In the Everglades there are certain times of the year when moccasins will gang up together, and they can be rather aggressive at these times. I have been hunting around ponds (and would skirt several) and not see any; and then approach a pond where there would be a moccasin every way you look. They tell me the same thing happens here in the mountains, but I have never personally seen it.

(11) Snake Leggings

My friend George joined me one opening day at "Fools Paradise" for the weekend hunt; he was very cautious about snakes. He had a pair of those snake leggings that were made out of canvas and a fine mesh wire; and he was very faithful about wearing them. I had graduated down to just using lightweight, high top tennis shoes for my preferred foot wear. George came in after the first day's hunt and took off the leggings and leaned them against the sink stand.

The next morning as we were dressing for the day's hunt, George pulled a lawn chair over by the sink, sat down in it, and reached for his canvas leggings. As he picked them up a rather large yellow King Snake fell out of them, right at George's feet. It startled him so much he toppled over backwards. The rest of the week end we kidded him about wearing something that attracts snakes.

(M) Hogs

Hog hunting in the Everglades was a big part of our adventure, and they contributed a lot of food to the Boyer table. There is no better eating than a fresh ham off of a feral hog. The mountains have a few, but in the Everglades in the areas I hunted, we killed as many hogs as deer. In most states they are not considered a game animal, and we could harvest one in the summer. A small one made a special treat for the family. We stocked our lease with trapped pigs from a nearby ranch. Then we left them alone for two years and we had all we needed for our consumption. Some of us used pit bulls to hunt them; mostly we would harvest one while we were on a stand waiting for a deer. They look docile and will usually run from you, but under the right circumstances, they can be extremely dangerous.

The Pitbull is Luke

Ding My Nephew

(a) Biggest Boar I Killed

It was during deer season and I had chosen a stand that was only about eight feet above the ground. It was right on the road that cut through a rather large cypress strand. Years ago it had been a section road for when the government divided up the land into one hundred and sixty acre plots for homesteaders. It was a good spot, because it was on the dividing line between the strand and the palmettos. The actual stand was placed where (at this time of the year) you had to wade to it. I always left my buggy on the other side of the strand, and walked that old road that last ¼ mile through the heavy cypress, because I could slip up to the stand without making any noise. I practically had to feel my way across, because it was an overcast night and pitch dark under those trees. I had forgotten my flashlight at the cabin, but I had plenty of time before daylight. I had already gone about half way when I bumped into something furry. My rifle was slung across my shoulders, so I just reacted by pushing it away from me. It shoved back up against me hard, this time, and I shoved it away again. I couldn't see what it was but it was one of those moments you think about when you are alone in the dark in a creepy place. I know that my hair had to be standing up, because I could feel it crawling around on my head. Whatever it was, it suddenly decided to vacate the spot. It jumped off the road into the water and tore out across the strand. I know it wasn't a pig because they have real coarse hair. It wasn't a hound because it would not have long hair.

The hair didn't feel like bear fur, so I never did figure out what it was. I even looked real good for tracks, when I went back to the buggy, but all I was able to find was scuff marks in the leaves.

Anyway, I was in the stand well before daylight and listened to a bunch of noisy Ibis feed by in the water at daylight. It wasn't long after that that I heard a palmetto rustle behind me; I guessed that it was either a deer or a hog. It didn't move for a long time, but it had my adrenalin pumping. I heard something again. Then I heard that telltale chop that a boar hog makes when he is sharpening his tusks. Suddenly he breaks out in the open like a rabid dog and starts thrashing everything in sight with his tusks. That hog was mad and he was looking for me. I was glad that I was eight feet in the air. He was still tearing up the terrain, when I dropped him with my old 25-35. He had huge tusks and probably weighed 350 pounds. He had scars all over him where he had been fighting many times. He was colored black on his shoulders and rump and white on the rest of his body. When I cleaned him, the hide on his back was a good three inches thick. The hide was impossible to bend, so it was a real effort to skin him. I packaged the meat up and took it home, but none of us ever ate more than a mouthful. I learned from that experience never to kill a boar hog if you wanted table meat. I did kill small boars after that, by accident but I never looked for one.

(b) Mama and Babies

I had already moved to the mountains and still belonged to the club in Florida. I decided to go down to Florida for a week of hunting during spring gobbler season.

I walked a good distance to turkey hunt and had no luck, so I decided to go back to the camp for the afternoon. I didn't go my regular way, because I decided to cut between two cypress heads and shorten the distance. I was not being careful and stopped dead in my tracks when I discovered something I had never seen before. Right next to me was a nest about 3 feet in circumference. To look at it you would swear that it was built by a big bird, but that was not the case; this one was. full of baby pigs. They were about 5 inches long and were striped like a Russian boar's offspring. I stood there frozen, while my mind raced and I thought out the options.

"I wanted a pair of those babies; really bad, to take back to the mountains with me. Did I dare try and steal a couple? I knew mama had to be close and I was scanning the underbrush to see if I could spot her."

I stood there motionless for a good 10 minutes before I saw one of her ears flop to ward off a fly or something.

Then I looked around to see if there was something

I could get up on to get away from her if I grabbed two of her piglets. I was too chicken to attempt it. I sure didn't want to kill her because I couldn't take care of all those babies. There was nothing around that I could climb up on, so I used my better judgment and left them alone.

(c) Injured Pig

I had gone out to the camp by myself and had unintentionally left some supplies in the truck where we parked our vehicles. I didn't need them that first night, so I decided to hunt in the morning, and then go back to my truck around noon to pick up the other supplies. I was about a third of the way back to the truck, idling along on one of those old dividing roads, when I spot several pigs milling around under a tree that was alongside of the road. They hadn't seen me or heard me, so I shut the buggy down and reached for my rifle from its rack behind the seat. They were a good 150 yards in front of me and the steering wheel made a perfect rest for my rifle. From that distance they looked to be about 60 or 70 pounds. I had to wait 20 minutes for one to turn its head so I could get a good shot. I had gotten so spoiled that I always tried to get a good head shot so it would drop right there and none of the meat would be wasted. Just according to plan I fired and one dropped right in the road. I cranked the buggy back up and drove on down there.

I thought to myself, "*I don't want to clean her now; it would be so much easier back at the camp where I would have running water."*

I decided to pull her down into the water alongside the road and cover her with palm fronds so the buzzards wouldn't spot her. She would be cool and it would give me enough time to go on to the truck, pick up my supplies, and pick her up on the way back to take her on to the camp. I was gone about an hour and when I returned I looked in the water and she was gone!

I couldn't believe it! "*Where had she gone? I was positive she was dead and yet she wasn't here."*

I searched around the pond to see if I could figure it out. On the far side of the pond I found the answer. Apparently my shot had knocked her out and paralyzed her front legs at the same time. I found where she had exited the pond; laying down on her front end and pushing with her back legs until she had managed to move away from the pond. I knew that she would soon die, if she hadn't already, so I followed her trail. I got about 50 yards from the road and I saw her laid out and another pig was standing right beside her.

I said to myself, *"Oh s--t that's a boar and he looks mad. This guy is coming my way and I don't have my gun with me!"*

I saw a myrtle bush close by and I dove into it just in time. I wasn't very high, but it was out of his reach; and there I sat for what seemed like an eternity. I don't know if he knew I had shot that sow or he just didn't like humans. When I got back to the camp one someone said, "You probably shot his girlfriend.

Jaime, My Son Guting His First Hog

(N) Bears

Bears are wild animals!

I make that statement to remind you they can be dangerous and to be cautious.

(1) Bear Experiences in the Mountains

We were a young family that had just discovered the beauty of the mountains. We were on our first real vacation and we had a week to explore. Jaime, my youngest son, was about five; and my oldest, Steve, was about eleven. We had rented a cabin for a whole week at Shady Rest Cabins in Hiawassee, Ga., and had spent our first night telling ghost stories. We brought a small boat and motor; we had even brought our family dog, Lonesome. Lonesome was a cross between a greyhound and a black lab, so she was fast and big. We made a mistake and decided to leave her in the cabin while we did our first day exploring. We had a wonderful time finding all the beautiful spots that were so foreign to a flatlander.

The most pleasurable experience we discovered was a spot called Moody Hollow. It is a waterfall that has a large deep pond at the base of the fall. We wore ourselves out swinging on the rope, and dropping into the water. We learned that first day to take warm clothes with us, even in the summer, so that if we got wet, we could at least get warm.

That first day we arrived back at the cabin well after dark. When we opened the door we got a big surprise! Lonesome had striped the sheets and blankets from the beds, pulled the curtains off the wall, and pulled every bit of toilet paper from the roll. Only then did we realize that she thought that we had deserted her. Luckily, we were able to repair everything, so no one was the wiser. We made our plans for the next day, and left time to return to Moody Hollow late in the day. Well, as it was, we didn't get there till about the time the sun was going down. It was too cold to go in the water, so we decided to walk up a side trail that leads to the Appalachian Trail. We had left Lonesome in the car, so I sent Steve back to let her out to join us.

Laurie, Jaime, and I walked slowly on up the trail. It was drizzling rain, but it was a beautiful end of the day. We hadn't gone very far when we came upon a huge chestnut log that was lying across the trail. It was so large that I could barely see over it. I had always instructed my family to walk quietly and slowly, for you will get a better chance to see more of Mother Nature.

As we approached the log, I heard something on the other side rustling around on the ground. I picked Jaime up, motioned for him to be quiet and I told Laurie to come up closer to me. As I peered over the log to see what was making the noise, a huge black bear stood up on the other side; he looked me right in the eye (from about six feet away). Now he was about a foot taller than me and his head was at least two foot wide. The thing that caught my eye (and is etched into my memory) was that all his whiskers were black as coal, except for one that was snow white. All I could think of was that I was caught with my pants down. I didn't have a thing to defend us with, and all I could think of was my two inch long pin knife in my pocket, that Laurie had given me for Christmas. She wasn't making it any easier for she was jerking on my sleeve asking me what I was going to do.

I was trying to stare down the bear and he wasn't blinking! I know he had to be able to smell my fear. Here I was staring at an animal that had to weigh, 300 pounds or better, with a baby in my arms and a noisy wife behind me; I didn't have a clue as to what to do.

All of a sudden the bear dropped down and disappeared from my sight. I thought I heard him running down the mountain. I got brave, or stupid, and hustled my family around the upper end of the log, so that we could get a glimpse of him going down the mountain. We were standing where the bear had been standing and we were trying to see him running away.

Guess what? The bear hadn't gone anywhere; he had switched places with us, and was now standing up in our old spot glaring at us again. Only now we were cut off from the car! This stare-down went on for several hours or seconds, depending on which side of the story you were on. The bear looked back over his shoulder and spotted Steve and Lonesome coming up the trail. Although Lonesome was a woose, the bear didn't know that. When she barked, that broke the spell and the bear took off. When we got back to town and started telling about our experience, everyone told us all the bears had been killed off years ago. I could tell that no one believed us. It was our first experience where the locals thought of us as "different" because we came from Florida.

(2) Jethro's Story

This story is a figment of my imagination. It was an assignment by my writing class after we read in our local paper a man was found nude on the steps of the University of Georgia experiment station.

Jethro hated bears and to him he had good reason. You see, Jethro kept bee hives and he always had a problem with the bears destroying his hives. However, Jethro was not having problems with the hives that he maintained on the edge of the woods on the experimental property grounds. He had seen a female and cubs near his hives. He made up a story and told the Department of Natural Resources that the bears had been in his hives. He applied to the DNR for a permit to move the bears. They responded with a trap and caught a large momma bear and two yearling cubs.

Jethro, after quite a bit of sipping from the contents of a canning jar, had to be on hand to witness the capture. Seeing them in the culvert pipe he decided to take out his frustrations by agitating them. He would jab at them with a stick. The bears would respond by tearing at the end of the trap, reaching and trying to grab him. They were growling and screaming with both revenge and fear in their actions.

The DNR man, Jim, put a stop to the taunting saying "Jethro, you better stop, before you or the bears get hurt."

Jethro would feint toward the culvert and stamp his foot, trying to agitate them. He was real brave letting them know who was boss with them in the cage and him safely outside. Jim was hooking his truck to the cage and the commotion was more than he wanted.

He finally said "Jethro! You have two choices, stop, get in your truck and leave, or I am going to take you and put you in a cage.

Jethro responded, under his breath with some sort of unintelligible grumbling, as he slowly moved toward his truck.

Jim didn't care for Jethro very much, he had his suspicions about him hunting out of season with a crossbow. To this point it was only suspicion, for Jethro was one of those crafty mountain men that believed the mountains were put here for him, and all the game was his to harvest any time he wanted. Jim finally got his trap-trailer connected and left the bee hive spot with his captives. By this time, being a compassionate man, Jim was showing more sympathy for the bears than Jethro and his hives.

As he pulled out on the highway and headed south toward Neil's Gap and the other side of the mountain, he thought to himself, *"If I take these bears miles away from here, they are going to have a tough time trying to find food in a new area. They haven't given any trouble to anyone but Jethro, and I really think most of Jethro's problems are imaginary. The employees around the experiment station have told me how they can almost hand feed the bears, so why should they be punished because Jethro doesn't like bears? I'll just turn East here on 180, and find a side road where they won't be far out of their feeding range."*

It wasn't too many days until the bears were back looking for handouts from the employees at the station. They all were abuzz about how fast the bears found their way back from the other side of the mountain.

It didn't take Jethro long to discover they were back either. Jethro had a piece of plywood nailed in an oak tree, alongside of an abandoned corn field near the station where he would take his crossbow and kill a deer when his supply ran low. On the way to the stand he saw the fresh tracks where the bears had been gleaning for leftover corn. Jethro was infuriated.

He thought "Well I'll just take care of this myself."

He went back to his cabin, to his beekeeping shed, to assemble his plan. He had a five gallon thin plastic jug that he had salvaged from the garbage can behind a restaurant, the kind that fry grease comes in. Over the years he had poured dirty honey into it, and he had accumulated several gallons in it. He couldn't sell the leftover honey with particles of trash floating in it, so he figured it would be good bait for the bears. Jethro went back to the field with the jug tied on his back. When he arrived in front of the oak tree, where he wanted to spread the honey on the ground; he leaned his crossbow on a bush and proceeded to try and remove the bottle from his back. Jethro hadn't noticed the old plastic bottle had already started to split. He had to lift it over his head to set it down, from the awkward way he had tied it on his back. Just as he got it over his head the whole bottle burst, spilling all the honey all over him. He was in shock! He was a mess!

He picked up a stick and tried scraping it off on to the ground, but it only made a bigger mess. Jethro's dilemma was, this was all the bad honey he had, and he had to go through with the hunt. He knew bears feed mostly at night, and it was getting later and later. He decided to continue his hunt, (no matter how messy he was), so he got on up in the tree.

He had tied his flashlight on his bow, so he could see to shoot when the bears came. He hadn't been there long when he heard some rustling on the ground. He stood up, without making a sound, and eased out on the plywood for a better shot. He could see the bears, fairly well, for it was a bright night.

He didn't turn on the light. Just as he was about to fire, his feet (slick from the honey) went out from under him, and down he went. He lit flat on his back where his head struck a root, knocking him unconscious.

Momma bear heard the commotion, but when she sniffed into the air, all she could smell was a big gob of honey, and she led her cubs to the site. The bears worked on Jethro until they had stripped all of his clothes off, as they chewed all the goodness from the tatters. Jethro was not seriously hurt from the fall; but the bears had managed to scratch him up pretty good, flipping him over and over like a pancake, trying to get at the honey. Just about the time the bears were finished cleaning up the honey, Jethro woke up and realized what was happening to him. He groaned and tried to rise up. Momma bear put her big paw in the center of his back and easily pinned him down. He was frightened and let out a bloodcurdling scream! It was hard to tell who was frightened the most, Jethro or the bears. They both took off in different directions, with Jethro ending up at the experiment station, waiting for the first employee to arrive and get him some help.

Jethro's dilemma was how would he explain this?

Here he was buck naked. He was hunting out of season, on government property, at night, with a light, and with bait. Wow! Was he in trouble?

This was one time the truth wouldn't work.

(3) Tree Shaker

I love to turkey hunt and I had picked a spot to set up a good blind. I was looking up a cove that where I was just below a ridge. I used an old chestnut root that had been pushed aside to build a logging road. It was perfect to lean back against, and proved to be rather comfortable. By habit I carry a length of camouflage material to stretch around in front of me; and I wear the same material over my head, so I blend in very well with the surroundings. It was one of those still spring mornings where all the birds seem enthralled with life, and they were telling the world about it. The only birds that weren't sounding off were the turkeys.

I had called several times and had gotten no response. I was sitting there just enjoying the beautiful morning in between my calling sessions. To tell the truth, I had just about fallen asleep when I caught a movement on the ridge out of the corner of my eye, and it was dark. It was just a glimpse, and I really wasn't sure if I had seen anything. However I froze and kept my eye on that spot, for I have learned how to play the game! An old gobbler will slip along very cautiously, and if you aren't observant you will never know he is around. This guy was heading my way, and I never try to call when they are. As usual, it took forever before I saw any more movement, and then it was just a glimpse again.

I thought, "If he keeps moving in that direction he will break out from the underbrush directly in front of me 30 yards out."

I slipped my old double barrel around to that projected spot and waited for him to appear. My heart was pounding! I could see my heart beat in my eyes as that adrenalin rush surged through my body. Surprise!

He came out at that exact spot, but it was a bear instead of a turkey! He was really big and he was interested in something in a small rotten log that was lying on the ground. He did not see me because the wind was in my favor, so I watched him for several minutes. I had my mouth-turkey call in my mouth; I decided to call on it and see how he would react. The second I called, he froze and stood motionless for a long time. I called again, and he slowly turned his head and looked in my direction, then he flared his nostrils to try and wind me. He was looking right at me, but he couldn't make out what that lump on the ground was. I called again, and this time he stood up and tried to see me better from the greater height.

Then he did something that really surprised me. He

walked upright about 20 feet to his right and placed his paw against a poplar tree that was about 10 or 12 inches thick, and started shaking it violently. All this time he was still looking directly at me!

My mind was racing, trying to plan ahead. If this scenario starts to turn bad,. I only had two shells in my gun. They were only # 4 bird shot; and that is no good against something like him, unless you are only feet away. All this was racing through my mind when the wrong things started to happen.

The bear dropped back down on all fours, and started coming toward me. I really didn't want it to come to the point of me killing the bear, or him hurting me; so I jumped up, hollered and waved my arms around. He stopped, and stared at me for a few seconds, and then he wheeled around and ambled up the mountain, without ever looking back.

Mama and two half grown cubs going after a bird feeder. The danger is not knowing they are there and stepping outdoors between mama and her cubs.

(4) Stones Overturned

I was walking a ridge early one morning, calling every so often, trying to get a gobbler to answer when I noticed something strange. All the rocks had been turned over not long ago. I thought "*It must be somebody looking for lizards to fish with.*"

But then I thought, "*No they wouldn't be looking on the ridge, maybe on a creek bank, but not up here. They sure were doing a thorough job though, for I couldn't see any stones they missed.*"

I had walked about a half mile, all the while following the ridge and pondering about the stones, when I came upon a thick patch of laurel that forced me off the ridge. I was about 50 yards off the ridge, when I heard and saw a commotion in the laurel bushes in front of me. I froze (where I was) to see what was making the disturbance. I had barely stopped, when a little farther off the ridge and probably 35 yards in front of me, was a large white oak tree. I watched as three fifty pound bear cubs climbed that tree like they were black squirrels. I instantly knew what had turned the rocks over.

I also knew that I was in a very dangerous position, because I didn't know where Mama was! Once the cubs found a comfortable spot on their limbs, the woods quieted down and I had to think fast. I knew Mama knew exactly where I was, but I didn't have a clue where she was, and that was dangerous for me. I knew that she had to be somewhere between me and the oak tree, or she would have already attacked. My problem was that the tree wasn't over 40 yards from me, and I couldn't see her. I decided my best move was to retreat, but I did it v e r y s l o w l y. I faced that tree as I backed back up that slope, (one careful step at a time), toward the top of the hill. I was glad my son wasn't with me, for he wouldn't have missed the opportunity to scare me while all this was going on. I hadn't gone far when the change in elevation allowed me to see her under the tree. She was standing erect on her back legs, and had her head cradled between her two front legs, and her chest was all the way on the ground. The body parts that impressed me were her eyes, and her ears that were lying back against her head. She meant business and I knew it! I continued backing up that hill, and when I reached a point that she thought I was safe, she relaxed, and started loping on down that mountainside. How she communicated with those cubs was a mystery, but they scrambled down and followed her, leaving me a happy camper.

Bear Tearing Down Feeder

(5) Bear at Home

I built a small pond and then built my house so that the back porch actually hangs over the water. The pond is about a half-acre and I left the foliage, large oaks and maples, in place; so it is a lake in the middle of the forest. The deck is 28' x 20' and it is my favorite spot to write. It gets me away from the honeydews. Yesterday while I was writing this manuscript, a doe and her fawn stepped out of the woods and waded out into the water for a drink. I have a Peacock that sits on my picnic table when I write, and he was less than a foot from my laptop and so content he was dosing.

Some people think us rather strange from the critters we keep. At this time we have 8 rat terriers, (one is even three legged from an accident), two cats, the peacock, six huge coy in the pond and a pair of pigs from the Florida Everglades. We did have a big catfish in the pond that my Granddaughter caught when it was 6 inches long and she was 3 years old. Last year during the drought, my pond lost half its water and a bear tried to catch him in the shallow water. He died when the scratch from the bear got infected and all the family was saddened, for he had become quite a pet. I was able to weigh him at that time and he topped the scales at 42 pounds. The bear keep us on our toes and we have to lock up anything that they can eat, including the garbage.

One afternoon my wife came up to me excited and explained, "There's a bear on the dam!"

I grabbed my camera and followed her outside. From where we were, we were looking across the pond and sure enough there were bears on the far end of the dam.

Our rat terriers were trying to get up enough nerve to challenge them and they were inching their way across the dam. Apparently it was a mama bear and a two year old cub; because the smaller of the two weighed around 175 lbs. Mama didn't like all the dogs approaching her, so she instructed the smaller one to go up a large oak that was growing on the end of the dam.

She turned and went up and over the hill that was at the end of the dam with all my dogs in hot pursuit. When the bear ran, they got real brave. I got the bright idea to go across the dam and get under the one up the tree and take a picture of him up through the branches.

I told my wife and granddaughter to stay on the far side of the lake, while I went across the dam to where the bear was.

I was standing under the oak trying to get my camera to focus up through the tree limbs, when all my dogs almost knocked me down coming off that hill; they were just a yelping. Right behind them was Mama Bear, with her ears laid back, charging and grunting with every step. Needless to say I vacated that spot and almost overran all the dogs, as I tore back across that dam.

I had a brief thought of diving in the lake, but then I thought, *"I can run faster than I can swim."*

Mama stopped just past the oak tree, but I could have sworn she was right behind me all the way cross.

When it was over my granddaughter said, "PaPa, I didn't know you could run so fast."

Our 42 lb. Pet Catfish Bear Injured

Everglades Bears

(7) Agile Bear

My first encounter with a live wild bear was in the Everglades about 1965. I belonged to a hunting camp that leased about 5600 acres, which was located just south of the Big Cypress Indian Reservation. If you were to draw lines from the most desolate roads to the center of the most uninhabited parts of the Everglades, where they intersected, would be our lease. It was a two hour drive from Miami, to the place where we left our cars, and transferred our gear to our swamp buggies. Then it took us about 1½ hours by swamp buggy to get to our camp. To give you an idea of how large a piece of land this is; we had to fence it in and it was 13 miles around the property.

On my very first visit to this lease, (when I was contemplating joining,) I discovered a large bear track in the center of a road, alongside of a cypress swamp. I followed the track for a ways down the road when I noticed that a panther had come out in the road and followed the bear for several hundred yards. To give myself a little perspective of how large it was, I placed a standard size beer can in the pad. Although it was laying crossways in the pad, it did not touch either side. At that time it was legal to hunt bears in the Everglades, so this was one of the determining factors of my joining the club. I never got to see that particular bear, but he sure let his presence be known.

During the off season we fed the turkeys corn, and he would continually figure out how to rob our feeders. The most chilling thing he ever did was to come into our camp, while we were there, and look into our camp kitchen window. The window was over six feet off the ground. He stood up and peered into the window, while placing his front muddy feet on the plywood alongside the window. I had walked by the window on the way to eat supper, and the tracks weren't there. This camp was always lit up like a tourist trap, because we had a large generator, and when it was on, all the lights come on.

On the way back to my cabin, I immediately saw the paw prints on the wall and brought it to everyone's attention. I even took a marking pen and outlined the paw prints, so all future campers were able to see what was wandering around in the woods.

The only sighting I had of a bear was when I was coming in late one afternoon. My swamp buggy had a small engine, and I had it muffled down to where it was real quiet. The thing that was different about the sound of the buggy was the noise that the chains made. Instead of transmissions, I used chains and sprockets to get power, and it did sound very different from the other buggies in our camp. I looked off to my right and saw about sixty or seventy yards from me, a bear scampering up a large pine tree that was growing near the cypress. He apparently couldn't see us on the ground, for there was a palmetto patch between us and him. When he got to the first limb (which was about 60 feet off the ground), he propped himself on that limb, and peered over to see what the strange noise was. It didn't take him but a second to decide he didn't like our looks. He turned loose from the tree and dropped free-fall for at least 50 feet, before he dug his claws into the tree to stop his fall. He stripped bark away from the tree for seven or eight feet and left huge scars that were there for years. I gained a lot of respect for the power of bears (from that single incident,) both from his climbing the tree like a squirrel and the power it took to catch himself in a fall like that.

(8) Dumb Luck

I did help load a really large bear onto the back of a buggy which a greenhorn hunter killed by his stupidity.

I was a visitor to a camp that was established in the Loop area of the Everglades and we were going to hunt deer with dogs. I was introduced to someone's brother-in-law that had never been hunting before. He had just bought a Remington five shot automatic 30/06 rifle and knew nothing about guns, and it was very obvious he was a greenhorn in the woods.

I thought to myself, *"This is one that I want to be far away from when the hunt starts."*

We all knew the favorite routes the deer take when running from the dogs. So early in the morning, before the dogs are released, we were taken to these spots and left to wait for the deer.

Everyone was reminded of the rules of the hunt. "Don't leave your stand until the hunt master blows his cow-horn or the buggy picks you up; telling us the hunt was over."

As each hunter was left at his spot, he was cautioned about which direction he could shoot. High powered rifles will carry over a mile on flat grounds, so we were cautioned not to shoot toward another stand. Lucky for me, I was placed on a stand that was a couple of miles from the greenhorn; so I felt fairly safe. We started real early, for we had a lot of ground to travel to place six of us on stands. The driver of the buggy was to be the hunt master for the day, so he was in control of the dogs.

It was just cracking daylight as I heard the buggy stop running in the distance. I could hear the door to the dog box as it opened and the dogs barking with excitement as they were being released to start the hunt. The dogs had just gotten out of the buggy when I heard five quick shots from a high powered rifle somewhere between me and the camp. I wondered what that was about, for it wasn't yet light enough to sight a gun on anything; and it sure wasn't light enough to identify a buck from a doe. I soon forgot about the shots, for it was only a few minutes later that I heard old Satchel open up with that high pitched scream that let you know she is looking at a deer. As luck would have it, they got on the trail hot and heavy, but they took the deer the other way, and away from any of our stands. I could hear the chase for about 45 minutes, and to a dog hunter, it was music to my ears. To me that is one of the things that brought me to the woods, for I had been listening to dogs hunting Coons, bobcats, and foxes since I was a little boy; this was a good vocal one.

It was a still morning and there was a fog that was laying close to the ground, magnifying the sounds of the dogs as they were working hard to keep those deer on the move. Soon I knew that they were going the wrong direction and before long, the sounds disappeared into the distance. I knew I was in for a long wait, so I found a comfortable spot in the shade, leaned my head against a root and took a nap.

I don't know how long I had been laying there when I heard a pat pat pat of something coming through the pond towards me. I eased my head up, just as my dog (Satchel) cleared the grass and spotted me. It wasn't long before I heard the buggy crank up and start back towards me. As we picked up the hunters on the way back to camp, we were all remarking about the excellent chase we had heard that morning. When we got to the greenhorns spot, we couldn't find him. We didn't understand what he could have possibly have done. We had cautioned him about not leaving, yet he wasn't there. We hollered and hollered, but there was no answer. We decided to go on back to the camp; maybe he had decided to walk back. When we got back to camp, he wasn't there. Now the problem was getting serious and we were all worried. We spent the rest of the day scouting in a big circle, trying to find some sign of where he had gone. We decided to go back to the camp, build a large fire, and shoot a gun in the air every so often to see if that would attract him.

It worked! About two hours after we built the fire, up strolls the greenhorn with no rifle, soaking wet, scratched all over his face and arms. He was scared almost to the point of crying.

After everyone asked him the same question, "What happened?"

He finally told his story.

He said, "I stood right where I was told for a while. It was really scary to me, for I kept hearing noises that were really creepy sounding. That small cypress pond that was directly in front of where I was standing, the one that you told me the deer always skirted when they were running from the dogs, was especially noisy. It sounded like a hog was rooting around in the center of the pond. I thought it wouldn't hurt to slip over there and see what was making the noise, so I crouched down and eased into the water and cautiously worked my way closer and closer. I could make out a black shape of a large hog rooting around in the water, so I eased my gun to my shoulder. I couldn't see the sights, but I took the safety off. When I did that, hog turned into a huge bear that stood up right in front of me. I shot until my gun was empty and all hell broke loose. That bear was screaming and growling, as it was uprooting trees, and I thought it was chasing me. I turned to run and tripped and dropped my gun in the water. I tore out of there and got good and lost. I have been trying to get back here ever since. I am just grateful that you built a large fire and kept shooting off those guns, so I could find my way back."

We all looked at each other and almost laughed out loud at the ridiculous story.

We all said, "Let's go find your gun" as we winked at each other.

When we arrived at the spot, we found his gun right where he said, but what amazed us was the pond had been the scene of what appeared to have been a battle. We took our lanterns and after a short search, we found the bear partially submersed in water with four holes in it.

Getting it up on the buggy took a feat of

engineering, for he was a monster. Back at the camp we hung him on some old antique scales that registered up to 600 pounds, and he was larger than they read. Some people are just lucky when they go hunting and this guy happened to be one of them.

(O) Alligators

(a) Charlie and Elsie

One law that the old Florida Cracker ignored was the ones that had to do with alligators. A whole lot of men spent time working for the government, because they couldn't let easy money slide by in hard times. They were protected, but the crackers thought of them much in the same way as mountain men looked on making whiskey. Alligator belly hide brought several dollars a foot. To anyone familiar with the glades, it was easy money. The buyers came regularly from Louisiana and once they found regular hunters, they would even place orders as to the size they wanted. Our home was in a housing project, and our next door neighbors were a couple that were raised around Felsmer, Florida.

If ever you could classify a person as a swamp man, the husband was it. He even shaved every morning with his Jack knife and he didn't think it unusual. I knew it was going to be interesting living next to them when he offered me a drink. When I accepted, he went over to a five gallon tri-pure water bottle, tipped it over, and poured me a Dixie cup full of moon shine.

Their escapades and stories gave me real incite to gator hunting and frogging in the glades. The husband (Charlie) was an average size man, and he was friendly to me when he discovered that I liked to hunt. Elsie, a large woman with crossed eyes, was as sweet as she could be. She loved my first born son, Steve.

Charlie and his brother bought houses near each other and worked for the same farming corporation. They both drove D-8 bulldozers (barefooted), and cleared land for this company. The company had to watch them fairly close for they also had airboats and spent all the time they could in the glades.

I went to the glades with Charlie several times and he was really good at catching frogs. Frog hunting is done at night, with the use of a powerful spot light. Charlie would spend part of the evening sliding his boat sideways in the grass to knock it flat. Sometimes clearing out several acres, so he could return the next night when the frogs would be sitting up on these clumps of grass. The boat has to be traveling fast enough, so that it doesn't push a wake in front of it to warn the frogs. The gig is on a short pole, and it consists of four large fish hooks that are straightened and fastened to a piece of round stainless steel tubing.

The barbs are facing outward so that one can strip the frogs off the grass without snagging on anything. The gig is held out in front of you, as you are sliding along at a fairly good clip. When you approach that white belly gives them away. They guide the boat to the left of the frog, and let the momentum pierce the body, and swing it up in one motion. They stick the frog down a tube in between the driver's legs; strip him free of the gig, dropping him into a burlap bag at the bottom of the tube. It takes a lot of practice.

While they are frogging, it also gave them a chance to fill the orders for the gator hides. Charlie used a single shot 22 rifle, and he was really good at killing a gator without it even quivering. He used that kind of gun, because he wanted something he could throw away if he had a game warden after him.

He would wait for a rainy day and he and Elsie would go on a fishing trip. There were only a few boat landings and the game wardens always had them covered. It is never any trouble catching a good mess of fish in the glades, so they would do that first. Then they would go to the salt barrel, and Elsie would take off her big black oil cloth rain coat, and Charlie would wrap those gator bellies around her, tie them off securely, and she would put the oil cloth coat back on.

When they got back to the landing, Elsie would climb out of the boat and go sit in the car while Charlie bragged about the fish and loaded the airboat. I always knew where they had been when Elsie got out of the car and went into the house wearing that big black rain coat before she took it off.

(b) Gator and Buggy

Steve, my oldest, Art and I were on the way in to the camp on a Friday night when Art asked, "If you don't mind, if I see him tonight, I'm going to shoot that small gator we have been seeing every weekend."

It was archery season and Art had brought his shotgun in case we ran up on some pigs.

I made him promise that he would fry him up for supper before I said, "OK."

At that time the route into the camp was through the Indian reservation and we had to go through some deep water as we crossed through the slough. It was 3 or 4 feet deep in places, but no trouble for our buggies for they all had good ground clearance. This small gator had been hanging out in the buggy road, for some time tempting Art.

I worked for the same company as Art. I have to tell this on him as an example of his reputation and the type of food he liked. We both worked on a housing project west of Hollywood, Florida and it was built around a lake. I came up to a house one day and discovered that several Muscovy ducks had been accidentally closed inside the house I was assigned to work on. The old gentleman that was a laborer on the job came up at the same time as me and helped me shoo the ducks out of the house.

He grinned and said to me, "Them duck don no how lucky dey is that Mr. Art ain't the one that came here. Them ducks has to learn to walk rather lightly when Mr. Art is around."

Art always enjoyed his food and we always kidded him that he would eat anything that moved.

Well anyway, sure enough as we started through the water, Art spotted that tell tail red eyes of a gator. He shot and the gator disappeared.

I said, "Let's not drive up to him and muddy the water. Steve, take the flashlight and walk up to where the gator was, and see if you can see him."

Steve took the light and eased up to where we had seen the gator go down.

I asked, "Can you see him?"

Steve answered, "I can see him real plain. But Daddy he isn't a little gator, he is a big one.

I asked, "How big?"

"He's about ten or twelve feet at least."

I said. "Can you see where he was shot and can you tell if he's dead?

Steve said, "I can see where the bird shot tore some skin around his eye, but I can't see if he is alive or dead."

I told Steve to ease on back to the buggy. We rigged a pole and rope so we could put a loop around his head and drag him up to dry ground. With the three of us shining flashlights, we were able to slip a noose around his head. Art and I got back in the buggy and Steve stayed behind the buggy, as I eased ahead, and tightened up on the rope.

All hell broke loose! That gator didn't like the rope around his head; and as soon as he felt it, he started that rolling that they do. Steve was making tracks to get out of its way as it rolled up to the buggy. I don't know if it was biting at Steve or at the buggy, but the gator got hold of the tire and mashed it flat, when he bit down on it. He managed to keep a good clamp on it (for a few seconds), but the pressure soon overpowered his bite. It made a springing noise, as he gave way to the tire. I only ran with eight pounds of pressure and I guess that was the reason he could mash it like that.

We drug him on to dry land and I told Art, "There ain't no way I am going to butcher that thing tonight. Let's get the rope off him and turn him loose."

That was easier said than done. To put it mildly the

gator was pissed. The simple thing would have been to cut the rope; but then he would have been dragging that nylon rope forever. So we persisted and finally we got it off him.

By then all of us were a muddy mess and I told Art as we finally loaded up to go, "Don't get any more bright ideas!"

(c) About Gators

Florida now has an annual drawing to see who gets to hunt gators. After the state got really tough on poaching, the alligator population got so large and numerous that they have a lotto, to see who gets to hunt the "nuisance" gators. Nuisance gators are the ones that have gotten so big they become dangerous to people. The hunters are told (by the authorities) where harvest it. It has become very profitable for the lotto there is a dangerous gator and they are allowed to winner. He can sell the hide, the head, the feet and especially the meat. Before, the habit was to only eat the gator tail; but now all the meat is sold and eaten.

In the spring the big old bull gators come out of their pond or place where they feed and live, and travel quite far searching for romance. This is the time of the year people find them in their yards or under their cars, and they panic.

Good Sized Rattler & 5 1/2 Foot Gator

Before the Palmetto Expressway was officially opened and there were only a few cars using it, I saw two ladies (out of their car) standing beside a huge gator that was apparently trying to cross the road. I stopped my glass truck and got out to look at him.

One of the ladies asked me, "What do you suppose killed it?"

I looked at her and replied, "Lady that gator isn't dead."

She said, "Oh yes it is! We have been here 15 minutes and it hasn't moved one bit."

I Said, "I wouldn't advise getting any closer."

She gave me one of those "Holier than thou" looks as I went back to my truck. I had a 12 foot length of aluminum on the truck and I carried it to where the gator was laying. I goosed the gator in the side, just above his rear leg. He swung that tail one way and his head my way and let out a deep growl. The lady that was so sure he was dead tried to move backwards, lost her balance and plopped down on the road on her butt. I know it wasn't over thirty seconds before they were both in their car and gone. I kept prodding him with the aluminum until he ambled on over to the water that was alongside the road and slid on in.

Most people don't realize how fast a gator can move when he wants to. The saying is: they can out run a race horse for a short distance; and I believe it from some of my experiences with them. A gator will lay up on a bank several yards away from the water for hours, waiting for an animal to go between him and the water. When this happens the gator is quick enough to catch the unsuspecting animal. **They will grab a human**

also, and especially children.

Small Gator Running Between Two Ponds

Dogs beware! They are the favorite diet of the alligator, which is the most common complaint from home owners that live on water sources. It is a good topic of conservation to look out the window and brag to your Yankee friends about the big alligator that lives in the pond or canal behind your house. Some people even feed them. Marsh mellows are a favorite treat; and once the gators discover that they like them, they will come to your call to get them. They forget **they are a wild animal** until the gator makes a meal out of mama's pet poodle. When that happens "They" are shocked back into reality. There goes the 911 call for someone to come and get rid of the dangerous animal.

(d) Ding and Gator Hole

Gators do a lot of good for the food chain by keeping waterholes open. They will start with a low spot in the terrain and keep it cleaned out, thus forming a pond. They will dig up under a tree in the pond and will create a cave with a place for them to breathe underground. If you walk up on one of these waterholes and surprise one of these wild big gators it will submerge and disappear. It always seems like (no matter how long you wait) it won't surface again. They have retreated to the safety of their cave and will stay there for hours.

The Everglades are constantly changing and the water table rises and falls with the seasons. Sometimes it will be radically high water or the opposite, dried up sand. It always amazes me how people (who should know) always demand protection for the animals when one of these high or low water levels occur. This has occurred several times in my eighty years and Mother Nature always rescues the environment. Tragedy occurs **only** when man tries to give them a hand.

Anyhow, these holes provide a gathering place for all wildlife and a convenient feeding spot for alligators as they lay in wait for anything that moves. The lower the water, the more plentiful the activity!

On one of those summers, the water was

exceptionally low. Ding my nephew had accompanied me to my camp at Crooked Pine Ranch. It was primitive weapon season and we were scouting for signs of pigs or deer. We were passing one of those waterholes that was just off the section road we were traveling on and we decided to check the mud around it for tracks. We cleared the grass and were surprised that the hole was completely dried up. There was no water in the hole, only dried cracked mud in the bottom. The cave was even dried out.

I told Ding, "hold my rifle; I want to look back into that cave to see how far it goes."

It was probably three and a half feet deep and was hard when I jumped down. I leaned over and tried to focus my eyes back into that hole. I could see something there, but it didn't register what it was. It was about five feet from me and it looked like a watermelon. Just about the time I realized what I was looking at, it was the stub end of a tailless huge alligator.

At that instant Ding poked me with a stick and hollered.

Somehow I cleared the rim of the hole without touching anything. With that one poke with that stick, Ding paid me back for all the jokes I had ever played on him while he was growing up.

Theory on More Abundant Game

I learned to understand Florida lawless people, even though I never condoned their lawlessness. The same type of people lives here in the mountains. They had a tough upbringing, lived off the land and old habits are hard to break. They hunted when they were out of food and ate what they killed. Since I moved here they have been swallowed up by civilization. The odd thing that I have noticed is the return of the game. The squirrels were scarce and there wasn't hardly any deer. There just wasn't much of anything. The deer season was short and they never had a doe season. The DNR developed thousands of acres for a game management area on land adjoining mine and the old timers would not leave it alone. Whatever they stocked would disappear shortly after it was turned loose.

Now 35 years later, the deer are eating everyone's gardens; bear are a hazard to everyone, and you see flocks of turkey everywhere. You can't feed the birds for the marauding squirrels that get into the bird feeders.

What brought about the change? To me it's obvious. Up until the fifties, this was a small farming community; not the commercial type you see in South Georgia, but the small family farm. There isn't enough level land to have large farms. People had to hunt ginseng to pay the paltry taxes because if you weren't a mailman, county worker, sheriff or school teacher, there just weren't any jobs. The area is unique, for the government owns 60% of the land in the County, and most of it is steep.

About 1970 things began to change. The tourist arrived and like me saw and appreciated the beauty of the mountains. From the moment we saw it, we were determined to live here. Gradually people settled here and some were accepted; and a lot were resented for the migration, (not enough to not sell the land), but still blame all their troubles on the "Floridiots", as they call us. How did all this help the game population? Most of the newcomers were interested in preserving the beauty of the area, so they left the terrain as natural as they could. They feed the birds and animals, and enjoyed the beauty. What they did to help the replenishing of the game, was to watch out for it. No longer could locals shoot a deer anytime they wanted. They got reported. I don't even think there are a dozen families, anymore, in the whole area that would know how delicious squirrel, biscuits, and gravy go together. I know that if I were to harm one of the deer that frequent our property, my wife would make plenty of trouble for me.

I love to tease her and will say, "I need to put out some corn for these deer. I need to fatten them up because deer season is coming up."

I am a believer that most of the game laws are for good reasons and will help the hunter in the long run. Although some organizations mean well, they do manage to do more harm than they do good. A lot of these conflicts could be resolved, if more hunters would get involved in organizations that are concerned.

I suppose I could have been a better citizen and turned in anybody that I saw breaking any of the game laws, and I have, only when it came to the flagrant disregard of regulations. I remember once at “Fools Paradise” a doe was killed, (by accident) I was told. Two of the members brought it in and butchered it up to carry out to the road. They were real nervous and talked over how would be the best method to get it in the car and home without being caught. It could have been an accident or not, but if it was, I did admire them for not letting it lay and rot. I refused the request to help get it to the car. They understood, for they knew my stand on trying to follow the law, and my setting an example for my two boys.

They delayed for quite a while, discussing the pro and con of the attempt. Finally after about an hour, they decided to go on out to the road with the meat and they told me they would be back sometime around dark.

The deepest part of the trail back to the road was only about two hundred yards from the camp, and it was fairly easy walking to that point. It then was deep for the next hundred yards and then was shallow and open with scattered dwarf cypress for a good distance.

They hadn’t been gone long when I heard a small

airplane come overhead. I remembered that another friend of ours (that had been to the camp many times) told me he was going to try and find the camp from the air. I grabbed a red towel from the cabin and rushed outside the island to the prairie side, so that I could signal the plane from the ground. By this time I could see him banking to make another pass. I started waving the towel and he tipped his wings to let me know he had seen me. He made several passes coming pretty low, before he tipped his wings again, and turned back toward Miami.

I went on back on the island, figuring I would fix myself some lunch and take a nap, before I went out to my stand for the afternoon. I just sat down on a lawn chair to eat my sandwich when I heard someone running through the water. I knew it had to be the guys that had left here with the deer meat, for they were heading right for the island.

When they broke out onto the island, I couldn't believe that two men could change their looks so quickly. They were both soaking wet from head to toe and they were filthy dirty.

They said, "You didn't see that plane? It must have spotted us with the deer meat."

I started laughing when I realized what they were thinking.

"That was Whitey, I told you on the way out that he

might fly over this weekend. That wasn't the game warden; I could see him plain as day on a couple of his passes."

My friend said, "When he came by that first time we were right out in the open, and when he turned around to come back the second time, we started looking for a hiding place. We put the meat in a clump of grass, and we both got down in the water, under a fallen log and even ducked our heads under water as he went over. Every time he made a pass, we ran as hard as we could until we heard him coming back, and then we would hole up again. I have never been so scared in my whole life.

They left the meat where it was and decided to go back for it after dark, and take it home.

He said, "This will never happen to me again, if I didn't have heart trouble before, then I for sure have it now. Deer meat is delicious but it ain't worth going through that again or going to jail for."

As my minister says, "The Lord can get your attention in strange ways sometimes."

Correcting Bad Habits

I guess looking back over my life I have bent the law a little and done things I knew were wrong, but there are certain rules that I really believe in. Both of the hunting camps I was involved in were far from civilization and the game wardens hardly ever came to our camps. I only saw one game warden at either camp in my 30 year's involvement. There seldom was a doe season; yet some of our members were not above harvesting one for meat, and all of us would kill a gator every now and then for supper. I went along with feeding turkey in the off season, as long as our feeders were scattered out all over the property. I believe the biologist when they say it is dangerous to bunch up the turkey because it makes them more susceptible to disease.

Even though it was once legal to harvest a hen turkey our club noticed that the population was dwindling, so we on our own we decided not to harvest any more hens. It worked! In just a couple of years our turkey population picked up noticeably. Our club had a broad range of members in many trades. A couple of doctors, a banker, building contractor, carpenters, farmers, owners of a glass company and welding fabricators to name a few. No one was really rich until we allowed a new member to join. He was in the furniture business and was way out of our class. I liked him alright, but he had his own ideas about how to kill the turkey. He spent days and a lot of money building turkey feeders and filling them with corn, trying to lure all the turkey into one corner of the property. He built his blinds where he could shoot directly over the feeders. All of this is strictly against game laws and we reminded him he had to remove them before hunting season. He told us he wasn't worried about that because the game wardens were too lazy to get off the road. The ironic part of this story is that I never saw him bring in a turkey with all the money he spent.

One Sunday evening Tom and I went home early, and when we got to where we parked our vehicles I noticed a card under my windshield wiper; it gave me a great idea.

Tom said, "What are you up to? I see that evil grin on your face." I was in the process of gathering all the rest of the cards from the other cars.

I said, "Plan on coming early next week because I want to go around and put one of these cards in every one of those turkey feeders before our rich friend comes in."

Tom got a big grin on his face and said, "That will work."

The next weekend (after our deposits in the feeders) we were in camp for the big meal we always had on Saturday, when in walks the rich one and he had the fear of God on his face. He began telling about loading his jeep with corn and heading to his feeders to fill them, and what he found.

He said, "I pulled my jeep up to the first feeder and took the top off, when I noticed something white laying on the corn. I had to put my head down in there to see what it was; and I saw it was a business card. I read it while I was bent over in that can, when I realized it was a card from a game warden. I couldn't bring myself to look up out of that can."

By this time in the story, if I had looked at Tom I would have busted out laughing. I could hear Tom head to the door, coughing to keep from laughing. I managed to keep a straight face, but it was hard, as he went into detail about how he snuck out of the area without putting out any more corn. His fear was permanent, because he never set out any more corn during the season.

Fire Hunting

At our "Fools Paradise" camp we had a neighbor camper who got to where he fire hunted at night every time he came to the woods. We had asked him not to do it, but he thought it was manly and he wanted to go home with meat. He passed off our requests as a joke and we were at a loss as how to put a stop to it. He would run the deer off at night and we would not see anything during the day. It went on all year and the next year, I decided to put a stop to it.

We heard him shoot late one night and I picked up my rifle and headed to the woods. I was pretty good at moving around in the woods without a light, so I left mine in camp on purpose. I got within 200 yards of where he was shining his light around, and looked at it through my scope. I pulled the sight line about 10 yards to the right from where he was, and fired a round off. His light went out and it never came back on again then or any night after that. We saw him on Sunday when we were loading our cars and he never mentioned it.

Locating a Place to Hunt

Scouting For Turkey

The one thing that draws more hunters into turkey hunting is deer hunting. Stupid statement? Not really. If a hunter is in his stand waiting on a deer and a flock of turkeys feed near him, the first thing he probably does is look at them through his scope.

Then he thinks to himself, "*They don't look like they would be that hard to kill.*"

He then thinks, "*Maybe next spring I will give it a try.*"

It's a good drawing card that will make him return in the spring. If he doesn't plan on returning, he will talk about seeing the birds and will give you a clue about where to start looking. I keep my ears open, because hunters as well as non-hunters love to tell about seeing birds on their travels. You can spot them yourself in open fields, alongside highways, flying across highways etc. I located my favorite spot indirectly from my tax-preparer. She said in a casual conservation about seeing a flock stroll through her yard early one morning. I made no response, but that evening I looked her address up in the phone book. I found that she lived on a road that bordered the national forest, and I knew that this might be a good place to look. I have a county map on the wall that I use a high liter pen to mark any time I see or hear about anyone seeing any turkey. Sometime later on, I scouted that area looking for droppings, feathers, or tracks. Turkeys scratch the ground like chickens, and will turn over large areas of leaves on the forest floor.

If they are moving through an area looking for food, they will step forward, scratch once with each leg, and pause to see if they uncovered anything. Then they step forward again two or three steps, and repeat the scratching. They will move through an area like this until they find something that will keep them in one immediate area.

In the mountains they will turn over large areas under white oaks where squirrels have been feeding on acorns. I even once found a whole pecan in the craw of a turkey I was cleaning. They feed on the broken pieces that the squirrels drop, along with whole acorns. They love almost any kind of sprouts that come up from seeds, and will pull them up to eat seed and all.

I check areas around oak trees, cypress trees etc. to see if I can find any scratching. I also check around water to see if there are any fresh tracks. Most of the time you will only see the toe prints on hard ground, but you will become efficient at even spotting these if you take your time and really check the ground. I look for droppings, and feathers along old logging roads. They like to feed around and on new cut-over timber and they especially like the new grass that the foresters plant on their new roads after they finish hauling logs over them. In the early spring and the first of gobbler season the first grass to come up is always an attractive spot for turkeys to visit. They have been without any green in their diet all winter and I guess it is like ice cream to them. These spots are only good for about a week for grass soon begins to pop up everywhere. Turkeys are always accessible to water and most of the time will roost over or near water. I look along creek banks and in marshy areas. The Osceola strain of turkey in the Everglades will feed on grass seeds on grass growing out of the water. They can look awfully strange wading along in a foot of water, holding their tails up like a chicken to keep from getting it wet. I have a hobby of looking for ginseng and the time to find it is in the summer. Walking the woods slow and observant kills two birds at one time. Several times I have observed birds while easing along on the side of a mountain. Turkey love the same type of terrain where ginseng grows. This may sound strange but a lot of the time I try to think, *"What would the turkey do?"*

I will look at an area and try to guess which area or group of trees I would like to spend the night in if I were a turkey. Surprisingly, with a little experience a person can get fairly good at this. Ask questions of yourself. Is there a tree in that group that has limbs that would be comfortable for a turkey to roost? They seem to favor limbs that are a little smaller than the head of softball bat. But there are no set rules with a turkey. Is the area accessible to water? In dry areas they will roost over or near water. I have noted that they will usually end up getting a drink in the first hour after fly down. The birds in the mountains will sometimes roost on the high ridges and sail down the mountain to the lower valley.

The first time you hear it you wonder, "*What in the heck is that noise as they go by?*"

Other times they will roost at the head of a cove and either fly down underneath the tree or fly out to the paralleling ridge.

Turkeys like to roost in the same area and if left alone, some will roost in the same tree for several nights, and sometime even years. When you hear someone talk about a turkey roost, they usually mean a group of trees that the turkeys use frequently as a place to sleep. In the mountains they seem to use the top of the coves most often. They will pick a large tree near the top of the cove. Big gobblers will sometime gobble a few times, then sail out of the tree and glide to the bottom of the mountain. Other times they drop down right under the tree they roosted on, and then wander off. No one really knows why they make these choices, but it seems like the times I go up to the top of the mountain, they sail down, and when I stay down, they stay up. Go figure!

The roosts in south Florida are easier to predict, because of the flatter land. They favor roosting over water in the largest trees in the area. This is usually a large cypress tree along the edge of a pond or in a cypress strand. After you find the right kind of setting and find birds, you will get where you can look at, and just about tell where they are likely to fly up to roost. Turkeys can all be killed out in a particular area and have no birds for years. When they are re-introduced to that area several years later, they will pick that same group of trees as a roosting place. About the only thing that will change this is pressure from hunting or loss of terrain.

Scouting for Deer

Deer don't sleep at night like a turkey, so you have to be more careful when you are moving around before daylight, looking for a place to set up your stand. There are two main things that a deer does that give away the fact that they inhabit an area. They are called the rubbing and the scraping. Bucks are what most hunters are interested in and they are the ones that leave the signs that they have been there. Being observant in the woods takes practice. It also takes time to get to know an area. Don't be in a hurry. Observe the woods; there are a lot of telltale signs that will go unnoticed if you are in a hurry. Looking at a leaf covered forest floor at first glance looks all the same. If you look close you might see where a deer has spent time sleeping. The leaves will be all pressed flat where his body was curled up. It will leave about a two foot circle, and usually if you look closely, you will see where there may have been more than one. Tracks are hard to find on a leaf littered forest floor, but occasionally you will find droppings. They are about the size of rabbit pellets, but they are more egg shaped and a dark brown or black color. Droppings will usually be in a pile so they are easy to spot.

One of the funniest things I ever saw on a hunting show was a stunt pulled on Terry Bradshaw, the quarterback. The narrator of the show had obviously set up a stunt with rolled up small balls of tootsie rolls to simulate deer droppings. He was showing them to Terry, an admitted novice to hunting. He was standing under a tree explaining to Terry that you could tell deer were in the area by these droppings.

He said, "This is deer poop. You can see that it looks pretty fresh by its color and the fact that it still looks moist."

Terry was looking very intently and taking in every word as the narrator was explaining about deer sign.

He then said, "Now if you really want to see how long ago the deer was here, you can taste it and almost tell to the minute." With that statement he reached down and picked one up and popped it in his mouth.

The camera was on Terry's face and it was a classic. He first had a look of horror, and then he realized he had been had and shoved the man away.

The same as with turkey, you can tell when deer are in the area by their tracks. Florida has a lot of wet places where tracks are easier to find than in dryer country. Old roads are sometimes good ways for deer to travel from one area to another. A lot of the time you can tell where deer are crossing, because they will climb a bank in the same place, over and over, and leave a noticeable path at that point. White oaks are good gathering points for deer and produce their favorite acorn. I have a friend that has an area in the National Forest where he likes to set up his stand. He goes in the summer and takes a 50 pound bag of fertilizer and fertilizes two or three trees in a group that are right in front of where he looks. They produce more acorns and he harvests a good buck every year; so who knows, maybe he has a good system.

Corn fields, soy beans or any crop that deer like to feed on are the obvious. One unlikely spot that I found by accident that proved to be a feeding spot was a small shallow pond. It was about a hundred feet across and only about 5 foot deep in the center. Its surface, except for the outer edge, was covered with miniature water lilies. Five or six feet from the bank the water was muddy and the lilies were gone. I walked around the pond and found where the deer had been going in the water. I set up my stand and waited there at daylight. I didn't get a buck out of that experience, but I sure learned something that day. Four does came and fed on the lilies for over an hour. What surprised me was that they would put their heads all the way under water, to clip off the stems of those plants and eat stem leaf and all.

Deer lose their horns in the winter after the rut. Sometimes during the last of the hunting season, I have been dragging a buck by his horns and have it pop off in my hand. They grow new ones in the spring and they are covered with a fuzzy growth that must itch them something awful. A buck will frequent an area to feed, and I like to think he is advertising for a doe. A telltale sign, that you are in the right spot or close to where he is advertising, is when you spot a tree that he is using to rub that fuzzy material (velvet) off his horns. The average size tree that they use is about one inch in diameter. The bark will be rubbed clean off for an area of one foot off the ground, up to about three feet off the ground. Look around that area closely, for you know there has been a buck there recently if the rubbings are fresh. I had much rather find, old and new rubs in the same area; then I knew that bucks have been using that same area for more than one year. Once you find a rub, you really need to scout that area thoroughly. I like to hang a piece of toilet paper on a rub and start circling it until I find something else. Usually, a hundred feet or so away, you will probably find another. If you tie a piece of paper on this one, and circle it, you may find another. After you have found several, you will notice if they are following some kind of pattern; maybe following a ridge line, or a small branch, or even an old logging road. The trees they pick to rub can be hardwood or pines, but in my area they favor Virginia Cedars. They rub them so much; it will remove the bark so completely, they kill the tree. The theory is that the bigger the tree they chose to rub signifies the bigger the buck. That statement is one that I am not too sure of; I like to think the taller the rub, the bigger the buck.

Somewhere in that same vicinity you will also find their "scrapes," and then you know that you are in the right spot. Why they do this is known only to the buck, but they all do it. You will find a low bush that has an overhanging branch. That branch will be about four to five feet high and almost devoid of leaves. They will break the ends of a few of the branches. They don't seem to bite them off, just break them over on the tips. Directly under the broken branches, they will paw the leaves back until the ground is bare in a circle of about two or two and a half feet. They will urinate on that spot and then leave it. Somewhere a couple of hundred feet away they will repeat this process much like the rubs. I have watched a buck do this the weekend before the season opened. He tilted his head back and moved it around in the overhead branch, almost like it was giving him some erotic kick.

When you find a row of these scrapes, you can locate as high as a dozen, and they will follow some kind of pattern. From these signs you know that a buck is advertising for a doe, and he is going to check those spots sometime in the near future. The doe, when she is in heat and ready, will find one of those scrapes and also urinate on it. Then she will be close by waiting for the buck to find her. I always set my stand off to the side of their pattern, so that they don't notice anything strange when they are making their rounds.

I have always felt like persistence is the best ally in harvesting a deer. When I was young and had a lot of energy, I hunted in the Everglades. A better description would be in The Big Cypress. My area of hunting consisted of about one mile squared and I really had no reason to go any farther. There was plenty of game for the three of us that hunted together within that area.

We had an occasional bear stroll through; although we never killed one at our camp, they were there. There were several flocks of turkey that were in our area, and we always managed to have deer meat in the freezer from one of us. Hogs were plentiful along with ducks, fox squirrels, plenty of snipe and we could find a rabbit any time we wanted. My partners would start out in the morning with big ideas. About 10 am they would start thinking about the pot of beans or greens we had back at the camp, and that cool bed, and would head in for the morning. I got in the habit of taking something to eat and drink and I would stay up in the stand until late in the day. I made it comfortable so I wouldn't get tired.

One thing I wish they had invented earlier is the lap top.

Another thing I discovered is that deer have no set rules that they follow. If anything, they probably move around more frequently at night but other than that, when they get hungry, they eat and when they want to rest or sleepy, they sleep. If you are not there when they decide to move around you are not going to get a chance to get a shot. I shot a nice 6 pointer from that stand, three o'clock in the afternoon walking around out on a place we had burnt off the day before.

Tom and Art always accused me of being lucky but I always answered, "Persistent is the word to use."

"If you aren't in the woods you aren't going to kill anything."

I got a good back handed compliment once from my nephew's friend, Danny Creel, a good hunter himself.

When he was asked on returning to camp by one of the members where Sonny was?

He answered, "You see those buzzards circling over there? I'll bet good money he is somewhere right underneath them."

Danny Creel

Turkey Hunting Section

I am going into turkey hunting first, because admittedly, it is my favorite.

The Wild Turkey
(Meleagris gallopavo)

The wild turkey is one of the largest birds of North America; it is a native, ranging many centuries from Mexico to southern Canada. It was a staple food supply for the American Indian long before the European man made his way across the oceans. It has been worshiped in rituals by many of our native tribes. Its feathers are still used on ceremonial robes in proceedings by several Indian nations to this day. Its wing feathers are used to fletch and guide most of the modern arrows made today. It is a majestic bird that Benjamin Franklin, I, and several of our forefathers thought should have been the national bird. Now I'm talking about the turkey in the wild state, any comparison to the domestic bird is purely coincidental. Other than a few wild areas, large farms, and private ranches, the wild turkey population was almost decimated in the United States. In the early 70's biologist started to turn it around. Some ranches protected the birds by only letting select friends shoot them off the roost, so as not to scatter them.

The south Florida strain "Osceola" is considered to be the wildest by most hunters. When you scatter them over thousands of acres of public land, the odds really start to go down that you will ever see a gobbler, much less see them without working at it.

I was lucky enough, when I was a child, that I grew up in an area that still had a turkey population large enough to withstand hunting pressure. During the forties and fifties, turkey hunting was allowed at the same time as deer and quail season, and spring gobbler season didn't exist. I probably ran off more turkeys in my early attempts to call, than I got interested, in my feeble attempts. I can truly say that I learned to call turkeys by listening and observing. The scarcity of birds and not having anyone to teach me made it a long process before I got my first kill. Although it was illegal, some of the large ranches hunted turkey (much as we hunt quail), but preferred shooting them off the roost. Although a bird dog will work a turkey in much the same way as a quail, a turkey won't hold for a point as long as a quail. I have been quail hunting and I thought something was wrong with the dogs, the way they were working the birds. They would point for a few seconds, break point, move a few yards foreword, point, and continue again and again, moving farther. They would keep this up until finally the turkey would flush, leaving everyone surprised.

In recent years biologist have been very successful in introducing birds into areas that have been void for many years. I live in an area where a few old timers still believe it is all right to kill something (any time of the year), as long as it's for the table. To me, anyone who depends on game for the table hasn't caught up to modern times. Until we started protecting them with proper conservation and our new game laws, this lack of understanding, almost led to the downfall of a lot of game in this country. During the end of the Second World War, many efforts were made to re-stock areas, without much success. Pen raised birds were introduced; and they soon died off, because they did not know how to survive in the wild. Many different methods were tried (without much success) until someone tried the cannon net to trap wild birds, and move them rapidly in dark boxes to a new habitat. An area is picked where there are ample birds and bait is spread so that the birds become used to feeding at a certain spot. A long net (cannon net) is laid out in a line in the feeding area. One side is fastened to the ground. The other side is fastened to several small canons that are aimed so that they will pull the net in an arch over the top of the bait that is placed parallel to the net. The net usually has to be concealed with leaves to make it less noticeable. A triggerman is placed in a concealed blind, and he waits for the birds to arrive. The triggerman has to time firing the net until all, or most, of the birds have their heads down. The ones with their heads up will simply fly out from under the net. Some (with their heads down) will even make it out. The Wild Turkey Federation and volunteers have helped tremendously in re-introducing birds to a new habitat. Leaving the birds alone for several years, after introduction and protecting them, has allowed the rapid growth of our turkey population. When a new area is chosen and restocked, there is a good effort made to inform the public. Signs are posted all around the area, and rewards are offered for persons who report any molesting of the turkey.

When I first moved to North Georgia the process of re-introducing birds was just beginning and several of the old timers in the area were caught poaching for the table. The Judges were tough on the law breakers and the word soon got out to leave them alone. New people moving in, started protecting the birds. A "Change in attitude" re-introduced turkeys into areas that haven't had wild birds in many decades. Loss of habitat is probably the greatest danger the sportsman has of losing the privilege of hunting this majestic bird.

The turkey in the wild is sleek, and very seldom do you ever see a feather out of place. They are very agile, (can run almost 40 miles an hour), and fly even faster. I was riding a motorcycle across a freshly burnt field and happened to flush out a gobbler. I got behind him with him running, and I clocked him up to 40 mph before he came off the ground. I tried to stay even with him while he was in flight, and I was doing above 50 mph. He pulled away from me with no problem. The domestic pen raised bird would have had trouble flying two feet. A turkey has a fairly small head compared to his body size, with wattles or bare neck about a third of the way to his body. The hens' wattle is somewhat smaller than the gobbler and ranges in color from a pale blue-gray, to gray with a touch of red. In the woods they look gray like a weathered tree limb that has lost its bark. The hens' feathers are a lighter gray on her lower neck and shoulders; she has an almost perfect camouflage. Her feathers all over are somewhat duller than the male. Her body size is smaller, averaging somewhere around 10 lbs. (this depends on the sub species). The males' wattle is much bulkier and can change color like a chameleon. Most males will have a noticeable red color to it. In full strut a tom will be baby blue in color around the head, sometimes a little white, but mostly a crimson red. If you get a gobbler up close and you can see his wattle, it changes from a bright red to a duller light red according to his mood. The snood is a membrane that hangs down from the top of his head and it will droop along one side of his head or the other. His mood also seems to control the length of the snood. Fighting turkeys go for the snood and will hang on when they get ahold of it. The feathers on the gobbler range from a bronze to sometimes solid black, but always with an iridescent sheen like a piece of coal. Their feathers have the ability, like satin, to change colors, depending from which angle they are being observed. About middle ways of the back, the feathers start having buff tips to them and this continues to include the tail. In this same area the base of the feathers start changing to more of a brown on the base part, with a black stripe near the top, followed with a buff tip. The tail feathers, the part that he fans, are a motley brown at the base with the black stripe and buff tip.

I have described the wild turkeys coloration in general, for there are subtle differences between the five different sub-species that live throughout the United States.

When the gobbler is close to the hen, in full strut, he will always angle the front of his tail fan toward the hen. The wing feathers, (what are known as flight feathers), are very ridged; they are the gray and white that you always see on arrows. I recently had the opportunity to observe two turkeys, (one gobbler and one hen) as they glided past me. I noticed that on both of them, the wing feathers on the tips actually flared up on the end. I have a collection of turkey paintings, and I have seen many more, but I have never seen this feature illustrated.

The wild turkey has very keen eye sight and is very cunning. If they know to try and fly to escape would be dangerous for them, they will hide in a clump of grass or in a bush until they see which side you are going to walk past. After you have gone past them, they will escape by either flying or sneaking out of range with their head down. I have noticed the Osceola strain tends to choose to escape on the ground, whenever possible.

Most of the year adult gobblers will be found alone or in small groups of other gobblers. In the early spring when all of their feathers are at their finest, the mating season is triggered. The adult hens are still grouped with younger hens and some jakes may be with them. There will be a lot of fighting between the jakes and occasionally an older gobbler will put them in their place. The gobblers, when they are grouped with hens, are not in a gobbling mood; but are more interested in displaying their wares. They spread their feathers in full display and they pull their head back, almost into their feathers. He will take a couple of steps forward, dragging the tips of his flight feathers on the ground. As he steps forward, he will suck in air and hold his breath; when he stops he will blow this air out with a sort of puff. All the time he is doing this, he is pointing the surface of his spread tail fan in the direction of the hen he is trying to impress. This dance for the hen's affection is described as drumming. You have to be rather close to even hear this blowing or drumming. The hens that are ready for mating will choose the gobbler; when he approaches she will squat in front of him and become very still. He will mount her and it actually looks like he is trying to mash her in the ground by treading on her back. The actual mating only takes a couple of seconds as their tails entwine. He will dismount, and gobble triumphantly, and resume his strutting.

Most of the time, when it is time to roost, the big gobblers will separate and find their own roosting tree. Hens can be loners at this time but usually they will still be traveling in groups. The boss gobbler treats these hens as his harem. The immature gobblers (Jakes) will challenge his authority occasionally, but it is never a fair contest. The gobblers will separate in the late afternoon. Sometimes, after flying to roost, I have heard a soft low cluck from the hen. I believe she is letting the gobbler know where she is roosting. I used to think that any gobbler was fair game for my gun, but as I grew older I have altered my thinking. Although it is still legal to shoot birds off the roost in some states, I now only use roosting as a way to set up tomorrows hunt. The usual pattern is; the gobbler will gobble several times, very early in the morning, during mating season, announcing their territory, and looking for a response from the hen that they were with the day before. If they get no response from a hen they will usually fly to where they heard her call the night before or at least to the last place they were with the hen.

Early mornings will bring a gobble from him. Sometimes it is to re-locate the hen or hens and sometimes it is triggered by an owl hooting, a crow calling, a hawk screeching or any loud noise. When the hen starts her nest and laying, she no longer will travel with other hens. She will roost alone and join back up with the gobbler shortly after daylight. Sometimes she will call very softly at daylight, and other times she will fly down and go to where she heard the gobbler.

They will mate shortly after joining back together, and he will follow along strutting, until the hen sneaks off to lay her egg for the day. Sometimes he will gobble several times when he has discovered she has disappeared. This usually occurs about ten o'clock in the morning but it can be as late as one PM. After the hen has begun to set on her nest, she avoids the gobbler (or any company) altogether. The gobbler has had it pretty good up until now, and he panics somewhat. He will gobble longer in the mornings and will start wandering far and wide searching for a hen. This is the best time to call in a gobbler, sort of playing on his emotions.

Biologist try to set hunting seasons to begin with the egg laying time and end with the period when the gobblers are wandering, and the hens are setting on their nests.

On The Nest

Very Little Cover

Surprisingly a hen will lay her eggs in a very

shallow nest, almost in the open, leaving a clear view, for herself, in all directions. She will lay from 9 to 14 eggs before she begins to set on them continually. When she is on the nest, she is about as camouflaged as she can be. She fluffs her feathers out to cover the eggs fully and fans her tail flat on the ground; and when danger approaches she will even drop her head to further conceal herself. She will blend easily with the leaves with her dull gray and light brown feather tips. If a person or animal approaches too close, she will try to lead the culprit away from the nest by feigning injury as she leads them in the wrong direction.

Before she begins to set on the eggs continuously, she will lay one egg a day, very seldom skipping a day without laying one. She will stay in close proximity to the nest while she feeds frantically, fattening herself for her long set on the nest. After she decides she has laid enough eggs, she will not communicate with the gobblers and will actually avoid any contact.

The hen can lay three full nests from one breeding. By this I mean that she can lay one nest, have it destroyed, also have the second one destroyed, and lay a third nest. The eggs will still be fertile, all from one breeding by the gobbler.

This is bad news for the gobbler and has made him almost expendable. After he has completed his early breeding, (if you think about it), all of the gobblers could die at this point and it would not hurt the population of the flock. This is why the states, that have begun re-stocking, can have spring gobbler seasons many years before the overall population gets big enough to open a fall season and allow the killing of hens.

The hen sets on the nest, turning the eggs frequently. The eggs start hatching around 23 days after she starts setting around the clock. A couple of days before they hatch they start making a peeping sound, even before they come out of the shell. The hen starts bonding with them at this time, making a soft purring sound, with an occasional cluck. The little (poults) turkeys start pecking their way out of the shell, and momma will stay setting on the nest for as long as 36 hours, or as long as it takes all of the poults to emerge. She will not move very far the first day after she has left the nest. As the poults gain strength she will move faster and farther. All the time she is constantly communicating with them, and guiding them on what they eat, what is a danger. She will call them back to her when they wander too far, and sometime she will call them up under the protection of her wings for no other reason than to rest. Rain is very dangerous for young poults and can easily cause their death. At these times she will collect them under her feathers and sit down. The hen can sit for hours protecting the poults in this manner. Sustained bad weather will kill off most of the young poults and produce reduced gobbler numbers for a couple of years.

Young poults are led by the hen to areas where they

can find plenty of insects. You will find the hen and poults around grass fields, cut overs, and anywhere they can find insects. Insects are high in protein and are needed in the early life of poults. Later on in life and later in the summer, when the grass starts putting on seeds, their diet will switch over to mainly seeds and nuts. As the poults mature they lose the peeping sound and they will develop a whistling sound that has the same sequence and pattern as mature birds. They will keep this sound well into their first year, and sometimes their voice breaks much like a teen age boy.

Young poults hatch with some wing feathers; after a few days they are able to fly for short distances. The hen can sound an alarm and the poults will fly up landing on anything that will support their weight. If they are in the grass, and she sounds an alarm, they will hide in the grass until she sounds the all clear. The hen will roost on the ground as long as she needs to protect them from weather. After she can't cover them anymore, she will start roosting in the trees. At first they will all try to crowd under her on one limb, eventually moving out on the limb in a line. As they mature they start seeking their own limb. They never seen to be satisfied with the limb they initially pick, moving several times before they finally settle down for the night. Even adult birds seem to have difficulty settling on a comfortable limb. If left alone, hens will take up with other hens and form large flocks that will stay together throughout most of the winter. You can find jakes; (young male turkeys) grouped together, right through the spring and summer. Older gobblers are pretty much loners but they can be seen in large groups of adult males

Turkey Hunting

Turkey hunting can be rewarding or frustrating; you can make it whatever you wish. If you are impatient and have enough money, you can find a private reserve, hire a guide, and make a kill without much effort or much knowledge. If you don't have a lot of money, and truly enjoy a challenge, there are many public lands open all over the US. I am a believer turkey hunting can be the most rewarding sporting experience you will ever have. It will teach you to have patience like you never thought you could achieve. You will look at Mother Nature as you have never before.

During deer season, in late fall or early winter, the migratory birds have already left for the winter. The leaves have fallen, leaving the woods stark and cold. Most of the activity from small animals has disappeared; they have denned up and they are concentrating on keeping warm. In contrast spring gobbler hunting brings you in contact with nature at time of the year when the most beautiful sunrises are taking place. It is a time when our world is at its finest. Everything seems happy and full of life, birds are singing, and flowers are more vivid under an early spring, sunny morning. My wife doesn't like to hunt, but she sometimes accompanies me, taking along a book and pillow, sitting up against a tree, and getting her enjoyment from watching the woods wake up on a spring morning.

Turkey hunting is a sport where a so called dumb bird can make a complete fool of you before you realize what has happened. In the beginning of my experiences, I called up a lot of other hunters. It’s amazing the excuses a man can come up with, after he has just crawled a hundred yards, to find "Its- a-turkey" all right, but it’s "Not-a-bird" and it’s scratching on a piece of slate.

I had one fellow tell me, "He was just trying to see how close he could get before I noticed him."

All kidding aside, I realized as I got older that more and more amateurs were beginning to hunt. I soon discovered it’s a good way to get shot, playing games when someone is armed. It’s gotten to the point where there are more people killed or wounded during turkey season than during dear season.

When someone uses “I thought he was a turkey” for an excuse, I wish the Judge would ask, "Did you think the person was a gobbler or a hen?”

Accidents happen, but mistaking someone for a turkey is not an accident. Don’t forget, you are in the woods camouflaged and you are very hard to see, even by an experienced hunter.

When you see someone in the woods, ask yourself this question; "If they shot towards me could they hurt me?"

Always identify your position to them. The best way is to look out for yourself! If they are close enough for you to see, you aren't going to see any turkey for a while, anyway. Try to sit against a tree or rock that will cover your head and torso from your backside. Some people will shoot at any movement or sound when they hear a turkey calling. If you have your back covered, you are more likely to see someone approaching from the front, and you can warn them where you are. **Don't hesitate to do this if they are approaching you**. Besides, if your back is covered, it gives you a better chance to look behind you; without that turkey seeing you move, when he walks up behind you.

Hunting takes a lot of concentration. If you are always on guard and aware of what's going on around you, and if you follow a few simple rules; you will have a much safer trip. Errors in judgment from other people trying to hunt the same area as you, and a thousand other reasons can spoil a hunt; but the very worst thing that can happen, is to have some kind of an avoidable accident.

Persistence will pay off and will override errors in judgment and lack of experience, as you become more and more confident in playing the game.

After all, as one old timer told me, “It’s a simple thing to kill a gobbler. All you have to do to kill a gobbler is place yourself between where he is, and where he wants to go."

Turkey Hunting Equipment

If you don’t go prepared, about the only thing you will ever see of a big old gobbler in the woods, is his tracks, an occasional feather, and some droppings. I know there are exceptions to any rules, but this is one critter that doesn’t make many mistakes.

I’ll start with your head gear and work down. You will be sitting on the ground leaning against a tree, a lot of the time. When you lean your head back, you don’t want your hat tipping up in the air, so you need a soft brim in the back, or better yet, one with no brim in the rear. Without question you should always think camouflage when turkey hunting. Your head is really important, for everyone has a tendency to move that part of the body first. You have to move your head a little to see, so this should be concealed the best. I began hunting turkey before all the camouflage patterns. I started with the old olive green clothing, like army fatigues. Its common now, but I remember coming to work one morning in my new set of camouflage clothing, as I was taking the day off and we were going to travel that day to our hunting spot.

As I walked in the door an old black man, a friend of mine that loaded our trucks, looked at me and said, "It ain't working Boyer."

I looked at him with a quizzical look and replied, "What's that Otis?"

He smiled and said, "I can still see you."

All kidding aside, there are some real deceptive patterns being introduced every time I turn around. The color patterns that I have settled on match the colors of the woods in my area that occur in March and April when our season begins. My fall patterns for deer hunting are different.

The first face gear that I used was a piece of green sheer curtain material, but it was hard to see through. Later on I found that the terrazzo men received their colored rocks in small green nylon bags that worked perfect for going over your head. I sewed in an old pair of glasses, with no lens, to hold the eye holes in place. Next I wore a net that is like a small bag over the top. I pull the front of this up, and hang it over the bill of my cap until I know I have a turkey coming to me. Then I drop it down, covering my eye holes. This allows me to see well so that I can see any movement, and I don't miss anything that may be moving toward me. This second netting works very well as a mosquito guard for my face and neck. My last improvement is a "slip over" covering that has loose leaves sewn onto it. I really like this rig for it breaks up your contour and makes you look like a bush.

The best alternative to the netting is the camouflage face paint that you can now purchase. This is very popular, (especially among the younger hunters); but my experiences lead me to believe that turkeys react quicker to profiles and movement than to color. Sometimes a spring morning can be rather warm and the paint on your face can become unpleasant, especially if you start to sweat. I wear long sleeve shirts, (no matter how hot) and light weight gloves, so that I can operate the safety without taking them off. My belt was always dull with a buckle that didn't shine or have a bright color. I now wear suspenders most of the time when I am hunting. If my pants seem to require tugging up from ill-fitting pants or an ill-shaped torso like mine, you may be surprised how much easier it is to walk through the woods with a pair of suspenders on. I noticed when I stepped over a large log, I had to first hike my pants up before I made the step. This was tiring and I was constantly ripping the crouch of my pants out. Believe me you want to keep the repairs at a minimum that fall in your wife's department. When it comes to hunting keep your activities low profile when around your wife.

NEVER PRACTICE TURKEY CALLING WHILE YOUR WIFE IS IN HEARING DISTANCE!

My pants are camouflaged, brush type with deep pockets. The brush type is quiet and keeps you from getting scratched by briars. My favorite pair have zippers sewn across the pocket tops, so I am not constantly losing things out of my pocket. It's awfully discouraging to have to climb all the way back up a mountain, to find a favorite pocket knife that slid out of your pocket while you were calling turkeys. Some of the military combat pants have deep pockets with snaps or buttons that can prevent this from happening. There are pillows that hang off your belt, or the back of your pants. They make it more comfortable when you sit. I tried them, but I don’t like anything flopping around when I walk. My shoes are very important to me as my feet are hard to fit. I didn't have very much experience with cold weather when I first moved to the mountains, and I had a tendency to buy my shoes too tight. I soon discovered that with tight shoes you never can keep your feet warm. I now wear light weight, high top insulated sneakers or walking shoes. The insulated type doesn’t seem to be any hotter on warm days, yet they tend to stay drier on wet days. You may not feel comfortable wearing a light weight shoe in the area that you wish to hunt, because of the snake problem. Here in the mountains the weather is still cool enough that snakes are not usually moving at this time of the year. In Florida where they also had a fall season, the weather is warmer and I wore some kind of snake protection.

Today there are many types of ways to protect from being bitten, such as snake proof leggings, chaps boots, and snake proof pants. The decision, to wear or not to wear, has to be your choice depending on where you are hunting. On my back, I carry a small day pack like the kids use to carry their school books. Also over my shoulder I carry a Bota bag, for my water supply. My son sent me one from Spain, as a souvenir. The original had a tar interior and the water tasted awful, but I could see right away this was perfect for turkey hunting.

I now have one with a plastic or vinyl interior and it is covered with leather. The reason that these are better than a conventional canteen is, they fit under your arm, out of the way, and the water does not slosh around and make a lot of unnecessary noise.

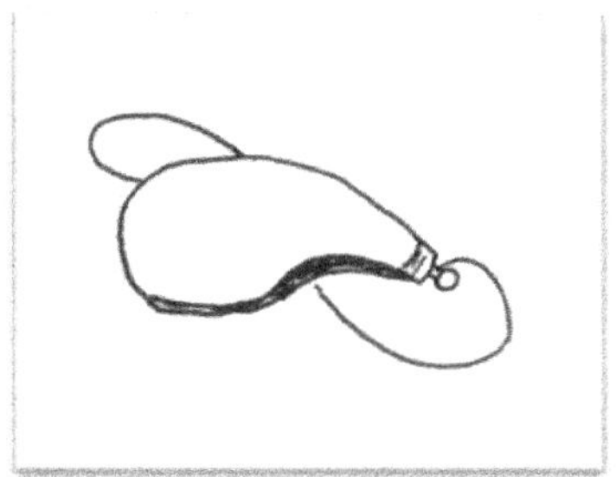

Bota Bag
Leather bound, plastic lined wine container. Fits around shoulder and above waist.

In my small pack I carry articles that I feel are necessary to have a successful hunt. In the small pocket on the back side of the pack, I carry; 3 to 5 shells. I usually load my gun with three legal shells. I have a small liquid filled compass that I use for more than finding my way. An assortment of turkey calls, a head net, my sharp bird knife.

A bird knife has an extra blade with a hook that is used to hook the entrails out of the chest cavity.

I carry a piece of heavy string about 18 inches long with a loop tied in each end, a heavy string about 10 feet long, a partial roll of toilet paper in a re-sealable plastic bag, and I carry a small squeeze bottle of insect repellent in a plastic bag. I also carry my gloves in this compartment when I am not wearing them. I used to carry cigarettes and chewing tobacco in this compartment, until I quit both twenty five years ago. The only sense that a turkey doesn't use when he is out smarting you is his sense of smell. Cigarette smoke is almost impossible to conceal as a turkey has eye sight that may even be better than an eagle. I never could master a mouth call with a wad of tobacco in my mouth anyway, so quitting didn't bother me when I was turkey hunting. I was calling with a box call one time with a wad of tobacco in my mouth. A turkey came in from behind me, not making a sound, and stepped out right in front of me. It startled me so much I swallowed the tobacco, I almost choked in the process, and the coughing ran the turkey off in the commotion. I ended up sick to my stomach. It wasn't long after that I quit.

In the large compartment of my backpack I carry a military surplus poncho that is camouflage. I prefer this over the olive drab. I used the olive drab color for years and it seemed to work fine. I used to use the cheap plastic ones, but they tear so easy on briars that I finally bought a good one. I try to buy everything in what they call camo green; mostly because that was the first camouflage that I ever saw. My son, who hunts with me, has everything in treebark pattern; so we don't argue about who has who's clothes. I also carry rolled up netting that I use for a blind, a piece of foam rubber (18 inches square), inside a camouflage bag that will fit over the foam rubber. If I plan on staying past lunch, I also carry my food there. If I can help it, I never carry anything in my pockets that might rattle, I even hide my car keys at my vehicle, so I won't lose them in the woods. I carry the foam rubber to sit on, because my old fanny can't take those root knots, and rocks that always seem to be where ever you want to sit. The bag can be used to carry the foam rubber in and carry a turkey out. After you have bled the turkey, I put him in the camo bag head first; I then gather his feet, and tail feathers, and put them in the bag and tie them all together with that long piece of cord that I have in the small pocket of my pack. Next I tie the bag and turkey to the back of my pack and I am ready for that long walk to the road. You can carry a turkey for a short distance, by swinging him over your shoulder, but if you have to carry it very far with spurs cutting into your hands, you will have wished you had taken the time to tie him to your pack. If it's a rainy day I will also add a large fold up camo umbrella, the type that ties around a tree.

I also have a small pack that is similar in size to my original that also has a fold up seat made into it. The older I get the harder I find it is to get up from sitting on the ground, so this pack makes it simpler. I occasionally carry a small metal frame seat that will bridge some of those rocks. I usually know the type of terrain and how many natural blinds that I have previously prepared, so I have an idea what kind of seat I need. I carry a small fold up saw to trim brush away. I carried an anti-venom kit in Florida, but I eliminated that when I moved to the mountains.

Blinds

A lot of good natural places occur in the woods that offer good hiding places for you to call a turkey. Fallen over trees, old stumps etc. are some of the better ones that occur naturally. The only trouble is they never occur in a place where you need them. If I am hunting an area continually I have developed a habit that has paid off a couple of times. If I am having success in an area I will, after the hunt, before I go home, or back to the truck, I find a good spot and take the time to drag up old branches, rocks, anything that will make good concealment. I put these near where I have seen turkey, or where I have heard them fly down. It helps when you hear a gobble and you remember that very close is a blind that you built.

I also have the netting blind that I carry inside my pack. I purchased four yards of camo green netting and made a simple blind that works well. The netting material is 50 inches wide and I turned the side over about 1 & ½ inches making a hem that runs the full a length of the material. I double sewed it, and then I started at one end and cut little half-moons out of the edge about a foot apart. I next took about a 30 foot piece of olive drab parachute cord and threaded it through the hem, going past the end about 18 inches and I stitched it permanent to that end of the net. This lets the 18 inch loose end of cord to tie off to something to start my blind. When I start to set up, I establish my seat and where I want to watch. I sit down if I can and usually start on my left. I tie this end somewhere close to my left shoulder, about eye height. Sitting down, about as far out as I can reach with my left hand is where I want the blind to make a turn. I reach into one of those half-moon holes, at about that distance, pull out a loop of the cord and find something out front to it tie to. If there is no branch or small object to tie to, you can create one by leaning a limb against the tree. I repeat this procedure on my right returning to the object that I am leaning against. I end up with a U shaped blind with only the top of my head sticking out.

With a little practice you can learn to do this rather fast. The 30 foot cord allows you to reach objects well out in front without running out of cord before you finish. You can purchase a blind similar that has poles that go with it, but I find this type too bulky. I like the blind where I can just see over the top so I can scoot down and conceal myself even more when a bird approaches.

The Right Mechanical Call

Now to the mechanical call itself. There are thousands of different types of calls, and I am sure some turkeys have been killed in front of all of them.

The most natural call is the one that people make when they use their own voice. This is usually easier for children and ladies and it becomes difficult for men because of their voice range. The mouth call or diaphragm is the type that fits inside of your mouth. It uses a small rubber reed that you blow across. I like this one the best, for you can call with it without any noticeable movement. They are hard for the average person to learn to use. I practiced with one for years before I gained the confidence to use it in the woods under battle conditions. It is my primary call. In fact I remake, and constructed my own diaphragm calls, using light-weight aluminum, duct tape and latex gloves. I make a habit of carrying several types of calls every time I hunt. I have found that if one call doesn't work, you can switch to another kind, and sometimes get a whole different response.

Another category uses slate as a surface to produce a call. Another is Virginia Cedar wood. This is probably the most common and it gives a mellow tone. A call can be made by scraping a piece of cedar across a cedar box or a slate strip across a wood box. Or even wood against wood. The boxes can be oblong, square or round in shape and some substitute plastic for cedar. Some exchange the slate for aluminum, and some calls are made using cedar to cedar. Most of these calls have to be perfectly dry to operate. The end result is that they all turn out to be very effective calls. Of all these calls, I think these are the easiest to learn how to use. The next are the wing bone type. On the wing of the turkey, between the first and second hinge, starting from the tip, there are two bones parallel to each other. These are comparable to your own arm bones, the radius and the ulna. The smaller of the two, the radius, has knuckles that can be trimmed off square, the marrow cleaned out, and the bone dried. You can use either one, but the bone from a hen turkey makes the better sound for me. It could now be used as a short, (about five inches long) drinking straw, one end should have a slightly oval shape and this is the end to put to your mouth. Make a ball shape with your two hands; place the other end down into that ball between your thumb and fore finger. Using a sucking motion, (much like calling your pet) you can attain a sound that sounds very much like a turkey. It takes a lot of practice, but it is another call that can be used rain or shine. Some substitute their hands for a permanent type end. I have seen this type constructed from all kinds of materials: goat horns, coconut shells, cedar boxes, and etc. This call has been around the longest, for they have been found on ancient midden sights in many parts of the United States. You can substitute many things that are similar in size to the wing bone; drinking straws, cut to a length that suits you, work fine. If I am deer hunting and run up on turkey without any call, (where fall hunting is allowed) I like to cut a length of dried dog fennel grass and make a call. For me, the sound produced by this hollow grass makes the best sound of any of the wing bone type.

The cylinder type is a very easy call to construct; it is made out of a small container such as a small pill bottle or film container. Take the lid and cut a half circle hole through the top, consuming almost half of the top, leaving enough material on the top so that it will stay on the bottle. Take the bottle and drill a small hole in the center of the bottom, (about 3/8 of an inch in diameter), cut a small piece of latex, (about 2 inches square), and stretch it over the hole, leaving a slot about 1/8 inch wide. How taught, you will learn from practice. Hold this in place with a small rubber band around the lip of the bottle.

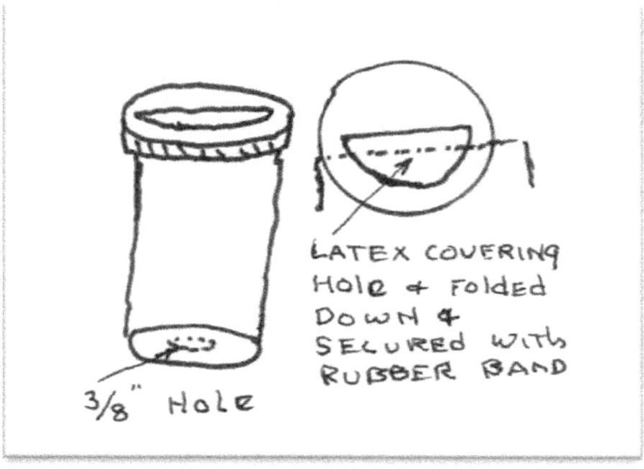

You place the latex against your lower lip with the larger portion of the container below the lip, blow lightly letting the latex vibrate against your lower lip. The sound produced, when you cup your hands over the container, can easily call a turkey. The nice thing about this type of call is that even if you had to purchase the materials, you can build it for about twenty cents. That's not as cheap as a drinking straw, but with a little practice you can learn to gobble with this call.

One of the most popular types of calls sold, is the elongated cedar box, that has two exposed sides. The top of this box is also cedar and is concave in shape. It is hinged at one end, with a screw through the center, and it has a handle on the other. Some calls are held in place, by rubber bands front and rear. Rubbing the lid on one side for the tom voice, or the other for the hen; and holding the call down and shaking it back and forth

Lynch Call

Hand Carved Cedar Box
Over 100 Years Old

for the gobble. You can reach a wide range of calls with this style.

The oldest I ever saw like this was owned by Dewey Bodiford, who lived in Sylvania, Georgia. He told me it was hand carved by his grandfather over a hundred years before. That would have dated it around 1880.

There are many different types of calls on the market, and I am sure all of them will work for someone. I believe that many will be invented in the future that will also work fine.

I always start someone new to the sport of turkey hunting with a simple slate call. It is the easiest to learn the basic calls, and hard to make a sound that will scare a turkey away. The type should be the one where you hold a slate covered box in your left hand, and have some sort of striker in your right, that you scratch across the slate producing the sound. After you become more involved, you would be wise to invest in some of the harder to learn calls.

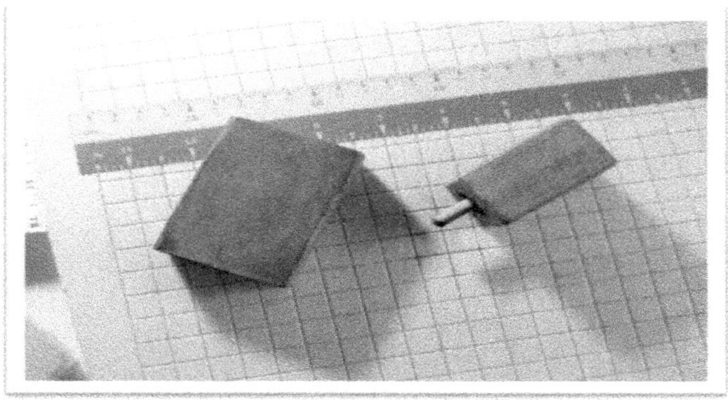

Slate Call I Make

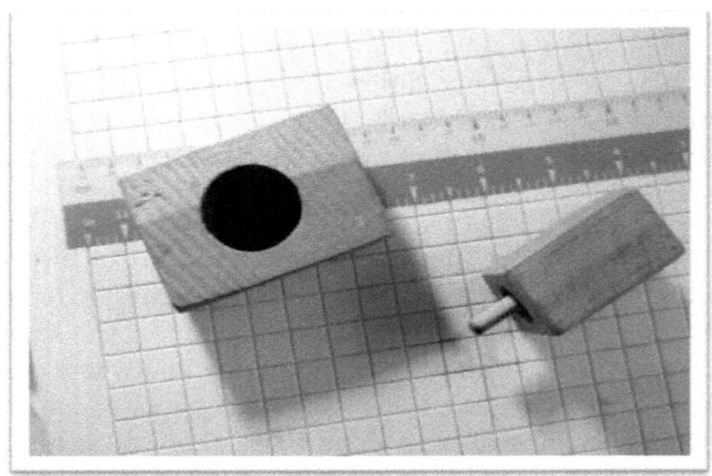

I have made about 25 calls that are similar in size to a standard pack of cigarettes. The striker is only about 2 inches long and I like them because they are small and they are very effective for calling a bird in closer, especially when a turkey is stubborn about coming closer.

Cleaning Your Turkey

After you have made a good shot and your turkey is flopping on the ground, one thing I do right away is to take my pocket knife, open the birds mouth and insert the blade up into his brain. I have a book on raising turkeys for the market, and it claims that to do this helps to release the feathers from the skin. Who knows if they are right? I do know that the other advice the book gave has simplified the time it takes to pick feathers off, so I do both, because this chore is not one of my favorites. You have probably heard your family tell of dunking chickens into boiling water so the feathers will come right off. Maybe you have done it yourself, but that would be telling your age. It works, but only one problem, a lot of the skin tears and comes off also. What this old book told me was to only heat the water to 175 degrees; submerge the bird under water for ten minutes, and then the feathers will come off without tearing the skin. I used to stand over a bird for what seemed like hours pulling every stubborn little feather out. I cut my time in half when I followed the book's direction. I have a fish fryer, the one with a big pot and strainer, that I use for heating water. I did get a deeper pot because the fryer pot is a little small. You have to be careful how much water you put in the pot for when you put the turkey in, it might overflow. Some hunters bypass this procedure and cut only the breast out of the turkey. They are delicious, but I personally like to cook a turkey the traditional way. To me that ain't nothing but being lazy. It just seems like a waste of a lot of good eating. I love the gravy as much as the meat. A fat Osceola turkey is as different tasting and better like the yard chicken is better than what you get in the store today.

One mistake that is made is in judging the weight of a wild turkey. The person who kills it always has a tendency to exaggerate the size. If one claims it to be 20 pounds, and in reality it only weighed 15 before it was cleaned, you end up with a 10 pound bird ready for cooking. Mama hears them describing the 20 pound bird, puts it in the oven and cooks it like it weighed 20 pounds. Then she ends up with a dried out cremated turkey. I found a set of baby scales at a yard sale and I weigh each turkey that is ready for the oven, so that it is not overcooked. Having eaten both the Osceola birds and the Eastern, I much prefer the Osceola for flavor. The birds that live in the mountains may be tasty, but the ones I have eaten are lacking something as far as flavor goes. My theory is that the Osceola has good food all year-round and mountain birds have to scrounge for food before the winter is over.

My favorite fried foul is a young turkey. I am not talking about this fad of cooking your Thanksgiving turkey in a deep fryer. A young five to eight pound turkey; cut up and fried like Mama used to serve chicken on Sunday, is a meal you will never forget. I really never understood why someone hasn't started a fast food restaurant that served turkey instead of chicken.

Blood Trailing a Turkey?

Turkey very seldom leave a blood trail, but I did have an experience where I could follow a blood trail. I was in Florida during the fall season working up-wind across a large pine and cabbage palm island. The fact that you could hunt deer and turkey at the same time kept me in turmoil all the time. I really never could make up my mind which species I wanted to concentrate on. The terrain in Florida is so varied that I finally settled to one specific stile. I didn't much care about sitting in one place hoping for something to amble by, so I did a lot of walking. I discovered that if I went out with a rifle I would end up in a bushy place and a shotgun would have been more practical. If I took a shotgun I would find myself out in the open where I needed the rifle. Besides that I never knew what I would find as far as fresh sign when I left in the morning.

I finally decided the only way to cure this was to carry two guns. I rigged up my Ansley Fox with the type of sling that has two loops, one fitting over the barrel and one over the grip of the stock. The rifle that I used was a Winchester model 94, in a 25-35 caliber. This gun already had a sling mounted so I didn't have to alter it.

Now when I was moving through the woods and I was in country with heavy cover, I carried the shot gun and slung the rifle over my back. I carried number 4 shot in the choked left barrel and 00 buckshot in the right barrel, so I always felt like I was prepared for any type of situation. Both of these guns are very light so It didn't take me long to adjust to the added weight. I ended up hunting like this for twenty plus years, so I got to where if I didn't carry the extra gun I felt like I was half naked.

When I am moving through the woods, I move slowly and I stop every few feet and look and listen. I had gone to this island because I had been seeing a lot of deer sign and traces of where a large gobbler had been feeding. I was slipping along with my shotgun in my hands, when I heard a Pileated woodpecker give out with his loud, half laugh, half cry, cackling call.

Immediately following his call I heard a tom turkey, gobble; as if to say, "let's cut out all that noise."

From the direction the commotion was coming from, I could visualize a small clearing that was between us. I quickly made my way to a location where I could slip up to the edge of the clearing. I found a spot where I could see in the direction that I had heard the sounds. There was no cover for me; I had to settle with sitting on the ground and leaning against a small cypress tree. The clearing was wider across than I had remembered, but I didn't have any choice at this point.

I thought "*Maybe I can call him across the clearing, if not, even though it's a long shot, I might be able to get him.*"

I knew that there was a game trail that led out onto this clearing and my chances were 50-50 that he was coming my way. I knew that I would have a better chance of him walking out onto that open if he didn't know anything was there. I decided to give him 15 minutes before I attempted to call at all. Well I waited and he didn't come. I pulled out my small slate call and made a soft call. I imitated a turkey hen feeding along talking to another hen or her brood. This was in the fall during deer season so a mating call would have been useless. I heard him answer with a cluck and he seemed to have moved quite a bit farther away. I decided not to try and move across the opening; to take my chances that he would turn and come back. I didn't hear anything from him again, even though I periodically continued making that soft purring sound that a hen makes when she is just feeding along. I had probably been doing this for about 45 minutes when I heard him putt one time. I looked and I could see his head peering above the palmettos on the far side of the clearing, just at the entrance to the game trail. He walked out in the opening about 6 feet and froze, staring my way. He didn't move and I didn't blink. This stare down continued, for a few minutes, (although it seemed longer) until he started giving his warning putt. He then turned and started back down the game trail. I knew it was now or never, I raised my gun and fired just as he disappeared into the palmettos. He didn't fly so I thought that I had got him.

I hurried to the spot that I had last seen him and no turkey! I found several feathers and a couple of small spots of blood. I knew he had to have been hit hard for any blood to appear that close to where he was standing. I had never heard of anyone blood trailing a turkey, but I figured I would give it a good try. Luckily the bird followed the game trail to where it intersected an old logging road and the blood spots were easy to see on the sand in the trail. The logging road however was covered with leaves and made it much more difficult to follow. It took me a while to determine which way he turned when he intersected the road. I finally got that squared away and noticed that he was headed for a big swamp ahead. Sure enough I found where he reached the swamp and apparently attempted to fly into it. I could tell this because I could see his tracks in the mud along the edge of the swamp. He brought his feet together and tried to push up to take flight, only to land several feet forward in a lump with a lot of wing tip marks in the mud. He then followed the edge of the swamp (where all I had to do was follow his tracks) until I discovered him where he had crawled into a bunch of ferns trying to conceal himself. He was already stiff for this hunt had taken me a couple of hours.

What did I do right?

I had gone prepared with the right equipment.
I thought out my game plan before I even attempted to call.
I took my time and tried to understand the signs I was looking at.

What did I do wrong?

I gambled the turkey was feeding my way when he apparently was feeding the other way.
I should have crossed the field.
I should have taken the time to set up better.

Heart Thumping

I have to tell this on myself. When I first realized that there were turkey in these mountains and got over the notion that, "No self-respecting turkey would be caught on the slopes as steep as these are."

I then had to condition myself to climbing, because I had always hunted on flat ground. I am sure that if I took one of these mountain boys and had him follow me for a day in the glades, he would be at a disadvantage. For sure, I was at a disadvantage when I started up one of these steep slopes. I had sore muscles that I didn't even know I had. It really doesn't make much difference whether you are going up, down, or sideways; you have to get conditioned for the difference. I like to hunt ginseng and found it was a lot easier to cover ground, if you walk around the mountain keeping yourself on a level plane. The only trouble with that idea is that your ankles get sore from bending one way. I soon learned to walk a short distance, turn, drop down a few feet and go in the other direction; so I was putting pressure on the other side of my feet. Going down is almost as hard as I found out at Brasstown Bald. The first trip to the mountains we decided to go up there for the view. The parking lot is long way below the tower, and you have two choices: ride the bus to the top or walk up a path. The bus cost money and we were short, so we decided to ride up and walk down to save a few pennies. Big mistake! The kids took it in stride. They had no problem, but the wife and I had sore shins for days, because we had never used those muscles.

I soon found that wherever I located a turkey gobbling, it taxed me just to get in range to call. If I started out on the top of a mountain, they would be calling in the valleys and when I went to the valley to start, they would be on the ridge tops. It is a challenging game; occasionally you will get it right because you will be in the right place.

One morning, just at daylight, I heard a gobbler sounding off and I was able to place his spot as being on a ridge that was a little east of where I was standing. In order to get within the range to strike up a conversation with him, I thought the best bet would be to climb the side of the mountain and join him on the ridge about two hundred yards farther along the top. I could tell he wasn't moving, and I figured he was probably strutting and drumming hoping to entice a hen. I knew that I was going to have to get with it, because he wouldn't stay there very long. I wanted to get to the top and set up my blind before I even attempted to call to him. I started up that steep grade and I could only get fifty yards before my body forced me to stop. My heart would be pounding and my legs hurt so bad that they would begin shaking. I have always been lucky though, after a short pause and I would recover quickly. I was a little apprehensive about taxing myself this way, because one of my old high school buddies had just passed away; he was the same age as me.

I was about half way to the ridge and had gone through several of these, "Climb and rest," efforts. I stopped once again and was leaning against a tree, with my heart pounding and my legs aching, when all of a sudden my heart started beating faster and picked up in tempo to where it was racing toward a climax. I dropped to my knees, grabbed my chest and was in the middle of asking for forgiveness. I knew this was going to be the, "Big One." After the initial shock of feeling my heart racing like that, I didn't feel any worse, and the pounding was going away normally.

I thought, *"What in the heck just happened?"*

It scared me enough that I just sat there quietly and contemplated my problem. My heart slowed down to normal, and I didn't feel any different, and that gobbler was still sounding off. I was just ready to get up to try again when I heard that same thumping, but this time I could tell it wasn't my heart. It was something in the woods! I carefully looked toward the sound and I could see a grouse perched on a fallen log; he was beating his chest with his wings. He would start slow and increase the tempo and then when he could not beat any faster, he would stop. I was embarrassed that I had jumped to the conclusion that the noise was my heart. I didn't tell the story for a long time, but when I did I found that others had similar experiences. The locals thought the tale was hilarious.

My First Experience with a Wild Turkey

Most of my chance meetings with turkeys were just that, "By chance."

My first encounter with a turkey was soon after the Second World War. I was invited by my neighbor on a quail hunting trip to an area, near LaBelle, Florida. The whole area had been a boon town in the early twenties. Parts of it had city blocks laid out with paved sidewalks, (all were over grown); but it was weird for a 12 year old.

It was called the three mile square and it was perfect for quail hunting. Most of the land was open, with several small ponds for water, and only a few scattered palmettos. We were to mostly hunt quail, but the first morning we were going to try for larger game in a cypress strand that ran parallel to highway 31.

There were three men on this trip and I thought I was in elite company: George Volker, my neighbor, Wiley Johnson, Mister Mills and I camped out alongside the highway (late in the afternoon), the day before we were to hunt. I had been quail hunting with Mr. Volker several times, but I barely knew Mr. Johnson and Mr. Mills. Whenever I sat in, while hunting stories were being told, Mr. Mills always ended up in one of the tales that were being told. He was quite noted for his hunting skills. He was in his sixties and still could walk most men into the ground, and he was a born story teller. Mr. Volker was one of those men that loved to tease, and he was always trying to get something on you that he could tease you about.

I had hunted with Mr. Volker several times for quail, but all of my experiences had been day trips, and this was my first experience with adults on an overnighter.

My boyhood camping and hunting friend (Bruce DeVay) and I had gotten to be fairly good at taking inexpensive food and doctoring it to where it tasted palatable. I learned the next morning that Mr. Volker was no cook! I didn't like coffee at that time and his method of preparing coffee almost ruined me for life. He had this large sloped-sided blue enamel pot, with no lid, that he would pour a whole pound of coffee into. For the first meal of the hunting trip, he would set the pot on the fire and bring it to a boil, laying a palmetto frond over the pot to keep it from boiling over. Thereafter all he would do was add water for the next meal and bring it back to a boil. That same black gruel stayed in that pot until we started home. He drank it black and all it did was get blacker. I never drank coffee after that until years later when I was in the service in Thule, Greenland, and I only started then to stay warm. The rest of the meals were just as bad. I noticed the other men carrying their own snacks with them when they left the camp. Mr. Volker was smart though, and very soon after that Mr. Woolsey, his brother in law, started going with us. It was his "Thing" to see how fancy he could fix meals over an open fire, and he was good at it.

We left the camp just as day was breaking, before the birds had started chirping. We had about a quarter of a mile to walk to reach a cypress strand, and I received brief instructions on the walk through the woods. I could shoot deer, turkey, or squirrel and that was about it. They picked a spot for me alongside the strand and left.

Now you have to picture this, I was eleven or twelve years old, and this cypress strand looked pretty scary to me. I was positive there were rattlesnakes all around me and I knew that I could see a panther peering at me from behind every bush. A large owl hooted somewhere nearby and the hair on the back of my neck started crawling around. It took all of my will power to keep from bolting, but I had one problem: I didn't know which way to run. I didn't want to mess up and not be invited again, so I toughed it out. Besides, it was daylight enough that I could see where I was walking.

I started to inch forward into the strand, and I think I really fell in love with the outdoors in the following thirty minutes. There were cypress knees everywhere, and the grass under the trees looked as if it had just been mowed. The cows had kept the underbrush to a minimum, so it was easy to move around. I could hear crows nearby and woodpeckers were hammering up and down the strand. I was standing there taking it all in, when I saw a furry tail twitching in a tree. I eased my old single barrel up and claimed my first squirrel. I was gaining confidence now and I was thinking ahead about my triumphant return to camp, when I spotted another squirrel and claimed him. Now I really was bragging to myself and anxious to return to camp.

No one had said what time to go back. I didn't have any idea what would be a proper amount of time to stay out. I decided to turn right down the strand and see if I could find one of the men. I hadn't gone very far when I spotted Mr. Mills squatted down in a crouch. He seemed to be looking at something.

I froze as I thought "*Well now I have messed up*", because running right behind him, I saw a gobbler going through the trees.

I just knew that any minute that he was going to shoot, but he just stood up! I realized why he was stooped down, as I saw him pulling his suspenders over his shoulder. It was a call of nature!

I like to think that I could have killed that bird easily, but I wasn't sure of what was happening, so I was cautious. I approached Mr. Mills and told him about what I had seen behind him. I don't think that he believed me until we walked over and found the tracks; then he had a good laugh about it. He also had killed a couple of squirrels, and he suggested that we go on back to camp and find something to eat.

We returned to camp to fix some sandwiches. The men decided to take a nap and hunt the dogs in the afternoon, when it was cooler. Mr. Johnson was one of those people that as soon as he lay down on his cot, he went to sleep and started snoring. Mr. George Volker waited several minutes, stood up, and motioned to me to stay quiet. He noticed some pigs rooting close to us and his mind started plotting. He took a short length of rope, fashioned a lariat on one end, and laid it on the ground in front of Mr. Johnson's cot. He placed some of our leftover food in the center of the loop and then tied the other end around Mr. Johnson's foot that was hanging over the edge of the cot. It wasn't long before one of those sows' smelled the food and came over to investigate. As soon as she put her foot in that circle, George snatched the rope and hollered. As long as I live I will remember Mr. Johnson sliding on one foot, his butt, and two hands down through the woods screaming, "George you SOB if I ever get loose, I'm going to kill you."

George picked up his gun and headed out to the strand. He said, "I'll be back when he cools down."

George hadn't been back long, when a logging truck stopped and the driver, asked if we were hunting turkey. He told us where he had seen a gobbler that had crossed the road in front of him. The spot he was talking about was about one hundred and fifty yards from our camp, so we set into action. Where he had crossed the road was mostly open country, with a few scattered gall berry bushes and some palmetto clumps. Mr. Volker took charge. He told each of us what to do. There was a large ditch alongside both sides of the road. He told us to get in the ditch, on which side of the road, (so as to conceal ourselves), and to move down the ditch to about where the turkey had crossed. We used hand signals, after we had spread out and crossed the road, all at the same time. We ended up about eighty yards apart, as we moved across the field.

The turkey was directly in front of me, but he was concealed by a clump of palmettos. He immediately spotted Mr. Volker, and started running around the clump, away from him, and directly at me. Mr. Volker fired, from where he was, and rolled the turkey almost to my feet. He paced the distance later and discovered that not only was he eighty steps away, but he had shot it with number eight shot, which is almost an impossible shot. The only shot that we found in the turkey was in the unprotected head and neck area. After cleaning and dressing, we took the bird to an ice house for storage, because we had no way of keeping it cold for a week. The gobbler weighed in at 14 pounds ready for the oven.

My First Kill

My first hunting camp, as an adult, my partner Tom and I built on a small island about two and a half miles from the nearest road in the Everglades. This at the time was on public land and you were allowed to build a small shack to get out of the weather. We had to wade through water all the way to get to this island, so we pre-fabricated a cabin nine foot by twelve foot so we could float small pallets during the highest water. We concealed the cabin in the vegetation on the island and made the path in on rocks so as not to give away its location to other hunters. This worked very well for we would hear an occasional person walking by and never suspect there was a cabin not fifty feet from them.

We soon discovered that it was fooling the deer also, we could hear them splashing along as they waded past the cabin, and we couldn't see them for the vegetation. After this happened several times I decided to build a tree stand in the water, about a hundred feet from the edge of the island. The water in this part of the Everglades (the big cypress) ranges in depth from zero depth to about a foot, and only gets deeper in the cypress strands themselves. I picked two trees and built a platform about sixteen inches wide and about twelve feet off the ground. I put a rail around about eye level when I was sitting down. I hung palmetto fronds down from the railing to conceal myself. I got in the habit of setting in this stand after I came in for lunch, for a couple of hours during the heat of the day.

I had been there about an hour one afternoon when I spotted a flock of turkeys feeding through the water about seventy five yards from the stand. I had a habit at that time of sitting in a deer stand and practicing on my turkey call, and I had been doing this off and on while I was sitting there. I don't think this bothers the deer unless they are real close. In fact several times I have had deer come close acting like they were curious about the noise.

At that time you could hunt turkey during the fall season and you could use rifle or shot gun, and I was there with a rifle. I had almost fallen to sleep when I spotted them and when I realized what I was looking at I went all to pieces, and started firing wildly into the flock. All I managed to do was scatter them to the four winds, I probably didn't come within five feet of any of them. I was sitting there in a daze really cussing myself out because I knew I had done everything wrong.

I had been trying to get a turkey since I was about ten years old, and I was just about in tears, I was so out done. As I was brooding there I hear a hen start up her assembly call about a hundred yards away. Shortly, another answers her in the other direction. Soon they are calling from all directions, and it dawns on me 1'm setting here with a turkey call on the platform with me.

Well nothing was going right today, for in my

nervousness I reach for the call and knock it out of the stand! It was the type of call that has the long lid that hinges on one end and is held together by rubber bands. The call falls the twelve feet and hits a cypress knee under the tree in just the right way to make one "putt" before it lands in the water.

Right there my luck started changing. A hen hears that one putt and comes running to my stand. This time I had calmed down enough that I was able to make a clean shot and ended up with a kill.

I always tell people that I tell this story to that I didn't call up the first turkey that I killed, God called it up for me.

This area was taken into the National Park Service shortly after I stopped hunting there and their do-good practices have absolutely ruined the whole area for hunting. They were not satisfied with acquiring the Everglades National Park; they had to take in all the areas surrounding it with their regulations. I went to the hearings they held before they acquired this area and personally asked if we would be able to keep our cabins and still hunt with dogs. They promised that all that would remain the same. First thing they stopped was vehicles. Then they banned dogs and then we were told to remove our cabins. The ones that didn't were burnt down, mine included.

What did I do right in this hunt?

About the only thing was to finally calm down.

What did I do wrong?

I don't recommend trying to kill a turkey from a tree stand.

They will always spot you as being out of place, and even if you don't move they will make a wide circle around you.

I didn't force myself to calm down.

Unless the turkey has seen you, you always want to move slow and deliberate. If I had taken my time those turkey would have been in range for five or ten minutes.

I shouldn't have laid that call down on the platform.

Brush Pile Gobbler

Not aiming can be costly, as I discovered on one hunt. I had been seeing turkey sign along the northern fence line of our hunting lease in Florida. I decided to investigate that area one morning at daylight.

We had cleared a fifty foot area along our border

with the Big Cypress Indian Reservation, so that we could erect a fence around our lease. This cleared area had cut through a fairly large cypress strand, and I figured that this would be a good place to sit and listen. I sat down out on the open grass, on the outside of the strand, so that I could hear in all directions. I waited for daylight. I didn't hear anything gobble on the roost, but I did see a gobbler sail out of a cypress tree and land on the other side of the brush pile. The bulldozer operator had left a row of piled up brush that paralleled the fence. It left a corridor about 50 feet wide that went for several hundred yards. It made good cover for me to ease up to take a look. I eased up to the pile of brush, put on my head net, and found a place that I could see up and down the fence without him seeing me. I slowly raised my head into position and saw a big gobbler feeding along the fence. By now he was about one hundred yards farther down the fence than where I had seen him land. I took out one of my calls and gave a real soft mating call. He immediately gobbled and started to strut. For some reason he continued on in the direction he was going. I tried another type of call and got the same response, he continued on in the same direction.

I thought to myself, *"I can use this brush pile for cover and crawl past where he is, and waylay him as he passes."*

The brush pile was only about three feet high, so I actually had to crawl on my hands and knees to get to my target spot. Luckily I had a sling on my shot gun, so I was able to place the gun on my back while I was scooting along the ground. I got to where I thought I would be ahead of him, eased up into the brush pile, and discovered that he had turned and was now where I had come from. The word I said to myself began with an S; it gives you a clear idea of how I felt.

I tried calling again and I still got the same response, he would gobble and strut, but I couldn't get him to turn.

I thought "*Here I go again,*" down on my hands and knees and back in the other direction.

By the time I got to where I thought I would be ahead of him, my knees were sore and I was exhausted. My hands had picked up several thorns, and I hurt all over. I eased up to the pile again and this time I found a hole where I was almost perfectly concealed. This time I had guessed right; there was the turkey, back to feeding, and he was ambling down toward me. I eased my gun up and slipped it into the hole, so that I would be ready when he arrived. He came into range. I was so confident that I was already thinking about how far I was going to have to walk back to camp with him. I was even thinking about how envious everyone at camp would be. I was being so conceited, that I wasn't keeping my mind on what I was doing. I didn't take a shot when he first came into range. I knew I had a perfect place for concealment and I decided to see how close he would come to me. I couldn't believe it; he had walked up within fifteen feet of me. I couldn't stand it anymore. I pointed the gun at him and fired. The turkey jumped straight up in the air and started cackling, then started running away from me. I panicked trying to untangle my gun from the pile of brush. I fired the second time wildly into the air, as the turkey disappeared into the underbrush. Analyzing what had happened later, I realized that I had simply missed at that close range. If I had taken good aim I could have easily have decapitated him. I imagine that at that close distance the turkey must have thought it was a rifle slug going by his head.

Later on returning to camp my fellow hunters wanted to know if it was me that had shot?

I said "No, it must have been someone over on the Indian reservation."

They also wanted to know why the knees to my pants were so dirty.

I said "I fell in a mud hole."

What did I do right on this hunt?

I located the correct area scouting for sign.
I didn't over call when the turkey refused to come.
When the turkey was coming to me I didn't call at all.

What did I do wrong?

I got my gun in a position that I couldn't maneuver it.
I lost my concentration when I needed it the most.
I didn't aim my gun properly.
I actually let the bird get too close before I shot. The ideal range is between twenty and forty yards. If you shoot any closer than that, and you do happen to hit it in the body you will destroy too much of the meat.

Jaime's First Gobbler

It was during spring gobbler season when my son, Jaime and I worked out where we could be at the Brier Creek hunting camp on the same weekend. We got in late Friday night and set up our tent in anticipation of the next day hunt.

Saturday morning brought no sign of any turkey in the area. Turkey hunting was new to the club and we had very little competition. Jaime and I roamed that property from one end to the other and only found old tracks here and there. That afternoon I sent Jaime to one end of the property and I went to the other to see if we could hear a gobbler sound off as he flew up to roost. Again no luck! I had not taken a vehicle with me and it was a considerable distance to walk back to the camp. It had become completely dark as my flashlight lit the road in front of me. Something caught my attention, so I stopped and looked.

Two gobblers had come out of the woods and had casually walked down the road the same way I was heading. I knew they were fresh tracks because I had gone the other way earlier. They walked several hundred yards before they disappeared off the road. I knew that several hundred yards farther there was a T in the road. I figured that if this was one of those weekends where they were not making any racket, this crossroad would be a good place to wait in ambush.

That night I told Jaime of my plan for the next morning. We would take his nylon camouflage blind and set it up where he could see both directions down that T in the road.

We gave ourselves an extra hour before daylight and found a good spot, where he was well camouflaged, and comfortable. I advised him not to call; just to be patient and they might continue walking down the road when they flew down from the roost.

Jamie settled in to the book he was reading and soon forgot what he was there for.

Just as I thought might happen, two gobblers flew down from the roost, and continued their stroll down that sandy road. Neither one had made a sound before or after they flew down and continued their walk. Jamie had read several chapters in the book and forgotten to pay attention to what was coming down the road. The next time he looked up, they were only feet from him and he said they were trying to decide which road to go down. He had to set his book down, pick up the shotgun, release the safety, and aim without spooking one of the most wary creatures in the woods.

He managed to get that done without either one noticing him in that blind. In the excitement Jaime made one of those mistakes that a lot make in the excitement. He aimed at the turkey's body instead of the head. Being so close he managed to kill the turkey, but we had all that shot to be careful of when we had him for dinner.

Like I have done before, he was so intent on the one that he shot; he did not even notice where the other bird went.

Way-laying a bird is not as exciting as being able to call one towards you. Turkey do what they want to; they eat when they are hungry, call when they want to, and sometimes you have to put yourself in a place where they are headed in order to be successful.

The Blind

The Turkey

Gil and the Gobbler

One season at Crooked Pine camp I was hunting with Gil Smith and we decided to split up and try to hear a gobbler on either side of the strand that ran through the lease. We got an early start and I drove him through the strand and left him off on the dry ground. I told him if we heard nothing I would be back to pick him up around 11 AM. I drove back through the strand and set up my blind well before daylight. Gil wasn't a member but he was invited often because he was a born story teller and a pleasure to be around. He was in his seventies and had all kinds of heart problems but he didn't let it slow him down one bit. He was from Maine and could tell a lot of tales about moose and bears and hunting in the north woods. He liked his booze but never over did it at the camp and then only participated after supper.

It was one of those perfect spring mornings and I just had a feeling that the gobblers would be sounding off. I was right! Just as day broke I heard a gobbler sound off and it sounded like it was right in Gil's lap. I was thrilled for him as he had told me he had never killed one. This bird was one of those that you dream of but rarely hear. Every few seconds he would sound off and the woods would rattle. I kept waiting for Gil to shoot and nothing! I knew I was too far away to hear him calling to the gobbler yet I knew he was fairly good at his calling. I kept waiting and waiting and no shot. There was not a sound from my side and all my attention was on the gobbler that was with Gil. I couldn't imagine what was going on with him and that gobbler. This old bird had been gobbling steady for over an hour and I couldn't stand it any longer, I had to go see what was going on. I didn't drive back, I slipped through the strand to his side and it took a good 20 minutes and that bird was still gobbling. When I reached the other side I could tell that he was out on the prairie and I had to be careful not to mess up Gil. I found a good spot on the edge of the strand where I could see most of the prairie without being seen. I gradually raised my head up above the cover and I immediately saw three hens feeding along in the grass.

I didn't see the gobbler at first but then I spotted him about 25 yards behind the hens as he came from behind a clump of palmettos. He was a big one. He would gobble, strut for a few feet and blow. He was doing this constantly following those hens. I still couldn't figure what happened to Gil. Then I noticed some movement about 50 or 60 yards behind this turkey parade. I realized it was Gil crawling along after them apparently trying to get a chance at a shot. The strange thing was that he would crawl a short distance, roll over on his back and I would see his arm go up in the air. He did this as long as I could see him. I didn't want to mess up his stalk and it was only 9:30 so I slipped back in the strand and went back to my buggy to wait. At 11 when I went for him he was already half way through the strand coming to meet me.

He was still excited and went into the story about how they flew down just on the other side of the small palmetto patch where I had placed him. His knees were dirty and he was apparently tired but still excited. He explained how he crawled around that first patch of palmettos as they rounded the next and they were staying just out of sight and he kept going hoping to get a shot any minute. I told him what I had done.

I said, "Gil I came all the way through the slew and when I got to your side I could see the birds and you for a while. I knew you were trying to get a shot but the one thing I didn't understand was why would you stop crawling, roll over on your back and raise your arm up in the air?"

Gil looked at me for a moment like he didn't know what I was talking about.

Then a grin came over his face as he said, "Hell, I was popping nitro pills to keep the angina down so I could keep going."

I just shook my head from side to side and told him he was out of his mind as we went back for lunch.

Turkey Posing as Stump

My wife and I were raising beagles at the time I was involved in "Fool's Paradise" and I would take my favorites with me when I went. I was out there one season with several 5 month old dogs and just getting them used to the woods. I was walking through twelve inch high grass with flat rock outcroppings scattered in with it. The puppies were milling around me not over ten or twelve yards from where I was walking.

I came around a large bunch of bushes and said to myself, *"if that cypress knee had a head on it, it would look just like a turkey."*

As I got beyond it with the dogs I turned to look

back at it just as that cypress knee pulled its head out from under his wing and slinked down in the grass and scurried away. That incident made me wonder how many turkeys I had walked by and had them pull some stunt similar to that.

Wild animals are smarter than you think. If you catch one out in the open and don't see him they are uncanny at fooling you. If there is a single tree anywhere near them they will use it to block you from shooting. They will run like lightning using the tree trunk as protection. You will see them look out with only their head until they disappear and out of danger. Another thing I have seen them do is hide in a bush when you are approaching and wait to see which side of the bush you go on. Then they will step out of the bush on the other side and either fly or run using it for cover. Those are the tricks that I am aware of, No telling what tricks they have pulled that I am not aware of.

Disappearing Turkey

I set up a blind once on a small creek because I had heard a single gobble on the other side of the creek just before dark the night before. I managed to call him across the creek the next morning but he crossed about a hundred yards down the creek and was approaching me from the side. I wasn't covered on that side so I waited until he was close before I turned. As I did, the bead on my double hung on a vine and in that split second I took my eyes off him he just disappeared. I couldn't believe my eyes! I even doubted my sanity. The land where I last saw him in all appearances was flat with no cover. I sat frozen in place while I tried to figure out what had just happened to me. I couldn't fathom how he had just disappeared. It was not until I got up and went to where I had just seen him did I understand. There was a ditch running on an angle away from me and it was only then that I understood. He hopped down in that one foot deep ditch and used it for cover to outsmart me.

These big old wild gobblers don't get big by being stupid.

When it is your Time, You will be in the Right Place

I bought a motorcycle, Honda Trail 90, for hunting turkey because it ran so quiet. They have a two speed gear box that in the low gear it is very powerful, allowing one to ride almost anywhere you can walk. It was not very good when the water was up, or at fool's paradise but at Crooked Pine it was perfect.

When my son's stayed home I rode it instead of using the swamp buggy. It was a whole lot easier on my body and didn't burn near the gas. I decided to use it one opening morning of regular season because no guests were allowed for the first two weeks. I liked to still hunt the first couple of weeks and not run my dogs so as not to upset some of the older hunters who did not like to hear the dogs. This particular morning I had gotten up a little early and got going even before some of the men had even headed to the cook shack. I had decided on a good place where there was ample sign of deer, hogs and turkey. The southeast corner of the property had been cleared in preparation for the new fence we had put up and it was right at the corner of a strand of cypress that the game had been using to travel back and forth. The fence to the property on our eastern boundary connected on that corner and went to the east. The largest cleared area was on our property and the bulldozer had piled up all the trees, that had been cleared, in a spot that was ideal for a natural blind. I had wedged and old kitchen chair down in between two of those logs and along with the rubber pad from my pack it was very comfortable.

I arrived to where I had decided to leave motorcycle at a perfect time. The sky was just beginning to turn gray and showing signs of the approaching dawn and I had time to get into my chair and become quiet before the critters started moving. I really expected to see a hog, so I was sitting there with my rifle in my lap and my shotgun lying right beside me. I heard a crow call off in the distance and the normal tweet birds giving their morning greeting but as the scene before me became light enough for me to identify things, I could see there were no deer or hogs within my sight. I became adjusted to the fact that I might be there for a while when I hear that telltale sound of a turkey flying down. Their wings sound like when you slap yourself on the chest with your hand. I knew from the sound it was on the other property.

What he did was fly out of the tree, follow the fence toward me, still in the air but low, and as he got to our fence he just cleared it and landed about thirty yards to my right. I had the rifle in my hand and I needed the shotgun and I couldn't move or he would see me. He was a big gobbler and was in no hurry to do anything other than preen himself. There was a puddle of water seven or eight feet from him and he went to it and got a drink. I knew from making several mistakes, that he would be gone if I tried to out move him and try to switch my guns. I had to remain frozen and wait for the scenario to play out and see if I got a chance. In super slow motion I was able to move the rifle out of my lap and lay it down on my left side. The only reason I was able to get away with this was because the log in front of me was blocking his view of what I was doing with my hands down low. I had placed my shotgun too far away and I was going to have to lean over to get it. That old boy just strolled around, scratching every now and then and pecking at some imaginary thing on the ground and I was a nervous wreck. He was slowly moving to my left down the fence line toward the north and would stop periodically and stretch his neck peer around what seemed like forever. He was so close when he would stretch his wings and shake his feathers I could hear them. There was one bush in front of him and depending on which side he went on, I just might get a shot. I knew the bush was pushing forty yards from me and it would be my only chance because that was the limit of my shot gun. My luck was right, he went behind the bush only one problem, he was just tall enough to see over the bush. My heart jumped it was now or never. The next time he put his head down to look the ground I made my move. In one fluid motion I had that shotgun up and ready. I didn't think he would ever come out from behind that bush. He still would raise his head and look around but it took him forever to finally walk out. I didn't miss. I only had to walk fifty yards with him back to my motorcycle and I was back at the cook shack in less than twenty minutes. There were still two men eating breakfast and they wanted to know what I had forgot.

Duck Hunting

Admittedly, I have not done enough duck hunting to be giving advice on the proper methods and habits of the different types of birds.

As kids, Bruce DeVay and I hunted Marsh Hens in cattails with a cur dog I used to have.

Milan Dairy Lake was an abandoned rock quarry that was deep at both ends and shallow (18") in the middle. We would wade in the shallow water among the cattails, Bruce carrying his 20 gauge pump and me with my long tom 12 gauge. We happened upon this method of harvesting ducks during the 1947 flood in Miami. The bird we were after was a type of gallinule that was speckled somewhat like a quail, only larger, and the meat was white. They flew very seldom and only just above the cattails. They returned to the cattails as soon as they had enough distance to hide again. They gave away their existence by a telltale cackle they used to communicate with each other. My old dog Reann caught on to what we were after and would do her best to flush one in the air so one of us could get a shot. We had to be quick with our shooting because they did not stay in the air very long. Taste wise, they are the best game that I have ever eaten. Better than young turkey, a barn yard raised young chicken or even leopard frog legs. The daily bag limit was ten a person, but we never came close to killing that many. I do remember killing an occasional Coot for meat on a camping trip when we were learning to camp out. It was not all that tasty but sure better than Spam.

My dad killed two ducks during WWII when we were on a trip back from Georgia. He spotted flocks of ducks floating off shore along US Highway One on the Indian River. My dad was a good fisherman and usually carried his fishing rod and Pflueger Supreme reel wherever he went. Along with his minimal tackle, he carried a single shot 22 rifle for retrieving his lures when he would get one stuck on branch on the far side of a canal. Several times I have seen him shoot a branch in half, to retrieve his plug. I didn't think it was anything special until I tried it years later and then I realized what a excellent shot he was.

When he found ducks close to shore he pulled the car over. Then we took off our shoes and waded toward the ducks floating on the river. The water hardly came to my knees, way away from shore and the ducks were not spooked by us being there. He got as close as he dared and then he had me stand in front of him. He told me to stand as still as I could and he rested the gun barrel on my shoulder. I thought he would never shoot, but when he did, he hit one in the head. Several ducks flew to a different spot, but Dad told me to stay where I was because the one he had shot was drifting our way and soon the others would calm down.

We didn't stand there long before he said, "I think they are close enough for me to take another shot."

He did and another fell over.

He told me, "Two will make a good meal for us."

He also told me they were Canvas Back ducks.

The only time in my life I bought a duck stamp was on an opening day hunting trip when Bruce DeVay, Tom Davis and I decided to go to Fish Eating Creek's game management area for opening week. We were all about seventeen or eighteen years old, because I was still in high school.

We were mainly after quail, but had bought the duck stamps because we had seen a lot of ducks on the prairie ponds all around the area when we had been there earlier in the year on a fishing trip.

We really had a good hunt and we had accumulated a good assortment of game. Fox squirrels were legal and we had several of them, Bruce shot a young hen turkey. We killed several cotton tails we ate some for supper. Tom even made us a stew from a soft shell turtle, which was a first for me. We also caught some bass for supper one night.

I especially remember finding a large number of Mallard ducks and the spot where we found them. I was sitting under some water oaks and I saw a bunch of ducks feeding on acorns in the leaves. I sneaked out of there and went back to camp and I told Bruce and Tom what I had seen. We decided to try and ambush them. It was not a big grove of oaks, so we decided to come at them from three sides, and hope they would feed close enough to shoot. We guessed the remaining birds would flush to one of the others. We had not been concealed long when I heard Tom shoot and here came the flock flying under the canopy of trees right at me. I cut one out of the bunch and turned them down toward Bruce. I heard him pump his 20 gauge twice and saw the remaining ducks winging it out over the prairie. We ended up with three that were so fat I don't know how they were flying. The one thing that discouraged me about ducks was the cleaning them. We had a mound of feathers before we were through with them.

We decided to go home on Saturday afternoon because we were running low on ice. On the way out we killed a pretty good size rattlesnake. Tom wanted the skin so he put the dead snake in a cardboard box and put the box on top of our ice box.

When we got to the checking station there were two men on duty. One told us to set our ice box inside because he wanted to check out what we got and add it to his overall list. Tom took the cardboard box off the top of the icebox and set it on the cab of his pickup. The three of us carried the icebox inside the building while the man was checking our cleaned game. The three ducks were on top and he remarked how fat they were.

Just about that time we heard this scream from outside and something slam into the building. The one counting, rushes out to find the other man lying on the ground, white as a ghost.

His partner asked, "What the hell is the matter with you?"

He pointed to Tom's cardboard box now lying on the ground.

He looked at us and asked, "What's in the box?"

Tom answered, “A dead rattlesnake”

The checker looked at his partner and said, “Serves you right poking around in their stuff!”

He grinned, returned to the icebox and continued counting. I don’t know where the scared one went but we didn’t see him again before we left.

The un-explainable thing that happened the following Saturday was when I opened the Miami Herald sport pages, the headlines read, “Duck season opens statewide today.”

It was an honest mistake both by us and the man at the checking station but I would be able to bet our names were not on that roster when it was turned in.

I have spent several cold days sitting in an airboat waiting for ducks to fly over, so I could get a shot at one. I have shot several wood ducks on our leases but to actually consider myself a duck hunter, never happened. My Nephew, Chris, has posted some really appealing looking barbecued duck breast on Facebook, and maybe if I had learned to enjoy the taste, I would have become more interested in hunting them. I did learn to dip the ducks in hot wax and chill, to remove feathers.

My Three Main Hunting Camps

Fool's Paradise

My first hunting camp was about two miles from any road. Once you leave the road, the Everglades are just about as primitive as they have always been. The last logging that was done took place with horses and log carriers that had wooden wheels that were ten or twelve feet high. Tram roads cut through areas where narrow gauge trains pulled the logs to a central point for shipment. There are no traces left other than an occasional small gauge spike and the old small roadbeds. To go through one of the deep cypress strands where the bigger trees were harvested, one can hardly find one of the old stumps, it was long ago and even they have rotted down.

My hunting partner, Tom Davis, and I usually walked in Friday night after work to an unusual area we had come across by chance. The trek from the road was not for the faint of heart. Other than one short dry spot, most of the year the entire path is walking in water. The depth ranges from a couple of inches to around three feet deep. The deeper area is where we cut through a cypress strand. It is really only a mile and half direct line from the road, but that direction is through dwarf cypress. It has a marl bottom that is horrible walking, because your feet stick to the bottom on each step. We had explored every possible route and we decided that even though the water was deeper at times, the path we had established was the most practical. At night when we usually went in, it could be rather hair-raising at times. It was rough walking with stumps and a slippery bottom in places. We wore head lights and naturally walked with our heads down, so we could see the ground ahead of us. Walking this way, we would occasionally bump into a low hanging wasp nest that always seemed to be just at the right height to bump into without spotting it with your light. They wouldn't fly, but would end up down your collar or on your body to sting you later. Snakes were always a danger; mostly all we saw was moccasins in the trail. Once, I stepped up out of the trail to say something to whoever was following me, and a small moccasin struck out at me and got his fangs hung up in my pants leg.

Tom said, "You looked like an Indian doing a war dance. I thought you had lost your mind. The amount of water you were splashing around looked like when someone has pitched a hissy fit."

Snapping turtles liked to lie in the path and it could give you quite a start when you bumped into something you thought was a rock and it started to move. Occasionally I spotted a small alligator sliding away. Several times I have stepped on a large mud fish, to have it scoot out from under me.

Art, one of my hunting friends, was always doing

something dumb or at least not like everyone else. You know the type, a great guy but he just couldn't do anything right. One evening on the drive out to the camp, Art asked me to stop at the hardware store so he could get a new bulb for his head light. We waited, while he changed the bulb, before we started down the path. We had walked about fifty yards and all of a sudden, Art's light starts to flashing like a turn signal. I don't know if you have ever tried to walk over stumps and rocks with a flashing light, but it is almost impossible to do. He had bought the kind of bulb that once it heats up, starts flashing. We gave him a choice, either turn out the light, and walk in without it, staying close to one of us; or stay a hundred yards behind us. He chose the latter and arrived at the camp an hour after us.

Another example of Art's character happened later at a different camp we called Crooked Pine Ranch, where we were buddies in a cabin. Art was a habitual complainer. There wasn't that much wrong with him but that was just his way.

We got up well before daylight and went to the cook shack for our early morning coffee and bull session with the other hunters that had come in during the night. On the walk between the cabins, Art was telling me his feet must have swelled during the night because his feet were hurting more than usual.

I said, "Probably so."

I was not really paying much attention for he was always complaining about something.

We rode in the buggy for several miles after breakfast and we both had to walk a couple of hundred yards to our tree stands; he was still complaining about his feet hurting. I drove back at eleven to pick him up for the trip back. As he was approaching the buggy he again complained that his feet were still killing him.

I looked down, as it was now daylight and started laughing.

I said, "Art, no wonder they are hurting, you have your boots on the wrong feet."

He laughed at himself as much as I did and he was always first to tell on himself.

Back to stories about the walk in trail in that always had surprises.

Once when I was on my way out in the day time with my Boy Scout troop, I startled a huge moccasin that was several feet in front of me. I didn't usually take a gun to camp, but on that camping trip I had taken a gun. I shot his head off and we drug him to the road. The book says they only grow to five feet. I draped this one across the trunk of my Dodge Dart and his tail touched the ground on one side of the car and the stump where his head had been folded up on the other side on the ground. That snake was probably twelve inches in circumference; considerably more than five feet.

The most dangerous thing I encountered on the walk in took place on an opening day. I had shot a buck

Art prior & his uncle, "Gad-about Gaddis" (The flying Fisherman)

first thing in the morning and we had brought it back into camp to get it ready to hang in our screen box. We were going to be there several days so I decided to take it on back to Miami, because we were afraid it might spoil. I put the meat in one of our small boats and went out with it to the road. I drove back to Miami, packaged the meat and got it in the freezer. By the time I finished and started back to the glades, it was late in the afternoon. As I was driving west, thunderheads were building and lightning was flashing around in the clouds like it was looking for a place to escape. It wasn't going to the ground, just flashing around in the sky.

By the time I got back to the path he sky was really wicked looking, but it looked like I had made it just in time. I slung my rifle over my shoulder and started that trek a little faster than I usually went. I had gone about a third of the way in when a flash of lightning struck the water not over fifty feet from where I was walking. I know it was too late to do it, but I threw my rifle about ten feet from me and flopped down in the water. That bolt was so close it looked eighteen inches thick and it had hair all over it. How it kept from getting me I will never know. I was wading in a foot of water and had my rifle up in the air like a lightning rod. I lay in the path for considerable time before the flashes subsided and I built up enough courage to move again.

The walk in almost eliminated the beer drinkers. Tom would sometimes go back to the road and drive to a place where he could buy a six pack and enough ice to keep it cold, but it was a lot of bother. Everything you were going to eat or drink for the two or three days you were going to be there, had to go in on your back if it was the dry time of the year. The wet season was the best, because we rigged these small boats that we could pull behind us and that made it a whole lot easier. We were afraid of drinking the water in the ponds, so we each carried in our drinking water and gasoline for our Coleman lanterns. The area from where we came out of the water, after cutting through the cypress, was unusually dry and higher than above sea level. Tom and

I had tried hunting a lot of different areas throughout the glades; this area was ideal for our type of hunting. During the twelve years I hunted there, I only saw tracks where two swamp buggies had cut through and it was too rough for an air boat.

I found traces of ancient Indians on some of the higher places. I began to realize that this trail we used might have been established long before we came upon it. I would guess that if you used the spot where we established our camp as a starting point, hunting was excellent for about a three quarter mile area in any direction, other than toward the road. We came to cherish our little area; in fact we named our camp "Fool's Paradise."

We, (all the camps in that area were squatters) tried not to infringe on the other's territory as a matter of courtesy. After twelve years, I had a chance to join a lease several miles north of there. I grabbed the opportunity for it was safer for my young sons.

We started out sleeping underneath a big plastic sheet that was pulled over a tightly stretched rope between two trees. This got old quick, because of the dampness and a mysterious critter (that inhabited this small island), who didn't like us invading its territory. We would have as many as six hunters camping out under that plastic, all in a line every night. Soon after we got to sleep, the critter would run the length of the tube across our bodies.

We would all pop upright grabbing our flashlights to try to see what it was. We never spotted it, but it continued this game with us as long as we slept on the ground. It wasn't the only strange thing that happened out there; I will go into that later. One of our group obtained a worn out 10 x 12 walled canvas tent, and we used that for one whole hunting season.

Over a period of time Tom Davis, Art Prior and I became the three who, continually returned together and formed the nucleus of the camp. Ding, (Harold Bell), my nephew got all his early training hunting there and he helped immensely with the construction. Bruce DeVay, George Kaufman, my cousin Ron Bell and others came occasionally, but they didn't participate every week end like we did.

Our building kind of graduated in the construction. We first built a wood floor to match the old canvas tent; this got us out of sleeping on the wet ground. We cut several small cypress logs and flattened one side, so we would have a nailing surface for the plywood we had acquired. This was a big improvement from sleeping on the muddy ground. We knew that the tent was only going to last one hunting season. We squared up the plywood as good as we could and measured the floor exactly, so we could pre-fabricate the walls and roof of a small cabin at home. Over the summer we accumulated the wood and supplies we needed. The sides were only five feet high with a peaked roof. I set the cross members to Tom's height so he wouldn't bump his head, for he was over six foot tall. We left two foot by three foot openings on the sides and the end of the cabin, stapled screen wire over the openings, and made plywood shutters that we could prop open for air. We found an old lightweight screen door and covered it with 1/4" plywood, leaving the bottom solid. We improvised the top so that we could slide it down for more air. We even painted that door and shutters lavender with some left over paint. The rest of the surface was covered with forty five weight tar paper.

As you went in the door (on the left), we built four cubes on top of each other that contained our kitchen supplies. Also on the left wall we had a shelf that held a two burner propane stove. The shelf actually ran the length of the fold up navy cot that was underneath it. On the back wall we had two cots, one over the other, and a single cot on the right wall with four more cubicles for each member's personal belongings.

I made this drawing of "Fools Paradise" before I located any photos. The time was before digital cameras and it was not wise to carry a camera because of the danger of getting it wet.

We started off with small "throw-away" propane bottles but Tom soon toted in a small twenty pound bottle. Later when we got more creative with our cooking and the water was down, Tom brought in a one hundred pound bottle that he carried in non-stop. I could hardly pick it up, yet he did the walk in record time. In the next ten years we never ran out of gas again. Tom, my partner, was a moose of a man and noted for his strength.

The inside of the cabin was nine foot wide and eleven feet long. I laid the whole thing out on the asphalt road in front of my home in Miami, and we floated the material into camp when the water was the highest. We spent almost a year floating wood, pipe, and materials to build the cabin. We even carried in a twenty foot length of galvanized two inch pipe and a one and one inch square piece of rebar; all the way back to that camp. The piece of rebar was a little longer than the pipe because we wanted to use it as a battering ram inside the pipe. We stood the pipe and rebar up through the branches of an oak tree that was growing on the small dry spot where we had established our camp. We climbed up into the tree and lifted the heavy rebar, dropped it repeatedly inside the pipe, and slowly the pipe sank down into the soil. When the pipe was down about five feet, we hit solid rock; and then the job got really hard. We would spend two or three hours each weekend, and it took four or five weekends to finally punch through the shelf of rock. We could tell we were making headway because we would measure the piece that was sticking above the ground. It was one of those things in my life that I just wasn't going to let whip me. We even carried a pipe cutter and threaded it, so we could attach a pitcher pump on the end to pump broken rock and sand out of the pipe. After breaking through the rock, we still had six feet left to get the pipe far enough in the ground so that our pump would be at the right level. When we finally got there, we had trouble getting clear water because we didn't have a cavity at the end of the pipe. Someone told us we could blast a cavity with a small piece of dynamite. Well we didn't have any dynamite, but we did have several old m-eighty fire crackers and their fuses would work fine under water. We ended up using one at a time until we had dropped three into the pipe. Then we hurriedly placed a cap on the pipe before they went off. We were prouder of that well than anything else we accomplished out there. When we finally got clear water, it tasted wonderful. I went to the trouble of collecting some water in a small bottle. I took it in to my doctor to have it tested to see if it was safe to drink.

He took the bottle out of my hand and asked, "Where did this come from?"

I explained and as I was talking, he walked over to the sink and poured it down the drain. He said, "People make water unsafe and animals don't. You would be just wasting your money."

Access to good drinking water sure made it easier on our backs.

The pump looked naked standing there alone so we scrounged up a double sink with chipped enamel that someone had thrown away.

The island we picked was sixty feet wide and one hundred and fifty feet long. We went to the far end and built our latrine. It was only a box with a back rest that sat over a whole in the ground. My nephew who was twelve at the time was responsible for adding the comfort of a toilet seat. We were on the way out to the camp and had just left home, when I spotted a toilet seat in a trash pile in front of someone's house. I had gone past it before I stopped. I called out to the back of the truck where, Ding, my nephew was riding.

I said, "Go and get that toilet seat it will be perfect for our latrine."

Now to appreciate what happened next you have to picture what stage Ding was in his life. He wasn't a bully, but he was one of those boys that all of his buddies respected; and he was the leader of the bunch. He turned bright red. I could tell what he was thinking. He was afraid someone he knew would see him going after that toilet seat. I told him to go ahead and get it. He slowly climbed out of the truck and with much reluctance went for the seat. When he had it in his possession and almost got back to the truck, I would pull away a few feet. When he would catch up again, I would pull away again. I pushed it to the point that if he could have, he would have whipped my butt. It was funny to us, but not to him.

The island was only one foot higher in elevation than we had ever seen the surrounding water come up. All around the edge of the island heavy (over head high) Coco Plumb bushes and Myrtle Bushes concealed what was in the interior. We cut the path onto the island on a curve. There was no way anyone would know there was anything there, even if you walked completely around the island. The interior soil was very rich, much like the potting soil you can purchase.

We found a square of Zoysa grass that had blown off a truck on the highway. We hauled that in and tore it apart. Then we sprig planted it all around the cabin and pump to see if it would cut down on the mud we were always tracking inside the cabin. It worked! In just one year we had a soft carpet all around the cabin.

Our hunting season usually started in October or November. Tom and I went out ahead of time and cleared a spot where we planted a good mix of greens. Art, our other hunting buddy, helped with this idea and it paid off in spades. By hunting season an assortment of greens were perfect for picking. On the first night in, we would strip the lower leaves off the plants and wash them before we went to bed. The next morning, before we left for the hunt, we would turn the stove on simmer, add a large chunk of smoked ham, and let it cook until we came back early in the afternoon. We had tree stands scattered around the prairie that was adjacent to our camp. It was really odd how that smell could travel upwind and reach you no matter which

stand you were in. I know that Tom and Art were out there, more for the enjoyment of the pioneer type of feeling that everyone felt when we were there. They were always in before me when that pot was simmering. We had some really good meals in that little shack and it made my life a whole lot richer.

We had two cast iron fry pans that were the same size. We could take the lower one and put a couple of sardine cans in the bottom to hold up our pie pan. The first time I tried this I was hankering for some biscuits and gravy. I had brought sausage, and Tom had some bacon. What I did was fry off some of Tom's bacon to get some grease. We didn't have any milk, but we did have Coffeemate. We had plenty of self-rising flour, so I mixed water and Coffeemate until it looked about like thick milk. I mixed the Coffeemate milk, bacon grease and flour until it looked the consistency of what my Momma used to make her biscuits. I made about ten dough balls and it filled up that pie pan. I set the pie pan on top of the sardine cans, turned the fire on real low, and put the other fry pan upside down over the lower one to form an oven.

Those were the most delicious golden brown biscuits any of us had ever eaten. We set them aside in the lower pan. Then we used the top one to make a fry pan full of sausage gravy; using the other half of the Coffeemate to make flour milk to thicken the gravy. We did this on a rainy day and the three of us consumed every bit of that gravy and biscuits, plus Tom's rendered bacon. We got to where every time we had some greens, we would make that pie pan full of cornbread. We reached the point that someone had the responsibility to bring in butter and Coffeemate every weekend.

One meal that was unusual was caused by an accident. One of us was assigned to bring in hamburger for the Friday night meal because it would be simple to prepare. Tom had it on his backpack, which was the seat and backrest of a common lawn chair. He had fashioned straps on the chair. It would carry quite a load and it was easy to tie things on to it. He had placed the meat package next to a small gasoline can. When we got to the camp, we discovered that the gas can had leaked and saturated the meat package with the gasoline. It was ruined, leaving three hungry men with nothing for supper. Someone got the idea of catching some of the crawfish that we always saw on the way in. We made a small seine out of an onion sack and headed to the slough. It was surprising how fast we were able to catch a whole bag full of them. We got the sand off them by putting them in the sink and pumping water over them. We heated up the greens pot and dumped them into boiling water; it surprised me how red they turned. I forget what we had with them, but as long as I live I will remember how delicious they were and how sweet the meat tasted.

Another meal that I especially remember was when I killed a small hen turkey. Instead of taking it home, we decided to fry it like chicken for the afternoon meal. We already had a pot of either navy or great northern beans on the stove that had been cooking all day. Tom had minced up an onion and we were about to sit down for a feast, when two of our friends came into the camp. Ray and George had been hunting our area all day and were on their way back to the road. They hunted turkey as a team and that is all they went after. We invited them to stay and eat with us. They both agreed, but George (A Yankee) balked at eating any beans.

We all told him, "Oh no, eat some beans or no turkey."

I noticed he was very tentative about tasting the beans but he ended up asking for seconds. Before he left, he got me off to the side and made me write down how I cooked them, because he was going home to tell his wife how to do it.

Our trips in and out over several years created a well-worn path that we had memorized. In many places the path was like walking in a trench. It got so familiar that on a bright starry or moon lit night; it was easy to walk in without any light. It had its dangers, but we were young and healthy, so we all looked forward to going there on the weekend. My nephew, who helped build the cabin when he was only eleven or twelve, still hunts that area; although the National Park Service burnt our cabin with everything in it. He is in his sixties now and his son is in his thirties. It was a great time in my life that I will always cherish.

We started concentrating on this area in the mid 60's and gradually decided to make it our primary hunting area. We actually floated in a test pallet with lumber to see how wide and how long we could successfully bring in. We floated or carried everything that was on that island and we were very proud of it.

Top-photo Tom-- Bottom photo Tom & Art

Tom and Art's widow's Marie and Dayce located these few pictures of "Fool's Paradise" and I am grateful. I only had one and it was terrible. These photos really don't do the area justice. Just outside this small island is a very large prairie that only occasionally had water on it. Across the prairie is a hardwood hammock that is inhabited with now rare colorful tree snails. Many clues can be found of an ancient civilization also lived here and saw what we were seeing. The whole area is splashed with a beauty that only our Supreme Being could create!

Marie & Tammy, Tom's Family

Crooked Pine Ranch

Crooked Pine Ranch was a lease that I joined that was part of the Collier holdings. The way I understand it, the original land was homesteaded and the government divided it into 160 acre plots. They offered it to the public with certain rules that they had to follow in order to gain title to the land. These 160 acre plots were actually divided by crude roads. Some roads were even pushed directly through swamp land.

The pioneers who tried to settle and claim these bits of land had everything against them; it was really rough going. Mosquitoes, rattlesnakes, panthers and miles from any help, forced them to give up. As they deserted their land, Baron Collier gave them a pittance for their homesteads. He ended up with thousands and thousands of acres. Some of these old dividing roads are still used to cut through swampy areas. Some of us mistakenly called them tram roads after the small train roads that were cut into the big cypress farther to the south.

The lease consisted of 5600 acres in the most remote part of the Everglades. We had three sleeping buildings; a cook shack, (16 x 24), a toilet with a bathtub, and a drilled well with a 1000-gallon tank for water. The camp even had a diesel generator. We had two Servel gas refrigerators in the kitchen with a large commercial size stove, a commercial butcher block, and

Old Dividing Roads

a table that sat 20 people. We even had an acre of grass that we kept mowed. There were parts of the lease that none of us ever went to, because there was no need and it was too dense. It was too rough; besides there was plenty of game on land that was easy to get to. I loved my "Fools Paradise," but my boys were getting bigger and I saw this as a once in a lifetime opportunity to join. The men that started the camp (ten years before I came along) were much older than I was. They were set in their ways and very strict about allowing alcohol, only after the day's hunt was over.

16 x 16 Cabins

Other than a gator tail now and then for supper, they understood and followed the game laws. In the 20 years, that I belonged to the club only one member was told to leave. It was expensive, but well worth the fun for my family. My wife loved to come in the summer and both of my boys loved it. We kept our freezer well supplied with wild hog meat, turkey, and deer meat.

There is nothing as beautiful as the bright night sky so far away from the reflective lights of civilization.

I was Scoutmaster of troop 210 in Miami and I brought the boys there several times, and they told me even after they were grown, that those trips were their favorite of all the places we went. Art Prior became a member first and invited me as a guest. One of us invited Thomas Davis so "the Fool's Paradise" bunch ended up in the new lease, about the same time the National Park Service burnt down our beloved cabin in the Loop.

Good day at Crooked Pine

Bruce DeVay became a member about a year later.

All four were assigned to the same cabin and it

provided us a stage for a lot of horse play. Bruce, Thomas, and I were school buddies and hunting buddies, and Art had been hunting with us for about a decade. There were a couple of doctors, a glass company owner, a banker, farmers and a metal fabricator, contractors and one millionaire. We were very diverse, but we were all there to get away from it all. There were no cell phones at that time, and the doctors especially loved that they could get away from phones. The members were also split in where they lived. Just about half lived in the Clewiston, Florida

Sonny Boyer-Bruce DeVay-Thomas Davis

area and the others were from Miami. Art made the mistake of infringing on the Clewiston doctor's time one morning and found out he didn't allow that. We had gone to breakfast when Art sat down next to the Doctor. We all loved Art, but he was a bit of a hypochondriac. He had a stiff neck, or he was starting a cold etc. etc., yet he could walk and hunt and keep up with anybody. This particular morning he started in on the doctor and went on for several minutes about all his aches and pains. No one else at the table was talking, they were busy eating their breakfast and listening to Art with his discourse.

The doc never acknowledged he was hearing a word, just nonchalantly continued eating his cereal.

After Art had covered everything he could think of he said, "Well Doc what do you think is wrong with me?"

The Doc laid his spoon in the now empty bowl and placed it in the sink. He opened the door to go out, turned to Art and said, "You have cancer."

That left Art sputtering and the rest of the men roaring with laughter.

A place on that property was the inspiration for my novel "The Pot," meaning the shared community cooking vessel. In fact, I named the Indian village in the story Crooked Pine Island, after our hunting camp. There is an ancient Indian burial mound on the property that was last used by the Calusa, around the time Columbus discovered the Americas. I daydreamed about how they must have lived all those years ago. My imagination and the beauty of our camp, inspired me to write the historical novel about their lives.

I even kept my membership up for a couple years after I moved to the mountains. It is gone now! After Barron Collier's estate was finally settled, the offspring notified us to vacate the property after 30 years.

Jaime Holds a Gator in Front of Our Cabin

Bruce Jaime Sonny & Thomas

Brier Creek Hunting Club

"Mouth of the Creek," CB handle

Brier Creek

Brier Creek is a picturesque slow moving creek that ambles south through central Georgia towards the great Savanna River. The area around the creek was the site of several Revolutionary War battles. Where it joins the Savanna River, the western side was the central area of land that comprised the hunting camp that I was lucky enough to become a member. At first I was invited as a guest, and eventually I was invited to join. The club had several large plots of land where they leased hunting rights. Most of the land had been cultivated for pine, yet it also had a lot of hardwood swampy areas that were unsuitable for pine. Along the Savannah River there are trees had never been harvested. It satisfied a long wish of mine that I could see the woods as they were before the white man.

During the 10 or so years that I belonged to this camp, first the cypress, then the hardwoods and finally big pines were cleared to make way for new slash pine seedlings. Sometimes, seeing progress advance has had a sad emotional effect on me.

Most of the people in the club were locals and probably would be described as rednecks by anyone from the north. They all drove pickups with a pack of dogs in the back and a gun rack in the window. What they really have become is, a people with a way of life that is becoming extinct. Hunting with dogs is what they and their forefathers did; it was not a sport. They fed their families with what they harvested from the woods and the river. The dogs are family members and are treated with great love and care. Even though that area has one of the largest deer populations in the south and the deer have become destructive, the laws have now been changed to where the dog hunter is the one who is becoming extinct. The new laws are obviously designed to discourage the use of dogs to hunt deer. Progress again!

While I was in the club, it was well organized and a real enjoyment. Everyone gathered at the skinning shed around daylight and the discussions began.

Someone would ask, "Where do you want to run the dogs this morning?"

And the answer would be, "I don't care, where would you like to run them?"

These questions would go around to several of the hunters until it became comical, or someone would get

My Son Steve & I Standing Next to Huge Pine along Savanna River

tired of the banter and make a decision. It amazed me that when we gathered in the morning there was always one person who stepped forward and assumed the leadership. It wasn't a written thing; it was more of an

Big Pine Towering Over Other Trees

understood pecking order. The amount of people that showed up in the morning dictated which plot would be hunted. There were only so many safe places a person could stand and be safe. These spots were called "Stands," and the club had actually drawn maps and numbered each one. The longtime members knew which way the deer were likely to run and those spots were claimed first. After everyone had time to get settled on his assigned spot, the dog men (the ones who worked the dogs through the center of the plots) were the only ones who moved. They could be located by the "whooping" they were doing to the dogs. Everyone else had to stay where they were placed, until the hunt was over. No rifles were allowed, so if you stayed in your spot, you were out of range of the other hunters. Usually two or three plots were worked before lunch, and then everyone met back at the skinning shed.

The morning harvest of deer were cleaned, split and hung in the screened meat shed. This process was done by two men to each deer and for a good reason; if you wanted to get cut, just try to step in and help one of these teams. They had cleaned hundreds of deer and were very efficient at what they were doing. An amateur would just slow down the process. The afternoon hunts went the same way. They usually ended in late afternoon, allowing time to clean up the afternoon harvest, and for some to make it home for supper. The CB radio was a must if you wanted to keep up with the fast moving action. They were turned off during the hunt, but invaluable when relocating the dogs, or placing the hunters around the next plot of land.

I know some will think this is not a sport and unfair to the deer because it has always been a big debate.

If you have never done it, think about this; you are placed on a small road fifteen feet wide, with thick pine trees on either side. You hear the dogs strike something and they start their excited barking. You have learned that the deer are way out in front of the dogs and they are chasing them by smell only. You have to try and guess which way the dogs are going; imagine the deer a couple of hundred yards in front, and guess again if it is liable to cross out of that area near you. If you guess right and the deer does cross the road near enough for you to shoot, nine out of ten times you will be looking the wrong way. There is no way you can turn around,

Skinning Shed

identify, aim and shoot a deer running as it crosses a fifteen foot span. A deer makes very little noise running in pine needles and your only chance of shooting is if you hear a telltale snap of a twig, or see a flash of brown before it gets to the road. It's not like shooting clay pigeons where you know where they are coming from and where they are going; even looking the right way, you have to have lightning reflexes and be a good shot.

The meeting place was a power line that ran parallel to the road and provided a good clear space for parking, water, dog pens, shed and tables, and a power supply. For me it was a good camping area; only missing a toilet and I had a chemical one, so I was all set with my fold out camper.

Everyone who participated in the day's hunt was eligible for a share of the meat, but many did not want any. The different reasons they had were: no more space in their freezer, they didn't like deer meat, etc. The halves of deer were pulled out of the screen room and cut into ham, ribs and shoulders. It would be piled into separate stacks equaling the number who wanted meat. The hunters who actually killed a deer were given first choice at picking a pile of meat, the rest were numbered and each man drew a number out of a can for his share.

The hunting week was laid out so that some days were allotted for still hunting. Before the morning hunt and after the evening hunt, still hunting with a rifle was allowed.

The cost of membership was determined by dividing the cost of leasing the land they had available. It was expensive, but when you subtract the cost of a freezer full of meat, and enjoyment, it was a good bargain.

Slaughter Racks & Ready for Screen Room

Screen Room

Sorting Piles of Meat for Evening Lotto

My Camper and Camping Spot

Tom and Helicopter Ride

Tom almost lost his life, shortly after he joined the Crooked Pine Club, when he had a wreck riding my son's Honda Trail 90. He had not ridden a bike for years and tried to relive his old skills. We were getting ready to eat, when I saw Tom pushing the Honda back to the camp. He was obviously in pain when I rushed out to see what had happened. He asked me to help him into the cabin and sat down in a chair. I saw that his back had a large bubble on it and it scared me. I could see that he was in no condition to be ridden out in a jeep, so I made the decision to get a helicopter to come into the camp. I threatened the other members to not try to take him out by a buggy. I don't think anyone but Gil Smith and I realized Tom was seriously hurt. Normally it was an hour and a half to get to the cars, but Gill and I made it in my buggy in about forty five minutes. Gil had a bottle of booze in his hand when we left, but it was not there when we got to the phone. We found it lying in the road on the way back.

He told me, "Hanging on with two hands was more important at the time"

The nearest phone was at the Indian reservation where I called for help in less than an hour. I called the United States Coast Guard first and they got a helicopter on the way. They contacted Dr. Forbes and he was the one who returned my call. He told me a helicopter was on the way from Miami to Clewiston. They were going to refuel in Clewiston, pick him up and he was going to lead them into the camp.

He told me later when he got aboard they asked him to pin point the camp on a map. They set the coordinates in the autopilot and the helicopter flew straight there.

When Gil and I got back to the camp, we had only been there a few minutes when we spotted the helicopter on the horizon headed directly to us. As they were easing it down on the dry pond, in front of the cabin, my dog, Tiny, spotted it and came out from under the cabin like he was going to eat it up. He was real brave until the prop wash hit him; he returned to his spot under the cabin, and didn't come out until the helicopter left.

The Doc gave Tom a quick exam and inserted an IV. They had him on a stretcher and they were on their way in just a few minutes.

It was a good decision to call the Coast Guard because the doc told us if he had been taken out by a buggy, he would have never made it. He had several crushed ribs and a collapsed lung. If he had gone out in a buggy, one of the broken ribs would have penetrated his heart. He stayed in the hospital in Clewiston for a month, or better, before he was transported to Miami, and he didn't go back to work for months.

Swamp Buggies

Not so much in the rest of the world, but the Everglades have unique types of vehicles for hunting. South Florida has many swampy areas interlaced with high ground. Many boggy areas are easily traversed with what they call four wheeler's, although I don't think they would work where I hunted, because of the deep water.

In my day it was Yankee ingenuity at its best.

Yankee, in this case, meaning what servicemen were called during the Second World War. The first buggies I ever saw were utilizing the model T Ford and the worm drive rear end, because both rear wheels pulled equally. The model A Ford was probably the most utilized vehicle in a variety of combinations. The rear ends were pulled apart and welded so that both wheels pulled in unison. A four-speed and a three speed transmission were joined together to gain the lower gearing. One thing you didn't have to worry about was how fast you could go. It was mostly slow-moving because; stumps, roots, water and holes forced you to go slow. I have seen all kinds of tire rigs. Aircraft tires with chains were popular, duel tractor-trailer tires were often used; and some even ran them without air, bolted to the rims with holes cut in them to let the water out.

Thomas Davis's Buggy

Tom, my partner, used 24 ply aircraft tires and bolted strips of aircraft tires to form traction like a tractor. Tractor tires themselves were popular, but expensive. You could design your buggy to the area you hunted in. In the open grass country, a lot of full track and half-tracks, much like tanks, were utilized.

Mr. Volker, my mentor, built the simplest buggy that I've ever seen. He took a Ford passenger car rear end, locked the gearing, turned it over, and faced it backwards. He mounted a 10 horse Onan engine under his seat, and set it high in the air. Through a system of sprockets and a Cushman motor scooter centrifugal

George Volker's-(driver) Even Had White Sidewalls

clutch, a three speed manual transmission out of an old Willis automobile, he was in business. I don't have a picture of my buggy, but I used the same principle; only I used the running gear of the wartime jeep, where I didn't lock the rear end. With the four-cylinder engine removed, I easily mounted a sprocket on the protruding shaft and stabilize it with a pillar block.

I was lucky enough to find four turf tires that had been manufactured to the wrong size. They had 16 inch centers and they were supposed to be 18. He had the

Irene Volker & Her Son George IV Tuning a Model A

rims without centers, so all I had to do was cut the centers out of my jeep wheels, and weld them into his centers. Those tires were 1500/16 and the one thing I forgot was: with tires that size and the buggy being so light, it had a tendency to float. We learned to be real careful when in deep water. Bruce's buggy, (pictured)

Bruce DeVay's Buggy

was powered with a tiny Morris Minor four-cylinder engine and it used sprockets and a three speed automobile transmission. Several of the members at Crooked Pine Ranch used standard World War II jeeps, with large tires, that were mostly aircraft tires. The trouble with this was it put a lot of strain on the steering, universal joints, and axles. My buggy, by utilizing a centrifugal Cushman motor scooter clutch, made it impossible to put a sudden strain on axles and universal joints. The other members were constantly working on their Jeeps, while the only problem I ever had was, it was sometimes hard to start the engine. One member worked in an automobile junkyard and his buggy was assembled from parts of all different kinds of vehicles. Everybody had different ideas and I never saw two buggies that were the same.

Ding's miniature buggy- Crosley Powered Back to Back Transmissions

This buggy had the advantage of being small enough to fit in a pickup, but was limited in what it would carry. Sure beat walking.

The following photo is George Volker with his back wheel and axel and heavy duty rear end. He called this one the Muddobber. His hobby was building model A buggies and he always had several under construction. He sold one buggy to a man from Oregon and he drove it all the way out there. He eventually took an Army Weasel and adapted it to run in the open grass of the Everglades. This buggy was fast and it almost killed him when he threw a track off and rolled it on a runway in the lower glades. He was airlifted out and spent several months in a coma.

George Volker IV with 410 double and a Colt strapped to his hip

Random Stories about the Outdoors

Turner River Bridge

One of the places I loved to fish was from the Turner River Bridge on Tamiami Trail. I stopped there once after a hunting trip and saw several large snook lying under the bridge. That scene played on my mind and I studied on how to entice one to take my line.

I would catch several large shiners near my house, put them in the back of my pickup (with a battery aerator), and head across the trail before daylight. I knew from seeing the same thing (under the old wooden bridge at the end of Flagler street in Miami), it would not be easy. As a child I haunted that bridge trying everything I could think of to hook one of the big snook or bass that hung out there. I caught several small snook and I did manage to catch a ten pound bass, but it was a constant challenge for a ten year old.

At the Turner River Bridge, the trick was landing a bass or snook once he was hooked. There was a lot of piling under the bridge, and standing on the bridge made it almost impossible to land one. I had a short bamboo pole (with a clothes pin fastened to the end), that was part of a rig I used for fishing for Jewfish in the channels in the 10,000 Islands. I would take that pole and tie it off to the bridge railing, so the clothes pin was eight or ten feet away from the bridge. Then I would take my rod down the bank, leaving my 50 pound linen line on the bridge. I wanted to be where, if one bit, I would have a straight pull away from the bridge. I would prop my rod in a safe place and return to the bridge to rig my shiner. I didn't use any leader, even though I knew that snook could easily cut your line with their razor sharp gills. I was depending on forcing him to me (with strong line) before he could cut it with his gills, or wrap the line around a piling. I wanted that shiner to look as natural as it could when I dropped it in the water.

The idea worked perfectly! I had the shiner barely under the water, ten feet away from the bridge and about twenty feet away from where the snook were laying. I would go back to my rod and reel in the slack, to where it was taunt between the rod and the clothespin. With a slight pull, the clothespin would release the line, and the shiner would start drifting back under the bridge. I knew that trying to cast under there would only spook them. On my very first attempt, I caught a twenty pounder, but I soon found you might as well go home, because they learn quickly. I had a real monster on once, and he was the first to cut my line.

The bridge was like a lot of fishing spots, sometimes you would catch one, but most of the time you didn't.

The big ones I caught kept me coming back. Besides I was usually back home by noon and had plenty of time for my wife's "Honey do's."

Trip down the Turner River

Standing on the bridge looking south, I often wondered how far it was to Chokoloskee and how long it would take to go.

I couldn't stand it, I had to try it! One spring morning my young ten year old son and I decided to give it a go. I had an eleven foot aluminum boat and a five horse motor, so away we went. I told Laurie, my wife, that I would call her when we got to Chokoloskee and she could come after us. We loaded down with water, a small ice chest with sandwiches, and a few cold drinks. I had a map of the Chokoloskee area, but nothing that covered Turner River. We each had a fishing rod and my small tackle box. As usual, I had my compass and flashlight. Our life vests were our cushions, and I had the necessary equipment required; but I kept everything light, on purpose.

We left the bridge early and were able to use the motor intermittently. We only idled along, because the scenery was gorgeous and there was an abundance of animals and birds to observe. One curious little otter, about 6 months old, followed us for about a mile trying to entertain us. I wondered where his parents were. The first couple of miles were obviously a dug canal, and it looked like that. At this point we actually intersected with the natural river and it really angled more to the west. It was a marshy area and I reached the point of giving up and going back. Instead, I pulled the motor out of the water and started polling through the cattails. At one time we even got out and pulled it along. I had no idea how far it was through them, but between Jaime pulling on the cattails and me polling from the rear, we finally made our way through. There were several other places where we couldn't use the motor because of the dense mangrove roots, which reminded one of tunnels through the trees. One of the wonders that we saw was a huge shell mound that covered several acres. All that was visible were tons and tons of oyster shells. I realized later in life that it was an ancient Calusa Indian midden sight. I didn't know anything about the Calusa at that time, but it sure peaked my curiosity. One of the oddities that I noticed on the trip was the presence of both fresh and salt water fish. The water was absolutely clear, and I was seeing snapper and largemouth bass swimming along together. I had always thought that bass were strictly fresh water and snapper were only in salt water. After about ten or twelve miles of sightseeing, we broke out in the open waterand then things looked familiar. I went on to Chokoloskee and called my wife to come after us. Jaime wanted to fish while we waited for her, so we took the boat to a small hole that had a few snapper. We caught a skipjack trolling to the spot and I talked Jaime into using it for bait. I pulled up to a clump of mangrove roots and tied off both ends of the boat. I had an end wrench in my tackle box, with 300 pound test monofilament wrapper around it, and a large hook on the end. I put that skip jack on the hook, dropped it over on the mangrove side, and tied it off to the oar lock. We were both intent on catching a snapper, when I heard the oarlock jingling and I pointed it out to Jaime. I stood up and took a step toward the oarlock, when the whole side of the boat went under water'; pitching me and my tackle box up in the mangroves. The 300 pound line broke, sounding like a firecracker going off. It was an interesting day!

Catching Snook in the Old Marco Canal

The fish fries my folks had in the back yard created a lot of entertainment for me, because I was able to go with my dad on a lot of his fishing trips. One of my favorites was when we went to Marco Island to troll for snook. It was during the war, so he had to save up his gas stamps, so we could make the trip from Miami.

My dad had managed to acquire a clinker built dory. I was just a kid, but I remember it as holding just three people; so I would guess it to be twelve to thirteen feet long. The motor he had was an old Johnson and it was not in very good shape. He always had trouble getting it started, and it was a source of a lot of welts on my body. To start the motor you had to wind a cord around the fly wheel and pull it through. I remember it would always tax my dad to the point of exhaustion, (both mentally and physically) before Betsy or #%&## would start. What he called it depended on how quick it started. What put the welts on me was that long cord, with the knot on the end, as it was pulled through. It would snap me like a buggy whip.

We always launched it near the east end of the canal that ran from Royal Palm to the wooden bridge at the west end. We didn't have a regular boat trailer, just a high-side utility trailer, and it was a trick to get that heavy boat on, and off, and in the water with no ramp to launch it from. I don't ever remember seeing an ice box until after the war. We used a canvas bag (with a metal bottom and a drawstring top), that I guess was furnished by the icehouse. My dad would fill it up about half way with crushed ice before we started across the Tamiami Trail.

Once in the water, we would start trolling toward Marco Island in the canal with Johnson spoons, (a type of lure). His goal was to catch enough fish to have a good fish fry; and we always managed to do that. We never caught any big snook, like you can catch around the passes; they were always about five to six pounds. Some days we wouldn't catch a mess until just before dark. I didn't enjoy that experience, but I knew not to complain, for fear of not going the next time. The mosquitoes and sand flies would just about carry you off around sundown.

We would stop ever so often and behead the fish, gut them, and stick them "tails up" down in the crushed ice. My dad was never greedy about how many fish he would catch.

Sometimes he would look in that bag and say "I think we have about enough. Let's head on back across the Trail"

I guess a lot had to do with we didn't have a refrigerator yet. At home, we still had an old tin lined wooden ice box to keep things cold.

One of the things I remember about that canal was a huge alligator we would occasionally see. A man in the store (at the Royal Palm end) told us he was the one who had put two stakes in the ground, sixteen feet apart, on the spoil bank where the gator liked to lie. My Dad and I saw him there after we were told that. We could see he was well over sixteen feet. Later in life, I wondered if maybe he was a crocodile instead of an alligator, as the water in the canal was brackish. The nicest thing about getting old is the memories you have.

Archery Hunting Adding to Hunting Season

Kicking Pig

In my life time, the game commission caused me to take up different methods of hunting. At least that is what I convinced my wife. I was very satisfied with the length of gun season, and managed to spend most weekends and holidays in the woods during the entire season.

The first curve they threw on me was opening archery season three weeks ahead of the gun season. I knew nothing about bows and arrows, but I just could not sit at home on those three weekends and brood about the lost fun. My partner (Tom) had a long bow that had a pull of 90 pounds, and he was an excellent instinct archer. I tried to shoot his bow and the first thing I did was strip the skin off my left arm. Needless to say, Tom's bow was not suited to my strength and lack of skill. We, (Tom and I) had about a month before the first archery season in Florida was to open, and we had a lot to learn and a short time to prepare. I purchased a rather short 45 pound pull, laminated re-curve bow, and a dozen wooden practice arrows. The shop (where I bought it) gave me a short course on what I needed to prepare my bow for sights, and how to set them. I was pushing it on the money I was spending, so I opted not to get any more accessories. I knew I could make an arm guard and quiver. I had the main articles and I would return to the shop, just before the season, to get several hunting arrows.

Tom and I met for several evenings. He helped me set up my bow and set the sights to three different distances. Twenty five, 30, and 35 yards seemed like practical distances, so that's what I practiced at. Tom apparently had spent a lot of time as a child with his long bow, because he sure didn't need to practice. He could hit a can thrown up in the air, most of the times he tried, and it made me feel real incompetent.

With several evenings of practice, I progressed to the point to where I felt like I might be able to hit a deer, if they were still. What came as an unexpected side problem was the soreness that I was experiencing. Although I was in good shape, because of my trade as a carpenter, I was using muscles that I had not used in years. I was extremely sore from this new experience.

We were up bright and early opening morning and were in our stands way before daylight. My favorite stand was beside what we called a hardwood head, it had been very productive for me. I didn't have to wait long, just after daylight two does walked out in the open and crossed in front of me about 60 yards away. They circled, ambling along like they didn't have a care in the world, and they maintained that same distance from me.

Florida had never had a doe season in the Everglades before this archery season, and I was ready to harvest one. I must have seen at least a dozen deer that morning, which was one of the most frustrating days of my life. I had waited in that stand a hundred times, and I had never seen deer move around out in the open like that. I had my bow sighted in at the maximum peg, at 35 yards, and it was if they knew, I was helpless! I learned that day I had to rethink this bow hunting game. I never used it out in the open again; I stuck to game trails and heaver wooded areas.

The camp that we called Crooked Pine, located north of Alligator Alley, had a lot of wild feral hogs. I took my bow and went on a slow walk through the area, trying to catch some of them rooting. There was a fence line along the area, and I walked out to the edge to see if I could spot some hogs feeding alongside it. We had cleared a path about 50 feet wide when we put up the fence, so it was a good place to see for a long ways. I eased up to the fence and saw several small hogs (about 50 pounds) feeding along the edge of the palmettos. They were feeding my way, so I just stayed right where I was and waited for them to come within range. I was over anxious and I couldn't wait like I should have. I decided to shoot an arrow when they were still too far away. I guessed they were about 40 yards away. I put my 35 yard peg about 6 inches above one of their backs and let it fly. The arrow did just that, it went about 6 inches above the hog, hit a palmetto frond, and made a loud popping sound, scattering the group of hogs in all directions. One came right at me! I waited until he got to me and gave him a good kick out of frustration. He went sprawling and squealing; it frightened him so bad.

My frustrating morning wasn't over by a good bit. That fence line was about 3 miles long, so I decided to follow it and see what else I could stir up. I came to a place where the fence went through a cypress pond, where we had cut a road out around it for several hundred yards. As I was slipping along this road, where it was running parallel to the fence line, I could see several deer feeding. They were feeding in the same direction I was traveling. I knew that the road came within 25 yards of the fence line, about 100 yards further on, so I crouched down and went on ahead to where I could waylay one of them. I found the perfect spot! A large clump of palmettos that would concealed me until the very last moment. I was lying in wait.

Two does fed by without even looking up; and my heart was pounding. I could see glimpses of a buck's rack every once in a while through the palmettos. He stepped out into the open and presented me with a perfect broad side shot, looking me dead in the eyes as I let the arrow fly.

One thing no one had ever told me was, never send an arrow when the deer is looking at you. That buck took a little hop to the side, as my arrow went right on by him. He snorted, took two quick steps and over the fence he went.

Only Deer with Bow

I had given both my sons compound bows for Christmas. When I was moving to North Georgia, I mistakenly sent my bow on ahead, before I had completely closed out my business. Archery season was opening that weekend, and I didn't have a bow or arrows. As luck would have it, my younger son told me he had loaned his bow to a friend, and he needed me to get it for him. My dilemma was answered, so I went and got the bow. I also had to go by Wally World to get some arrows. I was a short of money, but I found a package of three wooden hunting arrows that were in my price range.

I had never shot a compound bow, but I thought, "*How different can it be?*"

I had built a comfortable plywood stand in the swamp next to a hardwood island. It was about 20 yards from a good game trail, and I decided that would be the place to wait. My buddy, Bruce, dropped me off well before daylight. He went on around to his stand that was about a ¼ mile from me, on the other side of the strand. It proved to be an exciting morning. I tied myself off to a tree. I was standing, because of the awkwardness of shooting an arrow from a sitting position.

I heard something coming along through the water and my eyes and ears were like radar, as I anticipated what was on the way. I didn't have to wait long for there came one of the biggest hogs I have ever seen in the woods. I pulled that compound bow back and then realized that my son had not put any sights on the bow. I had no idea of what elevation to hold it at. I guessed! I guessed wrong; the arrow went 4 or 5 inches over his back and hit a cypress knee. Probably that arrow head is still sticking in that cypress knee, because later I couldn't dig it out.

It took an hour for me to calm down. I nocked my second arrow and waited again. Sure enough I saw some movement coming along the trail. It turned out to be two deer, one big doe and a smaller yearling. It was legal to harvest the doe or the yearling, but I chose the yearling because I thought I could see nubbs on his head.

I guessed wrong again! This arrow went just under the yearling's belly, spooking both of them into a bouncing run.

I started humming that country tune they played on "He Haw" that went: "If weren't for bad luck I would have no luck at all."

Here I am standing in a swamp with one arrow left, 80 miles from a place to purchase one, with a borrowed bow, with no sights; and I was seeing **all kinds** of game. It wasn't over yet! I was standing there cussing myself when I heard something else coming up the trail. I couldn't believe my eyes! Here came one of the prettiest bucks that had ever seen in the Glades; he had a nice rack and was a light brown color. He would walk a few steps, stop, wind the air, and walk a few more. When he got to the point where I had shot at the yearling, he stopped for a long time before he moved. This time he turned towards the tree I was in. I had already pulled the compound back, and I was glad that it was a compound, because I would have never been able to hold my re-curve back that long. He walked right up under the tree and stopped; I let the arrow fly. I had to lean out over the edge of the plywood to let it go. I didn't miss this shot! I could hear that telltale thump. The deer bucked up and took off around a clump of bushes. It sounded like he went through an open space beside of the strand. I waited a good thirty minutes before I came out of the blind.

There was water over the ground (about 6 inches deep) and I had decided to circle around to try to cross his trail near where I had last heard him. When I couldn't cross the trail, I decided to go back to the tree, to go real slow, to try and find his tracks under the clear water. It worked! I was able to see them without too much trouble. I had not gone 50 yards when I found him lying up in a bush. What I apparently heard was him kicking in his death throws; and as he died the sound got fainter and fainter, making me think he was getting farther and farther away. This is the only deer that I ever had mounted. He was not the largest I ever killed, but I was prouder of this kill than any I ever made.

Only Deer with Bow

I can't use a bow any more. I had a four way bypass operation on my heart; and for me personally; it feels like my chest is going to pull apart when I use a bow.

James L. (Sonny) Boyer

Ray and George and Deer

I was once in a tree stand on a prairie and I had been there since way before daylight. It was getting close to noon and Ray and George, the turkey hunters, walked up behind me and stopped for a chat. They talked for a couple of minutes and then they decided to go on in for the day. I said I was going to stay a little while longer and stayed in the stand. They walked straight away from me, which was the way back to the camp. As I watched them walk away, I could still hear them talking as they moved through the woods. When they got a hundred and fifty yards out in front of me, about seventy five yards in front of me, an eight point buck stood up out of the grass. He was watching them walk away. I raised my gun to my shoulder, but I could see both the buck and the men in my field of vision. I couldn't shoot because the ground was rocky and I sure didn't want to take a chance. I knew that the path they were walking on took a sharp left about fifty yards farther on, so I had to wait until they got to that point. They made the turn and the buck continued to stand there. I had to wait longer for his rear was the only thing facing me. He was close enough so I just waited for him to move and give me a better shot. When the men got out of sight, the buck finally dropped his head and turned to the left, giving me a perfect shot; and I took it. He dropped right where he was. Ray and George immediately came back towards me and I pointed to the buck lying there. It turned out they had walked within 15 foot of the deer when he was lying in the grass, and they had walked right by him.

First Shot "Ever" with Hawken

Muzzle Loading Rifles

This is another season that was added to my hunting days, that at the time, I knew nothing about. Luckily I knew it was coming, way ahead of time and I was able to scrounge enough money aside to purchase myself a Thompson Center 50 caliber Hawken. I ran across a gimmick sales promotion and had to practically threaten a law suit to get the gun. I finally was able to get my Hawken Friday evening. The new muzzle loading, "Antique Weapon Season" opened the very next morning. I didn't even know how to load it and I didn't have the necessary powder, patches, shot, or caps. I had invited my nephew to go with me to my camp. He was working in a gun shop and was a muzzle loading buff. He told me not to worry; he would instruct me when we arrived at camp that night. We didn't have time that night, so we opened the box on my new rifle the next morning at four thirty in the morning. He instructed me, as he was loading my rifle for the first time. I wasn't going to be able to test fire it, but at least they are not dangerous to transport loaded. He rigged me a second and third shot in plastic bags and a couple of snuff cans, and away we went to our choice of tree stands. As I remember, my group was the only ones hunting that week end. It was a new idea and most of the other camp members thought of the sport as a fad.

It was a cool, damp, foggy morning, as I climbed up in my chosen stand with my new toy. I had picked this stand for more than one reason. It was just inside the woods on the edge of what we called The Big Slough. It was big enough that I could stand, and reload if I had too. Looking toward the slough from the stand, it was easy to see a well-worn game trail that skirted the deeper water. Hogs, deer and all game used this trail as they moved up and down that huge cypress strand. I was in the stand well before daylight and I had managed to find a comfortable position with my new odyssey.

When the woods quieted down from my moving around and getting comfortable, I immediately heard some movement from down the strand to the south. It was still dark and I was hoping that "whatever it was" was moving my way, and that it would not get there too early. It didn't work out that way. It turned out to be several hogs in the fifty to sixty pound range, and they were rooting and feeding on the edge of the trail. It was still too dark to sight my new gun, with the open sights, and the hogs looked more like fleeting shadows. I had one of those cocky moments, where I planned on how I was going to harvest two hogs; and I was plotting how to reload my gun in a hurry. After years of hunting, I knew better than to do this, for it never works out the way you want. Finally the sun was up enough for me to get a good shot. As I eased that strange weapon to my shoulder, I discovered, *"Oh shit! I hadn't put the cap on."*

I put the gun across my legs and reached for the caps, but I couldn't remember which pocket they were in. I finally found the baggie where they were. The first one I pulled out, I promptly dropped as I was trying to fit it on the nipple. Caps are tiny little brass things about half the size of a pea. I couldn't understand why a little cap could make such a racket, as it hit the plywood stand, rolled over to the edge, and fell ten feet into the water. It sounded to me like I had dropped a brick into the water. I held my breath for a few seconds and found the hogs had not heard it. I fished out another cap and managed to get this one on the nipple. I pulled my gun up, pointed in their general direction, and waited for a clear shot. I waited, and waited, until finally a spotted hog provided me with a broad side shot. He was clearly visible by this time and I could tell there were several others. I sighted in on his head, for a shot there keeps from messing up too much meat.

When I squeezed off the shot I couldn't believe the difference in firing this gun and what I was used to. When my modern rifle is fired, it is instantaneous, with the powder burn and it is loud, but quick. This report was loud, slow and lingering. It surprised me, but not as much as what was out in front of me. I heard the hog squeal. It sounded like several of them were fighting.

I couldn't see anything in the swamp any more. That shot had covered the whole area with a thick white smoke that was not going anywhere. I managed to reload the gun, but the smoke prevented my second shot. I don't believe the report startled the pigs as much as the one I shot did when he squealed. I stayed in that stand for a full thirty minutes before I went for my hog and the smoke was still rather thick.

First Date with my Wife

I have to tell this story on my wife, for she must have thought me a nut for this experience. She was an airline stewardess and she had agreed to accompany me to Homestead, after a flight, while I bowled in a league. Then I was going to take her to dinner. If I remember right, it was our first date and I could have blown the whole thing.

Well on the way back to Miami, on a rainy night, leopard frogs were jumping everywhere. I got this bright idea and sprung it on her. I decided to catch a mess of frogs, and go to my home, and cook them for our supper. Trouble was I couldn't think of a thing to contain those frogs, once I caught them. This was before pantyhose. It dawned on me that she was wearing stockings, and one would be perfect to hold the frogs.

It was an embarrassing moment when I asked for one of her stockings.

"But there were millions of frogs."

So here we go down the highway; her shy one of her stockings. Her driving my car, and me jumping around in front of the headlights catching frogs. The dinner worked out perfectly, and she loved the frog legs. We often remind each other over the years what a strange date that was.

Game Warden Running Into Canal

I never had an air boat, although I made many trips on them, both hunting and catching frogs. Most of the frogs caught from an airboat are the big bull frogs and they can easily be seen by their white chins. They are delicious to eat, but I think the leopard frog is the tastiest.

There is an area south of Florida City that has plenty of frogs, but it was not a good area for air boats. Years ago someone cut roads through the whole area. The way they did it was to take a drag line and dig trenches on either side, then pile the soil in the center to form a road.

We used to wild cat hunt with dogs through that area and I noticed there were always bull frogs sounding off.

I figured out a way to cash in on those frogs. I was a carpenter by trade and had built several boats.

I even built a kayak when I was 12 years old. I had seen the Seminoles polling their canoes up and down the canal near the house, and I thought if I had one of those canoes, I could catch a mess of frogs. What I did was gather up some scrap cypress and make a light weight frame of a kayak with a square stern; large enough for an electric trolling motor. It had a pointed bow. I fitted the floor so that I could stand anywhere on about 3/4 the length. I fastened the frame down to a couple of saw horses, upside down, so I could create a skin for the boat. I had worked with fiberglass before, so I kind of knew what to do. I bought a cheap bed sheet and stapled that over the frame. I mixed some polyester resin and put enough on that sheet to stiffen it. When that dried, I stapled fiberglass screen wire over the top of the sheet, and added more resin. Over the top of that, I put fiberglass cloth; and I used a closely woven cloth. I really saturated this layer until I couldn't see any bubbles. After that hardened, I turned it right side up and gave it a good coat on the inside. The whole thing weighed less than 40 pounds. I bought a 16 foot Calcutta pole and fitted an airboat gig on the end.

I never did get a trolling motor, because I found in the places I used this boat I really didn't need one. I built a little wire cage that I could slide frogs into, and I set my icebox on the floor for me to sit on. With a car battery and a head lamp, I was in business. When I tried it out, I found that I had to really creep along in the grass to keep from alerting the frogs that I was approaching. I would hear a frog ahead of me, and I would ease forward until I could spot them in the grass. I would slip the Calcutta pole out to within five or six inches, and then jab it toward them. I would usually get a couple of dozen in a few hours.

One night I was slipping along searching for frogs when I heard this vehicle tearing down the road towards me. It slid to a stop parallel to me, and put a spotlight in my eyes where I couldn't see anything.

A man started barking orders, "Put your light out, put your hands up, and come towards the truck."

I answered, "Who the hell are you?"

It must have ticked him off, because he jerked open the door to his pickup, called me a SOB, and then he came running right at me. The next thing I saw and heard was him, as he made a loud splash when he ran off into water over his head. It was only then that I realized there was another man in the truck, because I heard him bust out laughing. I think that man realized what had happened, he announced that they were game and fish officers.

I answered, "Why didn't you say so?"

What happened was, they saw me and thought I was standing on the ground, because they couldn't see the boat in the grass. They thought I was poaching gators, and they charged up on me thinking I might throw a gun away. After everyone calmed down and he had fished his buddy out of the cattails, everyone had a good laugh about it.

I probably caught more fish out of that little boat than any one I ever owned. I liked to fly fish and I discovered that around the shallow water flats and mangroves, anywhere around south Florida, you can find snapper holes right up next to the mangroves. You can't get to them with a motor boat, but that little pole boat could travel over those flats with only one inch of water. Snook, red fish, and snapper; all inhabit those havens along the edge of the mangrove.

Posing for an Art Class

I should explain this story. I tried to duplicate a story I wrote in journalism class sixty five years ago. I wrote it in the owl's perspective, and it was targeted for a more youthful reader. The drawing is mine, but I did the original in watercolor.

It was in the early spring that I had a strange experience. My mate of two years was comfortably setting on four eggs that she had proudly laid last week.

It had taken us almost a month to dig out our cool home, under the turf of a big field that bordered a large lake. We picked a spot to make our entrance that was next to a flat rock. There were several cows that used the field, and we had to be careful that one of them did not accidentally cave in our entrance, and trap us underground. Foxes and raccoons are always trying to dig us out, so we dug several false tunnels to mislead them.

We had designed the tunnels so that in a real heavy rain, if we developed a leak, these false chambers would act as reservoirs to trap the water. We knew that in this type of sand, the water would dry up quickly.

Our sand pile (in front of our home), made a good perch for either of us to guard our children. Close by, was a row of wooden posts that also made good guard towers. Sometimes these posts were used by the other birds. We have seen Blackbirds, Meadow Larks, and occasionally other types; but our greatest danger was from Hawks that constantly patrol the area. I and my mate have learned to scream very loud, to warn each other of any danger that was in the area.

There is plenty of food for us in that field and our eyes are so good that we can hunt day or night. One of us always stays very close to the entrance, so we can be in the tunnel to protect our children.

The day my strange experience started was in the late afternoon, about three hours before the sun went down. A young human, I had seen many times before, was coming on his metal wheeled machine down the path that went alongside the wooden posts. He and another young human usually went to a large tree and stayed for a couple of days, and then they would leave. This time he stopped, laid his machine down, and walked straight to our home. I screamed to warn our mate. I didn't know what he was up to, for he bent over and did something to our pile of sand. He started backing away from our mound. I could see he had not damaged it, so I had no idea what he had done. He kept backing away and I knew he was far enough that our home was out of danger. He was carrying a stick with him and when he was far away, he just sat down in the grass and sat very still.

I stayed on the post for a long time and periodically I would scream to see if he would move.

My curiosity got the best of me and I had to go to the mound and see if my mate was safe. I flew and landed close to the mound. I called softly to my mate to let her know I was there. She cooed back, so I knew she was safe. I hopped up on the mound to see if the human was still there. He was standing up, and then he jerked the stick backwards. I felt something tighten around my feet and I couldn't get loose. I was able to fly, but the string that he had around my feet was drawing me closer to him. I was screaming and awfully scared. He drew me to him, grabbed my feet with one hand, and pulled my wings in close to my body with the other. He talked to me softly and I soon realized he was not going to hurt me.

He carried me to his machine and placed me in a wire box where I could barely stand erect. He took me to the place where he slept and we waited for morning. When morning came, we traveled inside a bigger machine that made a lot of noise, but the human sat with my box on his lap and continued to talk softly to me.

We arrived at a large building and entered a room with many young humans; they all wanted to look at me. The one who caught me reached in my box, and snapped something around my foot; then he lifted me out into the open. He gently sat me on a perch that had a bowl of water on one end and a small pan at the other. Whatever was in the pan was some kind of food, but I was too nervous to eat. My throat was so dry that

I could not resist the water, so I took a long drink.

An older human came into the room and all the young ones, including the one who had caught me, sat down and began trying to draw me on a piece of paper. The one who caught me instructed everyone not to move fast, not to make loud noises, so that I would not become frightened.

He was right! I was feeling better already. The older woman instructed the younger ones that I would only be there for the day. After school, the one who had caught me, (Sonny), was going to take me back and release me at my home.

I knew my mate was panicking and I was very relieved to know I would be going back home. The children were amazed when I would look all around the room by turning my head, without moving my body. Most of the time, I just stood very still, staring out into their young faces. One child thought I was stuffed and not real, until I turned and looked directly into her eyes. The young people would leave when a bell would ring and a new group would arrive and take their seats.

The older person and Sonny, the one who caught me, remained with me all day. Between classes Sonny would tempt me with some food. In the beginning I would snap my bill at him and warn him with my most ferocious look. He was not intimidated by my looks, even when I grabbed his finger when he put the food too close. I did get a taste when I did that. I decided to take a small amount. It was rather good! Everything I did during that day brought ooos and ahs from the young ones. Even when I took time to preen my feathers, they all thought I was wonderful. I looked all around the room and there were many strange things that I had no idea what they were. The object that fascinated me was the window, the invisible barriers that kept the wind from blowing.

At the end of the classes, true to his word, Sonny lifted me off of my perch and put me back into the wire box. We traveled in the big yellow noisy box back to where he had slept. He got out his wheeled metal machine and we headed back to the lake. He laid the machine on the ground, opened my metal box, and placed me on his finger; as if it was the perch that I had been standing on in the class. I could not bring myself to fly at that moment; I just stood there gazing into his eyes. I did not know how to thank him for my freedom, so I remained perched there looking at him. When I did fly, I just flew to the next post and stood there for a long while looking into his eyes. I could feel the apology for what I had been through, and I accepted it as I flew to find my mate.

I saw young Sonny many times after that, but I never felt again that there was any danger, and I always greeted him with my scream.

Sonny and Joan 1937

Fish and Grits

As you can see, my sister at three was already being taught the finer art of fishing and by six years of age I was already a professional.

My dad was born in 1906 in Sparta, Georgia, early in the 20th century. He was one of six siblings all under the age of eight, when his father was killed in a wagon accident. His death left his mother in a terrible spot. They were tenement farmers and had no money, even though his father; (my great grandfather) had accumulated a 7,000 acre plantation known as "Fairplay." It was lost after the Civil War due to taxes. My grandmother's people and my grandfather's people helped when they could, by doing the plowing and the things a woman just could not do.

Having the privilege of knowing her, I know that the things that were done for her had to be few, for she was a proud and resourceful lady. She and the kids, three boys and three girls, struggled through life, eking out a livelihood with the very bare necessities.

As I grow older I realize the stories my dad told me of walking great distances to school and carrying a sweet potato, both for warmth and food for lunch, could not have been an exaggeration. There was no such thing as food stamps, or welfare. You had to get out there and scrape and struggle or you would starve.

At 16 years of age my father took his younger brother and struck out to Miami, Florida. He told me he could not stay there and see his siblings and mother struggle any longer. He went south to find work and earn some money to help the rest of the family survive. This was in 1925.

My Mother on the other hand was born into a family in Miami, where her father was a successful building contractor, but they were destined to lose everything in the crash of 1929. In 1931, when I was born, the economy had been on rock bottom for 2 years.

My dad was very resourceful. He tried many different adventures to make a living. He cut lawns, did landscaping, had a laundry route, and opened an old fashioned sundry store. My favorite was when he had a "Toms Toasted Peanut" route. He became the favorite of all the kids.

He managed to save enough money to put a down payment on a modest CBS home. It was in an old subdivision, just off Flagler Street, the main drag in Miami, Florida. In 1938, when we moved there, Flagler and 63rd Avenue was still a dirt road. My sister is just three years younger (to the day) than I and she had not yet began school, when we moved to our new home. I had already started school and had to transfer to a completely different environment. Riverside

Elementary, where I began school, was, in town, and had a typical Norman Rockwell atmosphere. I actually enjoyed school until I had to transfer. The kids in my new school were mostly poor and a very small percentage could even afford shoes. Fighting was the norm and every child had to establish his dominance over any new kids. The harassment never seemed to end.

Our refuge was after school and the protection of our neighborhood. There were twelve houses scattered over about thirty acres in a subdivision that had gone bust in 1929. We had wide streets with sidewalks and cast-iron lamp posts, only they never got around to paving the streets. Some of the blocks had no houses and were fenced in with cows grazing on them.

All the parents were very protective of all the kids and you could almost say they originated the "Block Watch Neighborhood." We were way out in the country, by any standards in those days. There were plenty of snakes, rabbits and wild game in the area. We, all the people that lived there, developed a closeness that was really unique.

The old family heads are all gone now and only us 80 year old kids are left. Amazingly at Christmas the messages arrive bringing everyone up to date on the offspring, newly arrived in the previous year.

Our yard was the largest in the whole group and just ended up being a gathering place for adults, as well as for kids. Saturday night was pinochle or hearts for the men. I can still hear the racket they made arguing back and forth. For the kids, our big yard was the background for all kinds of games, but Friday or Saturday was the weekly fish fry. I don't know how it originally started, but it was a favorite weekly occurrence. We had a big Valencia orange tree in one corner of the yard, and next to it my dad built a stone barbecue pit with a short chimney. He had a large rectangular pan, about five inches deep that was for frying fish and hush puppies.

Unlike the mountains, our source of fire wood for heating grease was a handy supply of coconut husks. The women saved their bacon grease during the week and all we needed was fish when the weekend arrived. One food supply that is abundant in south Florida is sea food.

Once, while eating lunch in a house under construction, I heard a new laborer from the north ask a long time black resident, "What does a fellah need to get by here in Miami?"

The old timer answered with a short pause, "All you really need to get by is a piece of string and a fish hook."

There was a lot of truth in that statement, as far as the history of my family. I don't know how much our lives would have changed without fish as a staple.

Our old stand-by was Black Mullet. Just a few large ones would be plenty for our weekend neighborhood fish fry. It didn't take much of a tackle box to be able to catch them, and certain times of the year the canal two blocks from the house had plenty of Mullet. Black Mullet are vegetarians and even have a gizzard like birds. Biscuit dough, as bait, very small hooks, a small cork and a cane pole was all one needed. My dad had a trick of scattering oatmeal on the water to attract them to the bait. A pound and a half fish will eat bait as small as a green pea. It really takes a keen eye and a soft touch on the cane pole to hook one, because of their small mouth and cautious feeding. Most of the old timers smoke them, but fresh caught fish are really delicious fried. There are now "Mullet festivals" all over Florida that attract tourists.

There was a good supply of Snook and plenty of Bass, Catfish and fresh water fish of all kinds in that canal. Truthfully though, my favorite was always salt water fish. Two of the favorites of our neighbors were when we caught a Jewfish and my favorite was fillets from a Barracuda. They claim Barracuda can be poisonous but we ate plenty of them, and no one in our bunch ever got sick.

On the night picked for the fish fry, the women would gather early with their contribution of bacon grease and usually avocado salad or coleslaw. Someone would bring tea, and even ever so often beer would be passed around. My mom prepared the fish and a big pot of grits alongside the pan of bacon grease. She used half flower and half yellow corn meal to coat the fish, after salt and peppering it. After the fish was coated to her satisfaction, she would mix in chopped up onions, a little bit of baking powder, and enough butter milk to get the hushpuppies to the right consistency.

This is where my dad took over. He started cooking when the grits were creamy enough to suit him. Fish just don't taste right without a good helping of creamy grits. He pushed the grits pot to the back, where they would stay good and warm, and added coconut husks under the grease pan until it was very hot. His unique way of judging that, was with a floating kitchen match. When it ignited, the grease was just right. He would ease those filets into that grease; where they would sink momentarily, and then rise to the top. By the time they surfaced, he would turn them over, and the bottom side was already a golden brown. By the time he was half done cooking the fish, he would start spooning in the hush puppies, using the same floating method.

At first some of the invited neighbors would claim they didn't like fish and the response would be:

"That's because you never ate any of Myrt's fish."

There were a lot of people converted to fish eaters in that back yard.

The very best fry we ever had was in 1947 when we kids caught a couple of hundred frog legs after a hurricane, and everyone really had a treat.

My family was not limited to our back yard fish fries. My dad would drag us out of bed before daylight and we would go fishing off of a pier or bridge. We would take what we caught down on the beach at daylight, and have fried fish for breakfast. He had a favorite place south of Miami where we would go in the evening. He would build a fire, place a grate and a piece of tin over it, and then he would wade out into the mangroves, and break off a mangrove root that had a bunch of oysters growing on it. He would lay that whole root on the tin and it would not be long before the oysters would start opening up. My dad made up a sauce to dip them in, but I got to where I liked them better right out of the shell. I'm sure my mom had something to go with them, but I just can't remember what it was.

These and other activities such as catching shrimp, hunting rabbits, or gleaming vegetables from the south Dade truck farms (after they had been harvested), were fun to a couple of kids. Food gathering always had a dual purpose, although at the time I looked at it as entertainment. My dad had invented a way to put good food on the table and entertain the family with practically no cost. We never knew we were poor.

Betsy and the Test Ride

I have always been one who hated for someone to tell me something couldn't be done. Well Mother Nature put that stubbornness to a real test.

We were a young family; my youngest son was still in diapers, and my first born son was only 6 when we decided to take on a recreational project. A pool was discussed, but we were afraid of the constant danger that would exist. We talked about adding a room onto the house, and several other efforts. We decided it had to be something the whole family could enjoy around the Miami area. Of course, having nothing to do with my love of the water, we decided on saving for a boat; because I told everyone how much we would enjoy it.

When I was in high school, I had an uncle that included me in his excursions in his large sail boat. I learned the basics of seamanship from him. He taught me the importance of a chart and how to plot a course. He would put me to a test by having me set a course at night. He would have the search light handy, and when I told him to, he would turn it on. He had better be able to see the channel marker or buoy we were headed toward.

I didn't put it together until later in life, but I suspect that my inclusions had something to do with the fact that Uncle Jack had to have someone to help with the chores on his boat. My uncle's boat had so much sail area that it was almost impossible to sail alone. Whatever the reason, it had a big influence in my life and they were great experiences for a teenager.

I had an idea of what kind of boat we should look for. I had to have something that could go on a trailer; so that left out sail boats. At that time kit boats were the only way to go; there was a multitude of designs to choose from. I had even helped a friend assemble one. I looked and looked, but I couldn't find anything that was what I wanted. I worked with a retired Coast Guardsman, who would tell me the designs that he liked, and what a small boat needed in design to accomplish what I wanted. After about a year of looking, I decided if I was going to get what I wanted, I would have to design and build it myself. I put my skills (from Mr. Ellis's high school drafting class) to use, and came up with an ideal boat for South Florida.

The largest beam that I could have, had to fit a trailer, which was a maximum of eight feet; so I made it 7'11" & ½".' The length was controlled by the size of the plywood that I could find, and that was 20' long. I rented space in a cabinet shop from a friend of mine, and he ended up giving me a lot of good suggestions. He also knew where to find the right supplies. I built the transom, laid the keel, and built the stem on two extra heavy saw horses that were bolted to the floor. I didn't have any ribs in this boat, as I used five stringers and the strength of 3/8" marine plywood to surface the bottom, sides, deck, and gunnels. I kept the bow high to lift the front over the waves, but I brought the gunnels low, so it would have easy access to the water. She was wide enough (that in rough water) the buoyancy would pick the sides up and keep her from taking on any water. I built a seat across the front, that was permanent, which had a built in ice chest. This really added to the strength of the hull. The boat had no wind shield, only a flat deck. I fiber glassed the hull in white resin before I turned her over and mounted two thirty five-horse Johnson outboards on the stern, for power. After I turned it over, I took it home so that I could have more time to work on it.

Finally the day came that we were going to take her out, only one problem. There was a hurricane, named Betsy, out there racing toward the Florida Coast. To say we were disappointed was an understatement. This had been a long project and we were all anxious to enjoy our efforts. Now this occurred in 1965. The system of storm warnings was not as good as today, but we listened intently to the forecasts. Late that afternoon, the weather man said the Miami area was safe; the storm was off the coast of Florida, due east of Daytona, and headed north.

My wife and I preferred to fish at night so (being anxious to try out the boat) we decided to go south. We launched at Homestead, crossed the bay there, and went to the mouth of Caesar's Creek. I had been there several times on Jack's sailboat and always wanted to fish there, but never had. There is an old metal ring driven into the rocks where Black Caesar, the pirate, tied his ship up so he could watch the Gulf Stream for prey. Everything went fine, the boat handled like a dream. It was much faster than I had expected and was real comfortable.

When we arrived at Caesar's creek we saw that it wouldn't be any fun to try and go outside in the ocean. The waves were monstrous out in the ocean, so I pulled in to the lee of the outer island, dropped anchor where we far enough from land to get out of the mosquitoes, and started fishing.

Laurie, not being much of a fisherman, decided sleeping was more appealing and made a pallet from the preservers. Steve, my oldest, and I were catching enough fish to make it a successful trip and we were enjoying the adventure.

Somewhere around 3 or 4 in the morning, we saw a boat headed our way; it turned out to be a Park Ranger or some kind of government official. The boat came directly toward us and started circling us.

The man running the boat asked us, "Are we ok?"

I answered, "Fine."

He circled us several more times and we could tell that he was talking to the other man on the boat.

He asked again "Are you sure you are ok?"

I answered again, "Fine."

They waved, turned, and headed out into open water. I thought about this strange meeting and could think of no answer for his actions. I finally asked Laurie to turn on the radio and see what the progress of the storm was. Well we got a shock; the storm had made a loop off of Daytona and was coming back towards Miami. It was supposed to hit somewhere around noon that morning.

I'll tell anybody that scared the hell out of me.

My mind was racing! *"What have I got us into?"*

Laurie was looking at me asking, "What are we going to do?"

The bay that we had to cross was about 10 miles in width; and looking out into the darkness, I could see that it was extremely rough already. I knew that to follow the shallow water around the edge of the bay was a bad idea, for if we ran aground, it would be a death sentence. Our only choice was to go straight across the bay. I put preservers on everyone; made them use the extras as cushioning under the deck. Then I had them crawl under the front deck and lay on their backs. I pulled the anchor, swung the boat around; it was so rough I could not see the blinking light on the marker at the entrance to the marina. I thought well its 10 miles away, maybe I will see it when I get closer.

The waves were so huge that I was going over one

and through the next, and I was taking on too much water. I told Laurie to hold the wheel while I went to the back and removed both drain plugs. It worked! As long as I stayed slow (which I had to), the water would drain as fast as I was taking it on. I cracked jokes all the way across that bay, trying to act as if we weren't in trouble; but I was wet and scared. It's really hard to stay on course, with buckets of water constantly splashing in your face, and the boat slamming around by the waves, like they were going to tear it apart. Needless to say (being a believer in Christ) I was praying all the way for my family's safety. He gave me a miracle! I wiped the water from my face once again, and there in the pitch darkness, was the entrance to the marina, dead in front of me. The light was out on the marker, but we had crossed that bay, as rough as it was, and managed to find it under those conditions. After I got the boat on the trailer and tied down, I patted her side and told her, "Betsy you did a good job."

Conch Key

Our parents, (mine and Bruce DeVay's), were really generous with the things they would let us do when we were young. Bruce's parents had three automobiles. The really odd looking one was a Cord, and his dad used that one all the time. His mother drove a Graham back and forth to White Belt Dairy, where she was the owner's secretary. At age fourteen, they allowed Bruce to drive an old Plymouth sedan. I believe it was a 1936, but I am not sure. My dad's car was also a Plymouth, and it was a 1940 sedan. I believe the 1936 Plymouth had belonged to Bruce's brother, who was killed in a parachute jump on D-Day.

We had to buy our own gas and no one had insurance on cars back then. We were pretty industrious (on ways to make enough money to get gas), so we could try out new hunting and fishing spots.

Our favorite spot was at Conch Key. We would work all school year to save enough to rent a cabin on Conch Key, at the beginning of the summer. The cabins were unfinished frame buildings with windows with screens and wooden shutters. They had one metal frame bed, a two burner kerosene stove on a shelf, a one faucet sink, and wooden drain board. The bathroom was a crude shower and an old toilet with an overhead tank. There was no refrigerator, only a small ice box. The rent was fifteen dollars a week and we always managed to scrape up at least 30 dollars, so we could stay for two weeks.

Conch key- Late Forties

Four kids, or better, used to go down and live in what we thought was paradise. We practically lived off of fish while we were there. There were sunken telephone poles at the end of Three Mile Bridge, and Florida Spiney Lobster were under them by the hundreds. We mostly caught lobsters for bait, and if we did eat them, we battered them like fish and fried them. At that time we all would prefer fried grouper or snapper any time. We fished the west end of Three Mile Bridge on the north side, and most of the time we would walk the full length of Three Mile Bridge trolling a feather or lure over the railing. When we would hang a big fish, we carried a heavy line with a gang hook on it to slide it down our line to hook the fish, so we could bring it up to the top of the bridge. It was always a surprise what we would hang into on that bridge. Big grouper and snapper were what we wanted, but we also caught amberjack, snook and occasionally a big tarpon. I even caught a kingfish one night.

There was very little traffic at night, but we had to watch out for the Greyhound bus because that driver was sadistic. We got to know about what time he was due, and we knew what we had to do. The bridge was barely wide enough for cars to pass and it had a curb about six inches wide on both sides. When we saw that bus coming, we would place our tackle box on the curb, climb over the railing, and hang on to the outside. That driver delighted in running over our tackle box or rod, if it was anywhere in the road. He would put his right wheel up against the curb (on purpose), and wipe anything out, as he sped by.

We had two hefty jewfish lines we kept baited and tied off to the west end of the bridge, and once hit the jackpot with them. We had caught a large amberjack that we cut into two large chunks, we then baited those lines when we finished our six mile trolling walk.

The next morning we had decided to fish off the seawall at the end of the bridge and carried the necessary gear to where we were going to fish. Depending on which way the tide was running, governed which side we fished on. This particular morning we were setting up on the far side. I told Tom I would go and check the jewfish line that was tied off to the end of the bridge.

When I got there and pulled on the line I realized

we had something big on the line. Most of the time we would end up with a big shark, but this time it was a jewfish. I called to Bruce and Tom, and the three of us managed to get him around to the ebb, at the end of the seawall. He was hooked really well and we attempted to drag him over the seawall, but he was so big and heavy that the three of us couldn't get a good grip on the rope.

I said, "Hold him there! I will go and get the other line and maybe with two lines we can pull him up."

I ran to the other line and guess what? We had a big jewfish on there also. What we decided to do was to go to the fish house and see if we could get a boat to drag them to a place we could beach them. The owner of the fish house made a deal with us. He would pull them both around to the fish house, lift them up on the dock, and butcher them for half the meat. Sounded like a good deal to us and, as it was, it took us half a day to accomplish the chore. The man from the fish house said his scales only went to two hundred pounds, but he guessed they were both over three hundred pounds. We took our share of the meat back to White Belt Dairy and put it in the ice cream room where it was forty degrees below. When it froze solid like a brick, we sawed it up on the band saw in fry size pieces that were perfect at our back yard fish fry's.

I spent a lot of time on that bridge and even on Seven Mile Bridge. I remember once when we camped out at east end of the Seven Mile Bridge. We pulled one of those kinds of pranks that only kids dream up. At that time the city of Marathon dumped their garbage off the seawall on the north side of the bridge. The seagulls were always waiting for their free meals and they would swarm by the thousands. Bruce and I got the bright idea of catching some of them. We rigged our casting rods with small lead sinkers tied to the end of our lines, and would cast it into that mass of birds. Just about every cast, the sinker would wind around a wing, and we would real in a seagull. In our warped minds, the only safe place to store the birds was in the women's restroom, that was set up for the tourists. When we got tired of catching them, we had thirty or better stuffed in the restroom. Then we sat on the seawall fishing, while we waited for some unsuspecting tourist to use the facilities. It was hilarious when a snooty Yankee opened the door and the birds exploded, trying to get out. When a lady would scream, it would set the birds off even more.

After serving my time in the service and returning to Miami, I decided to drive to Key West to visit my sister, who had married a Marine who was stationed there. On the way by Conch Key I couldn't stand it, I stopped, dove off the seawall and caught four lobsters to take to my sister for dinner.

I returned to Conch Key after my kids were born. I used to drive a stake in the ground, put a harness on my smallest boy, and tether him to the stake so he couldn't fall over the seawall.

When I got older and working, I would go on down

in the keys, (either Big Pine or Summerland) and put in my boat. I would run the channel out to Content Key and camp out on the beach. The water was so pristine and the fish were plentiful. It is a special place for my wife and I. We played like we were Adam & Eve on a deserted island when we camped out there.

I was five years old the first time I heard about "The keys," and that was after the 1935 hurricane. My mother and father's good friend, Aubia, was a native of the keys and he lived through that terrible storm. He lost his wife, brother-in-law and three children, who were swept out of the rafters in their house, that was destroyed by the storm. That storm killed seventy eight members of his family.

It is a beautiful area on this earth and I saw and experienced it when it was still pristine, but like many places, it now has too many people.

Lobstering

As I grew older I developed a real love for the taste of lobster and I spent a lot of time pursuing them.

"Spiney lobster" that are native to Florida and the Caribbean, have no large claws. They have a different

flavor than the New England type and most eat only the tail.

I loved to use a bully net and catch them moving around on the flats at night and I dove for them. In the early days, we gigged them using a spring loaded devise that snapped around the shell and locked the lobster on the gig. The government outlawed those and the two prong gig because it killed the lobster, or left too many injured to die later.

I was successful at my trade, but at times I almost hated to go to work. I decided I would try to see if I could successfully run a trap line for lobster. I read up on the laws, acquired my numbers from the state, and set about building traps. John (a friend of mine) went in with me. We decided to try it on weekends the first year, keep good records, and see if it was feasible to try it full time. We could have put out several hundred traps but we only built fifty for our experiment.

We started searching for a bigger boat, as I only had an 18 foot outboard, and we thought we needed a bigger one. The boat we eventually bought was a 28 foot Emancipator. It was a perfect size; with a closed in cabin, a large cockpit, and a canvas cover over much of the stern. The boat was in dry-dock. The salesman was giving us a tour of the boat, pointing out all the advantages as he was trying to make a sale.

He put his hand up to the canvas top and said, "This cover is really unusual, it is made from a dirigible skin."

I saw John really take a good look at it before we went on. We told the salesman we would discuss the boat on the way home and we would let him know our decision tomorrow.

Now John was a Georgia boy, smart, but at that time not very wise about the world. We both agreed the boat was a good buy and we would go ahead and get it.

Things dropped off in one of those quiet spells that happen. Suddenly John asked, "Jim, let me ask you something. What kind of a critter is a dirigible?"

We were ready for the opening season and had a buyer ready to take any lobster we would catch. When we put the traps out, we lost two over the side; so now we only had 48.

I picked an area to lobster in Card Sound that I was familiar with. We put our traps out in two different lines and I kept a log of the depth and bottom type. When we would pull the traps, if they had no lobster, we would move them to the same kind of place where we had caught lobster.

A lot of people got the old ice mold cans from the ice houses and put these cans on the bottom as hiding places for the lobster. These or fifty five gallon drums were very effective for catching lobster, but just like anything that works good, the government came along and said that's a No No. The lobster traps that one can see stacked on the banks during the off season are not really traps. They are a place for the lobster to hide in the daytime. John and I, on the day the season was to open, watched just before daylight as three lobster, apparently returning from feeding, come across the bottom and entered the trap. What we experimented with, and finally put into practice, was we would bait the trap with a fish head or can of sardines, when we first moved it or placed it. After we pulled it and had a lobster in it, we would not bait it again. When we pulled the traps we would put a short lobster in any empty trap to attract others.

The caprice or front shell of the lobster had to be three inches in length to be legal to possess.

"Shorts" *That is what small lobster are known as.*

On clear calm days, I could observe the trap on the bottom, in shallow water. I noticed that many times when there would be several lobster in the trap, a large one would be on top like he was guarding the entrance. One thing for sure, they go and come as they please and they are not trapped.

About half way through the season, we got so good at placing the traps that the guy we were selling to followed us. He thought we were taking lobster from other peoples traps. He told us we were bringing in more lobster than men that were running several hundred traps. After I showed him my log, and what we were doing, he got real interested and started running his personal traps the same way.

I had a theory that going at it as a business, keeping track of all the expenses, and doing it faithfully like an everyday job, was the only way to test the feasibility of doing it full time. I soon found my outboard (with the two 35 Johnsons on it), was a lot better for us to run the traps, for it was a lot easier to handle. We went out in some really rough water and my outboard did a fine job. I enjoyed the mystery of what was going to be in the traps when we pulled them. We caught small sharks, and all kinds' good eating fish. They went home with me for the table, along with all the stone crabs.

I loved the life and being in the outdoors, and we had paid for everything in that one season with only 48 traps. All our fuel (in the boats and the cars) travel expenses were paid. We paid for the 28 footer, paid the dockage, and our food and drinks on the work days, and ended up with several hundred dollars for pocket money. By the end of the season, we had lost another 3 traps from cut lines, so we only pulled 45 out at the end.

My problem was the sun. I had developed, and had to have 12 sun cancers removed. The sun was eating me up and there is no way to escape it on the water. My doctor even advised I move away from South Florida. His advice helped in our decision to move to the North Georgia Mountains.

Another Big Jewfish

Bruce and I and another boy (Jimmy Insco) teamed up for a 3 day fishing trip to Marco. We were going to camp out on one of the out islands that were north of Marco. Jimmy's father let him use his boat and Bruce pulled it over with his old Plymouth. We were going to be back in Miami in time for me to go to work Sunday at four PM at Tanners Grocery. When we got to the bridge at Marco, we parked the boat and trailer, and walked out on the bridge to see what we could catch around the bridge pilings. I did catch a drum that weighed about five pounds, so at least we had bait for my jewfish line.

We launched the boat for where we wanted to set up camp and then we did some trolling before dark. We made it in plenty of time and had a real cool spot under some cabbage palms. The wind blew across that tip of land and kept the mosquitoes to a minimum. I tied my jewfish line on a mangrove tree, about a quarter of a mile north of where we were camping, and baited it with that drum. We went on trolling and we checked the jewfish line just before we went back to our camp for the night. We checked it periodically for the next two days with no action. No crabs even went after the drum. We did a lot of fishing that first day and a lot of sleeping on the second day. Part of the day was spent with Bruce and Jimmy sifting through the sand hunting for cigarette butts, so they wouldn't have nicotine fit. I didn't smoke so it didn't bother me. We caught a decent mess of fish and all of us had enjoyed the adventure. We decided to have a good breakfast, pack up camp, and head on back to Miami. We almost forgot my jewfish line and actually had to turn around and go back.

When we approached the tree it was tied to, we could see the line was taught and the tree was shaking. When we pulled him to the surface his head was huge. We had a big problem though, the leader for the line was a 9 strand steel cable. He had frayed that cable and only one strand was holding. The fish was just about worn out, but there was no way we could pull him in the boat. What we did was pull him up to where Bruce and Jimmy could grip his lips, and the two of them held him while I ran a ten pound anchor through his mouth and out his gills. I tied it back to the main line. Then we were able to drag him to a beach where we could butcher him. It took us hours to get his head off and gut him. When we got back to the dock, we had to get help to get him out of the boat and load him in the trunk of Bruce's car. To keep him cold for the trip home, we put fifty pounds of ice into his chest cavity. We had not cut the tail off, but had to, to close the trunk lid. Needless to say, I didn't get back to Miami in time for my job.

Note; Hurricane Donna September 10, 1960 went right through that area and completely changed the landscape. I went there to fish and could not believe what had happened. The channels were completely different and the vegetation was gone. Everything was stark white.

Chokoloskee Fishing for Jewfish

From the trip where my young son and I almost turned over my small aluminum boat, I returned many times to fish for these delicious fish. I kept going back to that spot to see if I could catch another big one. I never caught one, but I had jewfish break several lines. One of the old timers showed me how to fish for them, and I was always able to bring home a couple every time I went out.

The waterways around Chokoloskee and Everglades City are called the Ten Thousand Islands. There are not that many in reality, but you will think there are if you don't pay attention and get lost. The natives learn the passages from childhood. It takes a lot of trips for a newcomer to feel comfortable enough to venture far away from the established channels. The smaller channels that worked their way in and out of these mangrove islands are the perfect habitat for my favorite, the jewfish. Most fishermen go for snook, redfish, trout and tarpon; and I did too (at first), but I soon found myself concentrating on the jewfish.

I would try and catch some fish I could use for live bait, and sometimes that would be more difficult than catching the big ones. I had a short (10 foot) heavy bamboo pole that had a clothes pin fastened to the end. I would tie off my jewfish line to the bow of the boat, leaving some slack in the line, run it to the clothes pin, and pinch it with the pin. I would hang live bait down about four feet. Then I would sit in the rowing seat and paddle to keep the boat drifting the right way. It was easier if there were two of us. I would use that short pole to move the bait in and out, trying to keep it as close to the mangrove as possible as we drifted along. Fish like to lie under the bank overhang and they will dart out for bait. I would catch them in the 20 -50 pound range when I went. I was afraid to tie off to the side after we almost turned over. When a fish would get on, I would take my hand gaff and hook on to the line, so I could land him. One trip I caught seven fish and the largest one was about 50 pounds. I had a large Styrofoam ice chest, so I put the smaller ones in the bottom of the chest, and lay the big one on top to show off. I won't ever do that again because when we stopped for a cold drink on the way home, it was gone when we returned to the truck.

I am glad I moved out of Florida before they stopped people from catching jewfish. It would have broken my heart to have to stop catching them. It was bad enough to know I could never go back and catch any, and it destroyed my dream of returning.

Spinning Rod

Shortly after I returned from the service and was still looking for my first job, I would go to Matheson Hammock and fish. It is an old beach complex that is a large pond in saltwater. It has a breakwater around it with screened inlets in places that allow the tide to keep the water clean. It is a popular beach and picnic area for the public. My dad would take us there when I was a very small child.

The whole area around Matheson Hammock has a lot of fish to be caught, if you only look. The pond (where you first turn off Cutler Road) has plenty of good size snapper that are always hungry. My aunt and Uncle lived right across the road from the park. It was easy to go over there after they had closed the gate and fish, as long as you were quiet. The south side of the beach was what they called "The wading beach." If no one was wading, you could see schools of bonefish tailing out there, feeding on the bottom. My family liked to picnic at that end because there were never too many people. I was there many a day and watched several schools of fish feeding on that flat.

In 1952 when I was released from the service, the spinning rod and monofilament line were just coming into existence. I had a buddy that was stationed in Germany and I had him ship me a "Quick" reel and a supply of line. From what I had been reading, this was the way to go. When I got it, I had to make a rod because no one had anything that would fit properly. I had the same problem finding lures, for they were the wrong size.

I made a mold out of Plaster of Paris that made a lead head the size of a dime. It was flat on the top and oval on the bottom. The hook was molded into the head, with the hook pointing at a right angle to the flat part of the head. This allowed the lure to skip across the bottom without snagging. I wrapped a good wad of buck tail hair to the back, and all I had to do was paint it with my mom's red fingernail polish; then I was in business. I almost blew up the kitchen trying to pour lead into a wet mold. I had to make a second mold and dry this one out in the oven before I poured any lead. I practiced with that rod around the house for several days before I went to Matheson to try and catch a bone fish.

I went early, to be there before anyone else was on the beach. As I parked my car, I looked out in the water and saw two schools tailing. I watched for a few minutes trying to determine if I could tell which way they were moving. I made a guess and waded out way in front of them; cast my little red head lure as far as I could, and let it lay on the bottom. The school I was planning on way-laying, turned, and went the other way. Before I moved, I looked around to see if I could spot the other school. I didn't see it at first because they were the same way as the sun was shining. When I did spot them, they were headed just right; so I figured I might have a chance. These fish were rather large; and I was really nervous as they got closer and closer to where my lure was laying on the bottom. I finally thought the time was right, and I twitched that lure ever so slightly, and then followed with several short spurts. I saw one of the bigger fish dart toward it. I could feel the tug on the line, as I popped that pole upright. I hooked him, or he hooked himself; then he tore off like a freight train. I only had a six pound test line on that reel and in a second he was out seventy five or a hundred yards, and it looked like he was still going. I could see the bottom of the spool when he finally turned and slowed down. After that he only made short bursts of speed as he fought to get away. I took it easy because I really wanted to land him. When I finally caught him, I went back to the car and weighed him on a pair of spring scales; and they showed 8 pounds. Not bad for a homemade rod and lure, and the very first cast it made in a fishing mode. I took him back out in the water to turn him loose, but he kept turning upside down. I sat down in the water and held him upright, while I pushed him back and forth. After about ten minutes, he finally swam away from me without turning over. It was a good feeling seeing him swim away and it was worth the extra effort.

Barracuda on the Flats

Outside of the swimming pond at Matheson Hammock, to the northern side, the water was very shallow. One could wade out about a mile to a peninsular. Bruce, my buddy and I camped beside it several times, and the fishing was good. There is a canal that was dug from the highway all the way to the swimming pond, paralleling the road. I assume it was dug to get the fill to make the road that ran to the beach. That canal was an excellent place to go and catch enough fish for supper. Now that area is a conglomeration of million dollar homes.

Crossing over to the camping spot, I had occasionally seen Barracuda lying in the shallows. Thinking about this prompted me to catch four or five mullet with my cast net nearby in the Coral Gables Waterway. They were black mullet and a little large for what I wanted to do, but I went anyway. I was only a short way from the beach, so I carried them in a bucket and then I transferred them to a wire basket and set them in the water. It was no more than five minutes from catching them until they were in the wire cage in the water, so they were still lively. I had a small reel (A

Penn 209) that had a 20 pound linen line with a short length of steel leader and a small hook. I wanted to keep the rig light so a mullet was able to swim away with my line. I went out halfway across the pond, and waded out into 30 inch deep water on the edge of grass. I hooked one of the mullet in the back and let him swim away from me, while I kept the line freewheeling.

I had been there about an hour when a man came out on the flats and stopped to talk to me.

He asked, "What are you fishing for?"

I replied "Anything that will bite."

He was standing there trying to make small talk when he spotted my mullet and he hollered, "You have one! Pull him in."

I explained, "That's my bait"

He looked at me with a strange look and then broke out laughing as he walked on across the flats. While he was gone I caught a four foot barracuda which I had put on a stringer on a fairly long line.

In about a half hour here comes the same guy back. As he approached me, he said with a sarcastic voice, "Catch anything?"

I replied, "Matter of fact I did," as I pulled the Cuda in and lifted it up.

His only words after that were, "Oh s--t" as he

picked up his pace considerably on the way back to the beach.

Hunting in 1947 Flood

In 1947 we had a flood in south Florida that was not like anything before. I was about 16 at the time, maybe only 15, because I didn't have my driving license yet. My buddy, George, was the same age as me. Our older buddy, Tom, had his driver's license; so we conned my father into letting us use his International pickup for a hunting trip.

We planned a trip for four days and we went 65 miles west of Miami, and set up camp in a wide spot in the road. The Tamiami Canal was parallel to the road and at that spot, about 20 feet from the edge of the road. None of the small islands that we were used to camping on, were available because of the high water. We thought we were lucky that we found this spot. There were two or three cabbage palms placed just right to string a line between. We stretched a tarpaulin over it for a shelter. Tom and George both had mosquito bars, but I had a jungle hammock that provided shelter and it had a built-in mosquito bar.

We found this spot in the early afternoon, so we spent the rest of the day laying out our camp. We built a fire ring and spit for cooking, padded the ground where George and Tom were going to sleep with palm fronds, and gathered firewood. We had camped out together many times, so we knew what had to be done to make the area as comfortable as possible. Tom was the driver and the oldest, so he made the hunting plans for the next day, while we prepared our evening meal.

We discovered the following morning that the water was higher than we could have ever imagined. It became a problem to even find a place to hunt. We ended up driving all over the place just trying to find a place out of the water. We were running low on gas so Tom decided we should go on toward Naples, and get some gas and ice.

We were really just kids doing just whatever we thought of next. We found a place to get ice and gas and we were standing outside drinking a cold drink. Two young boys, not much older than us, one black and one white, asked us if we would give them a ride to Miami. We told them that they could ride with us as far as our camp, but it was only 25 miles away. They had been working for Ringling Brothers in Sarasota, and had gotten laid off when they came home. Winter quarters for Ringling Brothers is in Sarasota, Florida and they were trying to get to Miami. We had found two places to hunt the next day, so we went on back to our camp with these two boys in tow. The boys thanked us and went on down the road, walking toward Miami. There weren't very many cars traveling the Tamiami Trail in those days, so it was not likely they were going to get a ride. We put some coffee on and proceeded to lay around telling lies about sundry things in our lives. We were just about ready to start supper, and we were going to fry some spam and potatoes, when up walks these two boys carrying two large black bass. They wanted us to cook them and they would share them with us. They had run up on somebody fishing and he had given them the bass. We agreed and ended up with everyone having a delicious meal of hush puppies, fried bass, and grits. A little better than fried spam!

The boys decided to camp out with us and go on to Miami the next day. The white boy got busy and piled himself up some palm fronds to lie down on. The black boy said "No way am I going to lay down there, where snakes can crawl on me."

When I crawled into my jungle hammock he said, "Look at him. He's going to sleep, lying straight out in the air."

I don't think he had ever seen a hammock before. True to his word, he stayed up all night walking up and down the road near the fire.

Around 2 AM, a panther screamed across the canal in the woods, and it made the hair stand up on the back of my neck. There was a commotion beside my hammock where the white boy was trying to sleep. He had jumped up, when the panther screamed, and was trying to run. The palm fronds were slippery and he was running in place, flipping those fronds out into the canal with each step, until he finally hit the solid ground and traction. All the time he was moaning with an animal-like noise, and the black boy had disappeared. When my buddies and I finally got up, we could hear both of them running down the road toward Miami. I have often wondered what became of them, because they never came back.

The next day Tom let George and I out on a levy we had discovered. We were going to slip down the levy to see if we could jump a deer off it. We walked for miles and ended up having to walk down an old road that was under water that was beside the canal. We knew that from the way we were walking, that eventually we would arrive back near where our camp was. We hadn't brought a thing with us to eat. We were both starving, because it was getting late in the afternoon.

I saw a small cabbage island that was out of the water, and only about 50 yards off the road we were walking. On it was a whole bunch of beehives.

I told George, "Let's rob one of those hives. That honey would taste real good right now."

George replied, "Not me; your crazy!"

I said, "I will. I've watched my dad do it a lot of times and he never got bit. Hold my gun and I'll go over there and get one of those racks; it ought to be real good."

The road was about a foot under water and there

was actually another road that led to the hives. I walked up to the hive I was going to rob, and tried to remove the top, but it would not come off. I reached down and picked up a rock, to try and bump it off. Big mistake! It came off, but with it came hundreds of angry bees. They were biting me everywhere. All I could think of was to run. I ran back down the road, and right past George, miss-judging where the road was, and ended up in the canal.

George was killing himself laughing at me. That's where he made his mistake, because the bees went after him. He ended up, dropping the guns and jumping in the canal beside me. By the time we got back to camp my face was swollen bad; George was practically leading me like a blind man, and he had knots all over his head. Tom is the one who laughed the hardest at both of us.

Milam Dairy Lake

It's a lake that you won't find on any map but it was my buddy's and my playground during the Second World War. I guess at the time, it belonged to the Government; for it was created by digging oolite and trucking the oolite to build the runways for Miami International airport.

Oolite is a base rock formed from coral that when compacted and wet, forms an excellent road. When it dries it is like concrete.

All of the removed material had been hauled away and there were no piles of rock left around. The lake is about ¼ of a mile long, and as I remember, about 3 hundred yards wide; and it was in the middle of Milam Dairy. At each end, it was very deep, because we never found the bottom. The middle was only about waist deep, and cattails had taken over. One small sandy road led from the lake, to Milam Dairy Road, and back to civilization where my home was located.

Flagler Street, the main road in Miami, had just been paved (two lane); and our street was still a rock road.

When asked where I lived, I used to say, "The eastern part of the Everglades"

There were very few homes beyond us to the west. The lake was about two or three miles from the house, and to us it was paradise. Bruce and I camped out there as much as we could. We would ride our bicycles, with our camping gear loaded to the hilt, on Friday after school, and return Sunday evening.

There was one tree at the far end of the lake. It was an Australian Pine and it was very large. Around large Australian pines, saplings grow outwards for several yards, and these made a perfect camping spot. We had a spot where we could bend several saplings over and tie them together, just at head height. This made a great framework for our tarpaulin, and the roof of our sleeping spot. We used pine needles for our bedding. At first we just endured the mosquitoes with smudge fires. We used packing blankets for sleeping bags, and the food we ate was always the challenge. We managed to take a couple packets of Lipton chicken noodle soup for lunch, bacon and eggs for breakfast, and a bag of grits, flour, and corn meal, along with bread and spices, for supper. These were our only brought-from-home, supplies. We didn't have any ice, so supper was up to us; and we could be proud of our ingenuity with our meals. The lake and the surrounding pasture was a treasure trove of supplies for two young boys with imagination.

Bacon grease was always saved for the supper meal. Fish were always our stand by if we couldn't find anything else. This will probably shock Sierra Club members, but our favorite meal was meadow larks. I know you have seen them; they have a yellow breast and what appears to be a black bow tie. They are about the size of quail and inhabit open fields and pasture land. One of us always took a single shot 22 rifle, and we got very good at plinking the head off one of these birds while they were setting on a fence post. We didn't skin them; we sat and pulled every feather like we had a chicken. We would split the carcass through the bottom and lay it out flat, then salt and pepper and flour them, till every possible spot was covered. We would place them in our bacon grease and brown them at a low heat with a lid covering them. All the while we had a pot of rice cooking away for the finished product. Sometimes we would have a swamp cabbage simmering alongside the rice. When those birds were properly brown, we would move the fry pan to a cooler spot on the fire. Then we would add a little water and flour mix, and let it simmer as long as we could stand it; or until they disappeared into rich gravy.

One of us would invariably say, "I wonder what the poor people in Miami are eating tonight," as we stuffed ourselves with tender larks and gravy.

Our diet was varied, for around that lake was plenty to harvest. Nighttime found us wading around in the lake after frogs that we would keep in a burlap bag till the next night's meal. Occasionally we would be lucky enough to get a small gator and that was a real treat. Later when we were older, Bruce got a shot gun and we were able to wade in the lake and shoot one or two marsh hens for supper. These were even better than the larks.

One of the best lessons I learned about mankind was on that lake camping. We both knew that it wasn't according to Hoyle to be eating larks, but we did it anyway. One day as we were swimming in our favorite spot, a tanker truck pulled up down the bank from us and started dumping something into the lake. We had to look. Low and behold, they were dumping bass into there by the thousands and they were all about 7 or 8 inches long. After the truck left, we looked and they were all swimming around in one spot. Now at that time, bass were supposed to be 12 inches to keep, but this was too much of a temptation for two boys. These bass were hungry! We caught more than enough for supper and started fixing our meal early. Luckily we had brought an onion and tomatoes from home, so we had the fixing for a good meal. I was glad for Bruce thought a good dish was to mix a lot of strange stuff together, all in on pot. He wanted to open a can of Spam and he could really contrive a mess when he cooked.

There were so many fish that I filleted each one and skinned them. I mixed flour and yellow corn meal and battered each small piece until it was completely covered. I diced up onion and mixed it with the left over flour mixture to make plenty of hush puppies. We even brought a small jar of butter and had placed it in the lake to keep it fresh. I had made a good size pot of grits that had been cooking on the side for about an hour, so they were as creamy as you can make them.

As we were cooking I saw a man coming down the road toward us. He wasn't in a hurry, just seemed to be enjoying his walk. He had on a pair of bib overalls and we assumed he was from the dairy. He had a little dog with him that was friendly and was busy checking out my little dog. We talked with him all the time we were cooking the fish and he was really a nice man.

We asked him to join us with our supper and he said, "You know what boys I'm just going to do that."

We had cooked almost a pound of bacon for breakfast, so we had plenty of grease, and I had it good and hot. I dropped those small pieces of fish in that grease. They settled to the bottom for a few seconds and as soon as they floated to the top, I turned them over long enough to see if they were brown. Then I pulled them out and drained them on a towel. Those small fish had no bones and that meal was one of the better ones I ever ate. We all enjoyed every bite. There was even enough left over for both little dogs. The man introduced himself sometime during the meal and I promptly forgot it, however I will never forget him as long as I live. After spending several hours swapping tales and food, he told us how much he enjoyed the meal and he had never eaten fish that tasted as good. He even helped us clean up the dishes. When he rose to leave he pulled his wallet out of his pocket. We could both see the badge flashing in the firelight.

"Boys I'm the game warden for this area, I'm sure you didn't know, but the next time you catch any bass make sure they are 12 inches."

He tipped his hat to us and disappeared down the road in the darkness. I could feel the hair on the back of my neck crawling and I know my face turned beet red. Needless to say that ended Bruce and I shooting larks or catching small bass.

His method of handling us was a lot more effective than if he had arrested us, and it was a lesson that has stayed with me my whole life. I know this sounds like we didn't respect the game laws. I really hesitated to write about my childhood escapades, but we were kids, and it was a different time. No excuses, but I did clean up my act.

The following short tales really have nothing with fishing or the outdoors but begin from things we found at the Milam Dairy Lake.

The lake was also used as a dump by the military, so we were always rummaging through it for anything we could drag home. One thing we found was a small crate that had never been opened and it had in it a small Briggs and Stratton engine that was brand new. We gave it to my neighbor, Mr. Volker. He mounted it on a bicycle and used it for transportation to go to work during the war.

Several times we found die packets from life rafts and we thought of many ways to use them. When you put them in the water, they would turn huge volumes of water a bright chartreuse color. We thought about taking some to our favorite hangout on Saturday, a huge pool in Coral Gables called Venetian Pool. We started there on our bicycles, but we passed something that was a lot more appealing. We had to go right by the world famous Biltmore Hotel. Out front on the drive-in road was a large fountain where the water was continually spraying into the air. That was just too tempting for several boys looking for entertainment.

You are supposed to put the packets in water and they will dissolve through the material. Well we didn't do it that way; we tore them open and sprinkled the die on the surface of the water. In just a few seconds the water that was spraying up in the air and was extra bright green with the sun glowing through it. We hadn't thought that the water going up in the air would be affected. We thought it would only be in the pool and that we would have plenty of time to make our get-a-way.

It was like a huge beacon; we knew the first car to come along would mean trouble for us, so we tore out of there and didn't slow down till we got to Venetian Pool. We thought we were safe and had gotten away with it, until we dove in the water and discovered we were leaving a green trail everywhere we swam. We left and made our way to the safety of our homes, but I was one who skirted that fountain for a long time after that.

Our most treasured find, was a female manikin that looked almost life-like. As well as I remember there were three of us the day we found her. All of our bicycles were fender-less, so we had a problem figuring out how to get her home. We finally decided to tie her on the crossbar of my bike, just like you were riding someone double. She had a blond wig and that's all!

Now we lived a couple of miles from Milam Dairy. Part of the route home was on Flagler Street, which is the main street in Miami. At that time our neighborhood was on the outskirts of town, but there was still plenty of traffic, for it was on the way out of town. I can just imagine what went through people's heads as they came along the road and saw three boys riding along on their bicycles, with a naked blond with long legs riding side-saddle on one of them. I know there were a lot of squealing brakes and running off the road, as people saw what they thought they saw. We hammed it up with everything we could think of to shock people. Our sides hurt from laughing by the time we got home.

Everyone in our neighborhood knew each other and every one watched out for their neighbors, it was a great place to grow up.

When we got home we hid her until night, for we had made some great plans for that night. We found enough clothes from the girls in the neighborhood to dress her, so in the darkness of night she looked very real.

The secret was out! By this time we had all the kids in the area tagging along, even my parents came along, and everybody had to have a hiding place before we sprung our surprise. Our first victim was a neighbor that lived across the street from our house. We took

"Nellie" the name we gave her, and laid her out near the porch of Mr. Bell's house. We took a garden hose and concealed one end next to her head and stretched it out to our hiding place. When everyone was set, someone knocked on the door and then ran and hid. Then I would start moaning through the hose.

Mr. Bell came to the door and flipped on the porch light. When he saw Nellie lying on the ground moaning, he jerked open the door and ran to Nellie with his arms outstretched going to her aid. About the time he realized he had been had, everyone started laughing. The crowd grew as Mr. Bell and other neighbors joined us, as we tried out Nellie on everyone in the neighborhood.

The adults had gone on home and three of us kids were standing in the street, when a car drove up and turned on a spotlight. We realized it was a police car and it scared us to death.

He asked us, "What are you kids up to?"

We explained what we had been doing and he listened intently, asking a question now and then. Without commenting he got out of the car and motioned for us to get in.

Then he said, "Bring the dummy and hose also."

He drove us about five minutes away and stopped, turned out his lights, and instructed us to go up to the house he was pointing to, and pull our act on those people. He said that it was his brother's house and he wanted to see how he would react. He fell real hard and we could hear the officer laughing all the way down the street. He finally took us home after he and his brother exhausted everyone they could think of to pull it on.

It was a fun night that that didn't cost a dime.

Things I Have Been Privileged to See

Fish-Eating-Creek

One of my loves is a wilderness area in Florida called Fish-Eating-Creek. I hunted there as a child with Mr. Volker, before it was a management area, and truly enjoyed it as a place to go anytime of the year to get away from it all.

It is a creek, but it is hard to tell where the creek flows, because it is made up of hundreds of small shallow lakes that meander through cypress (that has grass growing under them), and it looks like it is planted and mowed. Cypress knees are everywhere, with an occasional patch of oaks and cabbage palms on the higher islands. These islands make wonderful camping spots and one of them was where I initiated my Yankee wife to the serenity and peacefulness of camping out.

It has excellent fishing! Being a fly fisherman, I waded the edges of these shaded ponds and enjoyed the peace and quiet. On one quiet morning, I saw a half grown otter across the pond from me. He was paralleling me as I moved down the creek. He wasn't 30 yards from me and he was watching my every move. He definitely was curious about what I was doing. Occasionally he would climb out on the bank and stand up as tall as he could, so he could see better. This went on for over an hour. I would pause every now and then to watch him; it didn't make him nervous at all.

All this time I hadn't caught a fish, but this otter was making the morning interesting with his curiosity. I actually started talking to him as I worked down that bank, and was kind of surprised when I did get a strike. I turned my attention to the fish I had hooked, but I noticed out of the corner of my eye that the otter was standing tall again, watching the splashing of the fish as I landed it. It was only a small bream, but I figured it was a good start for breakfast. I looked back to see the otter and he had disappeared from my sight. I stood there for a moment thinking maybe I had scared him off with the splashing of the fish. Boy was I wrong!

Suddenly I heard a commotion in the middle of the pond. I realized it was the otter thrashing around. In a few minutes I saw him swim over to the bank and emerge out of the water carrying about a two pound bass. That little turkey had watched me all morning and had finally figured out that I was fishing.

It didn't take much to read his mind; for he was tossing that fish in the air and looking at me as if to say, "You caught a little one and look what I caught!"

Does this photo require any explanation?
From Alvin Lederer collection

Family at Pond for Performance

When water starts to recede in the Everglades, fish-eating-critters can be found easily around the many small cypress ponds that are scattered throughout the landscape. I had the family out for a relaxing weekend at the hunting lease we called, "Crooked Pine Ranch." We decided to slip into one of these ponds to see what we could observe. I instructed my two boys and wife on the way there, on what they needed to do, to not frighten anything we might find. I approached the pond with a breeze in our faces, so no animal would wind us.

I knew there was a good size alligator living there. It had a den under a pond apple tree, and I was hoping to catch him out sunning himself. We slipped very quietly through the big cypress and it was almost completely dry under us. I hand motioned my family to sit on a log that was in the shade and near the edge of the water, where we would have a good vantage spot. The whole pond had about a fifty yard diameter with the deeper side away from us. The pond was in full sunlight and we were sitting under some low hanging branches, so we were hard to see. I had never seen my two boys (six and twelve) sit so still. It was like they were expecting a good show and they didn't have to wait long.

Four adult otters came out of the grass on the far side of the pond and started playing a game with each other. Only they knew the rules, but it was really amusing to watch them as they tumbled and twisted and chased each other in and out of the grass. They played like this for ten or fifteen minutes before they disappeared back into the grass. About the time we saw the last of the otters, a yearling raccoon came out of the grass and started wading around in six inch deep water in front of us. He was obviously trying to find something. He had both of his front paws moving around in the water, moving them back and forth, feeling every little twig or object, examining it in detail. What looked ridiculous was, he never looked at them; he had his head up and was acting like he was looking everywhere, but in the direction of his hands. What I thought was hilarious, was the way he was holding his tail. Normally a raccoon is very much at home in the water, and never seems to mind getting wet. This one had a horror of getting his tail wet. As he wadded around in front of us, is tail was sticking straight up in the air, and he never once let it touch the water. This show was taking place less than ten feet in front of us and he never once paid any attention to us sitting there. I was just about ready to give up on him catching anything, when he made a dive out in front of him and caught a small alligator gar. You could hear it crunch when he clamped down on it. Mind you now, he never got that tail wet. He waded out with his prize and proceeded to eat it right in front of us, when we were not five feet away. All this time we were like statues, afraid to move, for fear we would stop the show. After he finished his fish, he ambled out of sight; but on the dry ground, he was carrying his tail like a normal coon.

We saw an alligator stick his head up and look around and a pair of wood ducks landed, but spotted something they didn't like and left. It was all a beautiful experience, but I knew we had seen the main show when the little ringtail was finished with his act.

Wildcat kittens

In Georgia I belonged to a hunting lease at the mouth of Brier Creek where it emptied into the Savannah River. Along the river there was still land that had never been timbered and it was just like I had imagined it to be. The trees were huge and they had forced out smaller brush and trees so that you could see long distances under their cover. The only thing under them was a soft cover of leaves on the ground and it was very beautiful.

I was attracted to this club because it was one of the few places left where dog hunting for deer was still allowed and it brought back many memories of my childhood and fox hunting.

One of the blocks we were working one day was in thick cut-over timber. I volunteered to cross through the thick underbrush and stand on the far edge, because I liked to be in that virgin timber. I worked my way through and found a spot. If anything jumped out of the thicket across the virgin timber, I would have a good shot. I had stood there about an hour and had decided they had not jumped anything and they would call that hunt off any minute. I saw a Weimaraner coming from the timber headed for the thick. It was about thirty yards from me and was just walking along. As it started into the thick it dawned on me that it wasn't a Weimaraner at all, it was a bobcat and a big one. I was standing there congratulating myself on seeing one in the wild, when I saw two kittens following about fifty yards behind. The mother was headed for where I came out of the woods. Obviously she had crossed my trail and she just disappeared into the thick. The kittens came up to the thick and then started calling for mom.

I tried to make myself part of the tree I was leaning against. I closed my eyes to where I was just looking through small slits and I was hoping my shirt wasn't showing my rapid heartbeat. I don't know if you have ever seen a domestic cat, when they look like they are silently cursing a mother bird as she dive bombs them? Well, one of these kittens came right up to me, looked up into my face and did that silent cursing. It was so close I could have touched it. They didn't mind the human smell and they weren't concerned with the sight of me, I guess because I wasn't moving a muscle or an eyelash. The whole episode lasted about ten minutes with them wandering back and forth in front of me, trying to get their mom to answer. They finally wandered on down the edge of the thicket and I could occasionally hear them calling, even after I couldn't see them anymore.

Driving home to the mountains that night I thought, I won't remember if I shot a deer this weekend but I will never forget this day's experience with two little kittens.

Calling to a Panther

Ding (Gene Bell, my nephew) is a big man and I have always admired his lack of fear. In sports he always played to win and he has always been a leader of his peers. When he married and had his children (a boy first and then a girl) I wondered what kind of a father he would make. You see he is one of those individuals that takes no guff from anyone and his adversaries know it, just from looking at him. Standing about six feet and 200 pounds, with smooth tan skin, blond hair, and high cheek bones that accentuate his eyes; he is impressive. His wife is the opposite; she is slender and tall, dark hair, and soft spoken. Even if he doesn't want to admit it; she knows how to control and tame his macho persona.

If you want to dream up the ideal family you couldn't find a better one. The children are both grown now. The girl, Melisa, graduated from college and the boy, Chris, lost a couple of years of school while he played baseball in the Cincinnati baseball farm system.

He also graduated from college and the family is proud of them both.

Ding was a product of a broken marriage and my sister's oldest. I took him under my wing, when it came to the outdoors and included him on my hunting trips.

We had some good times hunting in the Everglades of South Florida. It is still the most peaceful environment that I have ever found on this earth. I miss the crystal clear nights and smog free days of the Everglades. Our camp was what we called a "walk in camp" and the trail meandered about 2 miles from the road. Everything we needed for the weekend we carried on our back, so we learned to go light. We usually went in on Friday night after work, and most of the time we arrived at the beginning of the trail after dark. A lot of the time we waded in water the whole way, depending on the season. Our camping spot was on the first dry ground that we came to. To some it would be spooky, but we did it so often, it was a peaceful walk. We all carried head lights to see where we were going, but Ding usually walked in without a light of any kind. I tell this about him because I want you to understand that he practically grew up in the Everglades and there is very little that would be a shock to him.

About the time I moved away from the Everglades, Ding had become a grown adult and he has continued using that same trail to this day. I must say that it has changed, for the National Park Service took over the area and they have actually ruined the glades from the paradise I knew.

I still hear from him occasionally and yesterday he called with a story about turkey hunting that I thought I must try and put down on paper.

He said, "Sonny I had to call and tell you this because I knew that you (if anyone), would relate to my experience. Since the old camp has had all the turkey run out by the Park Service, I have been hunting along a cypress strand that is near Turner River and on the north side of Highway 41. I can use my four-wheeler here and have had pretty of good luck in this area. In fact I got a nice gobbler in this area two weekends ago. There were a lot of camps set up when I got there this weekend and I decided to go on through the strand and explore for a spot away from the other hunters. I probably walked for an hour before I found a spot to my liking to set up my decoys.

'I settled in and waited for the woods to come alive again before I started calling. Now you know that I wear one of those Walker game ears, because my hearing has gotten so bad.

Three panthers on the Loop Road

Photo by Heather Green obtained from the Lederer collection

'All of a sudden I hear a roar coming from down the strand! Now this was so close that the game ear was vibrating in my ear. I jerked it out, for I couldn't tell which direction the sound was coming from. There was no mistaking what it was, for I have heard the same sound at the zoo when the lions roar. It petrified me!

'For a moment I thought, *"I hope that panther isn't looking for a turkey breakfast!"*

'I could feel the hair on the back of my neck start to crawl around as my heart picked up speed! Then I heard an answer from the other direction up the strand. This sound wasn't a roar, but a "wuh", "wuh",

"wuh", and it had the same volume. I tried the call again and got the same results; what was probably the male roared again and what was the female answered with wuh, wuh, wuh. Now you know that screech that they portray in the movies when they show a panther scene? Well in real life, it is nothing like that; it was loud, and a roar like an African lion. My mind started racing and all kinds of thoughts were going through it. I'm not in too good of a spot sitting here and the first thing I'm going to stop is scratching on this call. They both cranked up when I called, and these two acted like they wanted to get together; here I am smack dab in the middle of where they want to go. I think to myself, maybe if I shot in the air (one time) they might run. But then I thought, that leaves me with one less shot in my gun and it is only bird shot anyway.

'Now you have to picture this, I was so close I could probably hit either one with a rock. If they smelled me they didn't seem to care, so I figured the best thing for me was to get my butt out of there. I eased myself to my feet, collected my decoys, and backed away; keeping my attention to where the noise was coming from. I backed up a good hundred yards, maybe more, before I had the nerve to turn my back to them. Even then all the way back to my 4 wheeler, every time I would break a twig with my foot, it would startle me. When I got back to the 4 wheeler, I picked up my cell phone to called Debbie to tell her about it. I went through the whole story, and do you know what she said?"

"You can come home now."

Greenland

The older I get the more that I have learned to stop and take a look at the beauty and wonders around me. From the lowest ant scurrying around with his busy day, trying to accomplish tasks that are a wonderment to me; to my beautiful cobalt breasted peacock strutting in all his glory. I look at these marvels and it enforces my belief in a supreme being. How could anyone look at such beauty and not understand that "it" is not an accident of nature? A Being, greater than man, had to design it, and He had a purpose.

But it's not just my bird that captures my belief. I have not been all over the world, but I have traveled enough, and seen enough variations on the surface of this earth to see that there is great beauty where ever I have been. As a young man I was sent to the far northern end of Greenland. I sat in class learning how to survive in this harsh climate; the instructors almost scared me in their descriptions of a barren wilderness, with no trees, and devoid of life. It took us three days to make the trip; I think the pilots were dreading going there.

As we broke through the clouds, circling to land, I could see a scene before me that would have taken an awfully good artist to come anywhere near to duplicating. The sea was grey and dead calm, and it had that antique look of an old mirror. Lightly scattered about the surface were icebergs that, from the air, looked to be from a washtub size to some that covered several acres. No one had ever described an iceberg as being beautiful, but there was no other way to express what I was looking at. They each had their own form, like so many miniature mountains, and looked ageless from the wear of time. From the surface of the water down to an endless depth, they were a brilliant turquoise that made them look like assorted emeralds with grey white tops. There weren't any trees on the land, just a mossy like vegetation; and it was mountainous and rocky. In sharp contrast you could see the ice cap at a higher elevation was a so brilliant white that it hurt your eyes to look at it. From the air, the ice cap looked like a big bowl of pudding that was spilling out into the sea in the low gaps between the mountains. They told me the cap was 10,000 feet thick and the surrounding mountains are only 4 to 5 thousand feet high. It was surreal though, for rather than the ice flowing like a mountain stream, the whole scene was dead calm and almost eerie from the calmness. Previously I had sat in study hall, gazing into an encyclopedia in my high school library, just dreaming about beautiful scenes like this; yet here I was, a flatlander from south Florida, gazing down at something that was indescribably beautiful.

My fellow travelers were well indoctrinated; for

after we were settled in, and had some spare time, I could not find one person to go out and explore our surroundings with me. There was in the neighborhood of 15,000 people on that base. Everyone wanted to stay in and complain about their bad luck on being sent there. So I explored by myself and have never been sorry for my adventures.

This was my first experience with a mountain; in fact I had never even been close to one. I soon gained a lot of respect for people who climb mountains, for as I gained altitude, my heart was racing and I was gasping for breath.

I headed to the top for two reasons: right on top of the peak overlooking Thule someone had erected a cross. They told me it was for a Danish explorer that had died years before; it peaked my curiosity. The other reason was that the peaks had snow on them, and that also was new to me. I was forced to slow down and take my time.

I always carried a small backpack filled with assorted things that I thought were necessities. I made it myself in the parachute loft, so it really fit my personal gear.

One thing I had in there, I soon found it to be useless, and that was my compass. I found out that I was north of where the magnetic north pole is located, so all it would do is get you good and lost, for every time I looked it would be different. I had my

Me- In Back of C-119 Flying Over Greenland

camera and flash, a small breakdown fly rod and a small case, (not much bigger than a pack of cigarettes) that contained a small amount of fishing tackle and fly's. I had some assorted C rations, string and a small knife, a canteen and ample extra toilet paper. I didn't carry any first aid supplies, for at 19, no one thinks about getting hurt.

About half way up the mountain, I was resting on a rock, just taking in the scene before me. I noticed a movement off to my left and at about the same level on the mountain. Using all my hunting skills, I very slowly turned my head and discovered what had caught my eye. Feeding along the mountainside was a flock of birds, about 20, and they hadn't seen me. I eased my camera out of my pack and snapped a picture. No reaction! These birds were similar to the shape of quail and moved the same, but they were three or four times as big, and they had an uneven coloring of white and brown.

I made up my mind to try and get closer to get a better shot, thinking, *"If they fly I can catch them in the air, and besides I already have one good shot in my camera."*

I moved ten feet closer and took another shot; still no reaction. Another ten feet closer and another shot. I couldn't believe it! I ended up wasting several shots moving closer and soon found out they weren't the least bit afraid of me. I never did make them fly and I got closer than I could get to my own bantams at home.

I continued on to the top of the mountain and discovered the cross had been placed there recently, for it was made out of modern lumber. I sat on the top for a couple of hours, ate some c-rations and actually fell asleep in the warm sun. I discovered a small lake up on the top and while standing there, looking at it, I saw the flash of something in the water. There was also two small ducks swimming on the far side that also had no concern about my presence. I don't know what kind of duck they were, but they weren't much bigger than a sparrow. I took my fly rod out of my pack, assembled it, chose a streamer fly, and cast it along the edge of the lake. It no more than hit the water, than I had a fish on. When I landed it, I knew that it was some kind of trout, but I didn't know what kind. I stood there catching and releasing them until I actually got tired of it; then I decided to head on back down the mountain.

The ground is so barren that it is easy to see anything that moves on the whole side of the mountain. I discovered that resting and observing on the way down, that there was a whole lot of activity to be observed from this vantage point. I saw a den of silver foxes, at least the four kits that were playing and scurrying around in front of the entrance of their den under a large rock. I could see what was probably their parents, digging around in a turned over garbage can, behind the mess hall. There were several large dogs alongside the runway that had their heads down moving along like they were grazing. I never did figure out what they were up to. On the way down I also saw several more coveys of what I found out later were Ptarmigan.

As I walked through the entrance doors of my barracks, I thought what a treat. I felt like I was the first human that these animals had ever seen, and I left them just like I found them. How wrong that instructor was!

Petting Fawn

I was at Crooked Pine hunting camp during turkey season and it had just broken daylight. I had emerged from some rather thick underbrush onto a field that was clear with no trees. I was trying to get closer to a gobbler that began gobbling just after daylight. I had already traveled about half a mile towards him and had about that far to go yet. I listened, and he gobbled again, and I knew he was far enough away that I could go across a field in front of me, and he would not see me. The grass was only four or five inches high and I was concentrating on that turkey as I strode out onto that field. I was about halfway across the field when I reacted away from what I thought was a large snake coiled up. I realized it was a really small fawn sleeping in the grass. I lay my gun down, and reached down and petted it and scratched behind its ears. It reacted by snuggling into a tighter ball. It never opened its eyes.

It was so cute! I reached under it and lifted it up and it snuggled up like a puppy would. My mind was racing as I thought of all the scenarios of my taking this little guy home. My boys would be thrilled to death to raise it, but we lived in a crowded neighborhood and it would be trouble for us and Bambi. See, I was already thinking of a name.

Mama was probably standing somewhere nearby

with her heart in her throat, thinking I was going to eat her newborn baby.

My boys will never forgive me because they both love animals, especially ones no one else has.

I couldn't do it, I set it back on the ground and it stood up and looked up at me. Its big brown eyes trying to focus in on my face, as its lack of balance caused it to weave back and forth. It suddenly bleated and tried to run from me. It was so young it kept falling. I went on in the other direction and hid where it couldn't see me. It only took a few more steps before it lay back down and curled up again. I smiled to myself and went on to try and find that turkey that was calling to me.

Scaring Deer

Another turkey season found me at Fool's Paradise camp at what is called the Loop Road area. I had been calling all morning and had not gotten any results, and I decided to try another area.

I decided not to use a longer path that led to an area I wanted to move to, and chose to go through a rather thick area that would have lead me to where I wanted to go. It cut through a maze of saplings that led me straight to the spot I wanted. This choice was normally under water, but at present was dry walking, and helped me make my decision to make the short cut. I was in full camouflage and must have been hard to see. About half way through, I stopped and took a break by leaning against one of the larger saplings.

One of the problems I was having was that the wind was blowing rather briskly and I was having trouble hearing anything. The area where I was heading was protected by a thick cypress strand and my thoughts were that I might be able to hear a turkey gobble better because of that protection. The wind, even inside that tangle of saplings, was blowing in my face as I was walking through. While I was stopped, out of the corner of my eye, I caught that telltale flick of a deer's tail about fifty yards ahead of me. My shotgun was leaning against the tree beside me, and I was comfortable, so I decided to watch her for a while. As luck would have it she was moving my way. She was cautious because of the wind, and would move only a few feet at a time. She would stop, look all around, flip that tail a few times, and then move closer to me. I thought it odd that she was moving downwind at all. Most of the time deer will move up wind when going from one place to another. As she got closer and closer I went into my freeze mode. I didn't move a muscle, and closed my eyes, all but a sliver to look through. I have done this with turkey, and it worked, but turkey can't smell. I just wanted to see how close she would get before she smelled me or identified what I was.

The place where I was standing was a small opening

of maybe eight feet in diameter. I couldn't believe it; she came closer and closer. She was so close I could see the moisture dripping out of her nose. She stopped about six feet from that opening and went through that routine again of flicking her tail and looking around. I thought surely she will bolt any second, but she didn't. She stepped into that small clearing and this time she turned completely around and faced the way she had been coming from. She strained her neck and was sniffing the air and flicking her tail. Picture this; when she turned around and looked back the other way she had put her butt within six inches of me. I couldn't stand it, with my odd sense of humor I couldn't miss a chance like this. I reached over and slapped her on the butt. She bleated, went straddle legged, and fell completely to the ground for a split second.

When she did regain her feet, she jumped straight up in the air, went back the way she had come about thirty feet, stopped and looked back at me, while she stomped her feet with that look on her face, "What the hell was that?"

She never did run, but she sure kept looking back as she left.

Pecking my Foot

I got up late one morning at Crooked Pine hunting camp and was almost too late to hear the gobblers. I was riding my Trail Ninety and got to the place I had been scouting, just in time to hear a gobble. I heard him fly down on the other side of a small pond. I eased around the pond and found a dry spot and scattered clumps of palmettos. I figured the gobbler must have flown down out in those palmettos and more than likely was too close for me to go any farther. There wasn't any cover for me to conceal myself, only some dwarf cypress growing next to the larger ones in the pond. I sat down next to one of those small trees, put my shotgun in my lap, and pulled my face covering down. Then I waited several minutes before I attempted a call.

I would wait two or three minutes between calling, but I wasn't getting an answer. The line of palmettos was probably seventy to one hundred yards from where I was sitting. I must have stood out like a sore thumb.

My hearing was excellent then and I realized I could hear the gobbler drumming and strutting in that glob of palmettos. He had to be with a hen for him to be strutting like that. I had no idea what to do in a situation like that. I was stuck; and I couldn't get up because they would see me for sure. I was too close to call, so I just decided to sit it out and see what happened. I sat there more than thirty minutes and I could hear him all that time.

Down to my right I saw two hens step out from the cover of the palmettos. They were feeding on grass seed as they were ambling along. I could still hear the gobbler, but he was some distance behind the two hens. At first the hens looked like they were going to feed away from me but they started to swing in an arch that was coming my way. As they got closer I saw the gobbler come out of the palmettos, in full display, about fifty or sixty yards behind them. My mind was racing and my heart was probably beating 100 beats a minute. I had multiple problems; I couldn't move to pick up my gun because the hens were headed right towards me. I couldn't move anyway, for I would spook them and the gobbler in turn. I was getting more hyped up by the second. I had gone into my freeze mode not moving a muscle and squinting my eyes, but my foot was lying out in that grass and it was not cooperating. It was shaking uncontrollably and I knew it was going to spook the hens. I just couldn't stop it, I was way too nervous.

The hens were within several feet of me now and suddenly one of them darted right at me. She saw a stem of grass shaking from my palsied foot and must have thought it was something to eat, because she started pecking at it. I couldn't believe this was happening and knew at any moment they would see my heart thumping in my chest. She gave up and they fed on away from me down to my left. The gobbler was still maintaining that fifty or sixty yard distance behind them. When he passed me he was only feet away from me and close enough for me to see him blinking. I had to wait until he was far enough away that his fan of feathers blocked his sight of me raising my gun. Even then I had to wait for him to turn before I could get a head shot. When it was over I was so weak-kneed I had trouble standing and walking.

Changing Environment

As I get older I start to remember things as they used to be. A recent sermon about the wonderful gift man and Adam received from our Lord started me day dreaming. Our minister used a simple child's book to illustrate what a beautiful place this old earth and universe is to live in.

My mind carried me back to early Miami during the war and shortly after. I was one of those kids that existed for things to do in the outdoors. Every waking moment I thought and planed what adventure I was going to have that weekend or the next holiday.

My Uncle had a large sail boat and he taught me sailing at an early age, so I was constantly exploring the southern end of Florida. I was a Sea Scout (as well as a Boy Scout), and even crewed in sailing races that took place around Florida. I remember one trip especially in my uncle's big boat; we were navigating in fairly shallow water and we had the centerboard up. I was out on the bowsprit watching the bottom, guiding him with hand signals. There were large clumps of coral that were showing on the chart. The area was in Card Sound, between Key Largo and the mainland of Florida. It was early morning. The water was crystal clear and it was so calm it looked like a sheet of glass. We were trying to get close to US Highway One, so we could pick up a passenger waiting for us. The Borrachita had an engine that most people now call a, "Hit and miss," and it was turning over so slow I could easily count the strokes. When I went out on the bowsprit the water was still about ten feet deep, but I could see everything on the bottom. Fish would scurry out of the way and coral and sponges were everywhere. As we moved into the shallower water I noticed something new to me. The most common sponges in that area were ones about the size of a washtub. They had a dark center on the top that was about 6 inches in diameter. In this shallow calm water I could see the sponges were pumping huge volumes of water out that dark spot and it was so powerful that it disturbed the surface. I am sure those sponges had a lot to do with how clear the water was because they were acting like a filter.

Thirty years later I went back to that same area; I moored my lobster boat in that same place. I think what lured me back was my memories of that beautiful experience. What I found, or didn't find was the sponges. They weren't there anymore. Gone were the large coral formations that we had to watch out for. I caught lobster in that area for over two years and I never saw the water as clear as I had that day thirty years ago.

As a teenager my buddies and I would row out to an island just off the mainland and camp out for the weekend. There the water was also crystal clear. We all pooled our money and purchased a flat bottom boat, with a 2 horsepower inboard engine. We made daring trips as far out as the Gulfstream. The water again was clear and beautiful. Once we saw thousands of jellyfish and you could see them several hundred feet down. We always caught fish. We camped on Key Biscayne before there was a bridge. The bay was a paradise for young boys and I for one made the best of it.

As I grew older I could see change begin to take place. It became harder to make a decent catch of fish. The shrimp were not as plentiful, and the water began to look murky. Miami went from a little over 2 hundred thousand people to where they were counting millions, and it showed. One of my buddies who shared these experiences with me was Bruce DeVay. He went to work for the City of Miami, after coming out of the service, and worked his way up to where he was one of the bosses in the Water and Sewer Department. He told me that when he went to work for them that there were sixty some raw sewage outlets dumping into Biscayne

Bay. His goal and the city's, was to stop this practice. He managed to clean up the bay by constructing a 10 foot pipe that carried treated sewage out into the ocean and discharged sewage on the reef. It helped solve the bay problem but we are now killing our ocean.

We only had a compass, (we didn't have a GPS), so we relied on markers on the shore to guide us to our favored fishing spots. We loved to troll for mackerel. I could find the area by lining up the Cutler Power Plant and the southern end of Soldiers Key to find the spot to start trolling. We could always catch a good mess by going to this area. When I moved to the mountains, roaming the bay was one of the things I missed the most.

A couple of years ago, on one of my rare trips back to Miami, my nephew offered to take me and my oldest son on a day's fishing on my beloved Biscayne Bay. I jumped at the offer! Both of my nephews were still catching snapper in a hole I had shown them years before. We caught three that morning, starting the day off right. We circled the bay clockwise fishing the grass in front of the John Derring estate, catching a lone trout before heading off the sea aquarium to try for red fish.

Our next move was down the lee of Key Biscayne to the channels between the lighthouse and Soldiers Key to do some yellowtail fishing. We anchored in a channel and started chumming, and soon we were catching them left and right. Trouble was, they had to be one foot long and all but five had to be thrown back.

I was living a dream and enjoying every minute of it. We decided to finish off the day trolling for mackerel, so I offered to show my nephew how to find my old spot. We pulled the anchor and headed south to a line off the end of the Soldier key, before we headed west back across the bay.

My mouth dropped open, I couldn't believe my eyes! Someone had built a mountain in Miami! Before, when I was this far across the bay it was hard to even see the shore of the mainland, other than a few buildings sticking above the horizon. Now there was this huge hill that looked at least a half a mile long and two or three hundred feet tall. It really threw me for a loop!

As I pointed, I gasped and said, "When did they build that mountain?"

David grinned back at me and said. "That's Miami's garbage dump."

I don't know when it was started but it didn't exist when I left 30 years ago. I came back from Florida happy with my memories of the day, but I can't get the sight of the mountain of garbage out of my mind.

One of the things that attracted me to the mountains was the beauty of the trees and their green foliage and I worry about the changes that I notice here. The dogwoods are diseased; something is attacking the locust trees in Tennessee and pine trees are devastated with pine beetles. For some reason the oaks are forming dead branches in their tops and no one seems to notice but me.

Every group has their idea of a solution for these problems, but I am afraid the solutions are all temporary. We all know, in our heart, the real problem is the population explosion. I am afraid only our Lord knows the answer to that problem.

Deja Vous

I tell this story because of the irony of the timing and repetition of circumstances. If "Twilight zone" was still in existence I think this would make a good episode.

One hundred years ago my Grandmother and my Grandfather were working in a phosphate mine in Polk County, Florida. She, Virginia Bell, (later known as Ma Bell), was the cook for the miners. I am not sure if my Grandfather, Charles Bell, was also a cook or just an employee. They were living in the woods and she was cooking over an open fire. The year was 1913, the year my mother was born. My grandmother had my infant mother dressed in one of those long night shirts. She had strung up a hammock between two trees in the shade, and my infant mother was lying asleep while she was preparing the noon meal for the miners. The hammock was low to the ground, so that if my mother fell out, it would not injure her. Ma Bell was attentive to her needs and kept a watchful eye on her baby. After changing my mother and seeing that she had gone back to sleep, my Grandmother returned to her cooking; then the unexpected happened. She was only several feet from the hammock when she turned to glance toward it, she saw a big hog had just picked my mother out of the hammock, by her nightshirt, and was headed toward the woods.

Ma Bell

One of the rare photos of her taken by a street photographer Miami- 1937

If you didn't know better you would think my Grandmother was full blooded Indian. She was very small built, high cheekbones, and I don't think she ever weighed more than eighty five pounds. By the time I came along everyone called her "Ma Bell." I would describe her as very independent and resourceful. She was a single mom at a very rough time in our history, not a weak person by any means. I was amazed at her skill when she walked across the street to an empty lot, with only a hatchet, and peeled out a swamp cabbage in about fifteen minutes. Try as hard as I could I was never able to do one that quick with a chain saw. She was quick to put you in your place if she didn't approve of your actions and wasn't bashful with her language. I tell this short description of her so that you can picture her reaction to the hog stealing my mother.

From where she was, the axe she used to chop the firewood was blade down in a stump, with the handle sticking up in the air, and in her path to the pig. At this point the hog was in no hurry, so this gave my Grandmother the advantage she needed. With lightning speed she ran toward the hog, snatching the axe off the stump on the way. The hog, seeing my Grandmother in pursuit, tripped momentarily on the nightshirt and it was his fatal error. "Whack!" went the axe and the pig ended up being the dinner, instead of dining on my mother. If not for the spunk, toughness, and alertness of my Grandmother on that day, my family would have never been.

I know this is an unusual story but it is a true one.

My Grandmother and Grandfather left Polk County and migrated to Miami in 1913, when my mother was still an infant, and settled in the Shenandoah area. This was before there was a bridge across the Miami

River. They had to take a hand pulled ferry to cross the river. The two of them became successful builders but lost everything in the 1929 crash. She had two more children, both boys, before they split; with my Grandmother raising all three with very little income. From that point on, all the children and descendants (and family history) have been centered around Miami. My mother's great grandson, (now in his thirties and a hunter like me), had never heard the story about his Great Grandmother's rescue from the pig by his, Great Great Grandmother.

The old hunting areas around Miami are becoming more crowded with the population increase. Chris Bell started applying for permits to management areas around the state. He found one close to the Kissimmee River, near and named after an abandoned town of "Kicco," He tried it a couple of years ago and loved the beauty of the area, and he has returned for several trips. He even arranged for a special trip where his dad and his uncle would meet at Kicco and hunt together for several days. This trip is the one that is so strange to me. The guns on the hunt are limited to shotguns and sometimes they only wound an animal. This happened to Chris, and he had to chase down a pig and finish it off with a tomahawk that he usually carries.

It dawned on me when I heard about the kill that it was similar to my Grandmother and her feat. Checking further I discovered this town of Kicco is located in Polk County, Florida; and the strange part to me is it was almost one hundred years to the day apart and very close to the same spot.

I don't believe things like this happen by accident. I believe it is part of the Lord's plan. He just did not let me in on it.

Chris Bell and the Hog Taken 2013 at Polk County Florida

Chris Started Early

Pets I Have Had

I guess the first pet I remember was Tony, my parent's dog. During World War II, Tony stayed by the front window of our living room, for over a year, waiting for my dad to return from Trinidad. He was part of the family and when he left this earth, it was my first exposure to the heartbreak of death.

My dad had an old touring car and while riding in the car, I heard some strange noises coming from the upholstered pocket in the door. When I peered in there I saw several baby chicks. Mom had left eggs in there and they had hatched. My dad made a cage and we raised them behind our apartment in town. I named them all and was a little upset when Harry disappeared and we had chicken for supper that night.

I was eight years old when my folks bought a new house, way out in the country. We raised chickens and rabbits for food. I picked out several as favorites, but soon learned they were only around temporarily. We had several cats and my folks always had a dog of some kind. At age ten, my dad went to the pound and rescued two dogs, one small and one about 35 pounds. I picked the bigger one and it was for me, and my dad picked the smaller one. He named them Boocoo and ReAnn, for "a lot" and "nothing."

Actually the French spelling is "beaucoup" and

"rien"

He swapped the names and called the little one Boocoo.

ReAnn was the ideal dog for a growing boy. She followed me everywhere. I roamed the woods and waterways and she did anything I would, including diving off the railroad trestle at our swimming hole. Looking back I realize she spent her whole life pleasing me. I built a kayak and she would ride with me until a duck or something would distract her, and then she would jump overboard and swim behind the boat for miles. I loved to fish, but all I had was a cane pole until my dad gave me a reel and showed me how to make guides out of clothes hanger wire. I used a Calcutta cane pole for the rod. I bought a bantam chicken for fifty cents because she had beautiful feathers, just right for making flies for my homemade fly rod. She ended up disappearing and turned up later with a dozen baby chicks following her. They wandered all over the neighborhood but always returned for food at dark.

ReAnn found a fox den and I brought home a baby fox that had not even opened her eyes yet. I was in the seventh grade about then and had a crush on a girl with the name of "Orchid." To tease me, my dad named the fox after her. The fox turned out to be as tame as a dog, all but for its love of killing chickens; she soon depleted my bantam population. We even took her to Virginia in the car when we went on vacation.

I caught a skunk on my dad's dare, tamed it to where I could hold it. I ended up having to get it de-skunked after a nosy neighbor got sprayed snooping around my animals. I had a collection of snakes. I caught mice and tree frogs for a snake farm.

I had alligators, snakes, raccoons, and a crow that followed me to school and got me in trouble calling for me outside of the school window. The alligator got me in trouble with my science teacher, when I brought it in to class as my example of something from the outdoors.

Recently while sitting in a community meeting a fellow member asked, "Did you go to Citrus Grove Jr. High?"

I answered, "Yes I did."

He said, "I thought so, you were the guy with all the animals."

Turns out he was a classmate from 1945.

I collected a pair of everything I could find in the canal near our house. I built a total of 32 aquariums and used freshwater clams to do the filtering of the water. I built most of the aquariums out of the old square five gallon cans. I cut the tops off, and cut a hole on one side, and pasted a single piece of glass using aquarium putty.

After Laurie came into my life, she and I hit it off with our love of animals. Our first pet together was a big dog, half greyhound and half Labrador. We named her "Lonesome" because she had been abandoned at the county's garbage dump. I found a baby squirrel, who Laurie nursed at school in between the classes she taught. She would lay the squirrel on my shoulder as I watched TV in my lounge chair. We had a pet white dove that would fly from window to window to find what room Laurie was working in. Then she would nestle in between the jalousies, cooing as she watched Laurie work. She figured out when we went to the ball field for Steve's ball practice. She would follow along the car and take up her position on the back stop, then she would follow us home. Our neighbor brought us a female redwing blackbird he had knocked out by accident. She flew loose in the house and ruled our household. She ate right at the table with us, and if you disturbed her after she went to roost, you were in for a cussing out by a bird. We raised beagles and later redbone hounds. My oldest son brought home an injured great horned owl. We nursed him back to health and later turned it loose in the Everglades. When we moved to the mountains, like every flatlander, we wanted to try our hand at raising a pig for food, so we got two and fed them with restaurant slop from where my son worked. I finally sold them. They could only carry one at a time in their truck; said their guess on weight would be 1200 pounds each. We have raised chickens, turkeys, guineas, ducks, geese and peacocks. One gobbler lived to be 12 years old.

A friend asked how much we would sell one of our

turkeys for and Laurie told him to go to the grocery to buy his turkeys, ours were not for sale.

We have a pond and have five Coy that must go 30 lbs. Until last year, we had a catfish that weighed out at 42 pounds. Mollie, our Granddaughter, caught it at Lake Winfield Scott when she was only two years old. As he grew in size, we named him Jaws; Jaws loved pizza crust. All you had to do was throw some pizza crust in the pond, and from whatever depths he emerged, he was at the surface of the pond within seconds. A bear injured him, when the water was low, causing his eventual death. We had peacocks and hens but are down to one Peacock that will sit right in front of me on our picnic table watching me while I am typing. I love to look at him for his beauty is my proof that there is a God. That kind of beauty is no accident, nor is he a mutation of evolution. A Supreme Being designed every wonderful feature of his exquisite body.

I bought a small rat terrier (CUJO) about 20 years ago and he was the smartest animal I ever had. He and his daughter would roll a tennis ball back and forth to each other, if no one would do it for them. Cujo went everywhere with me; he was my buddy.

He was poisoned about 10 years ago and people I meet still say: "I know you. You are the guy with the dog that hated Clinton."

You see I went on stage with him at a Republican district convention and performed an act that my son taught him. I would sit in a chair and call him up near me and he was as friendly as he could be, until I asked him what he thought about Clinton. At that point he would jump up on me, and get right in my face, and act like he was going to tear me up. We still have 4 of his great, great, offspring. I had a patch of kudzu and bought several goats to clean it up; they only took two years to eradicate it. One of my old hunting friends came up from Florida and brought me a pair of baby razor backs (we call them piney-woods-rooters). We turned them in with the goats and it stopped stray dogs from killing our goats. All the goats are gone now and for a while the pigs have had the pasture all to themselves. The boar looked ferocious, but didn't know he was supposed to be. You could call it "Hog Heaven, because all the neighbors bring anything edible to help feed them. Unlike the goats, when they have a large area like our pasture they have no vile smell. The boar had a stroke a couple of years ago; we nursed him with bottled water and pancake syrup about two weeks before he finally died. Now all that is left in the pasture is one female pig. A couple of months ago I got a call from animal control. The officer said he got a complaint that we weren't giving the sow any water.

I laughed and explained, "Over the hill there is a creek running through the pasture, and she knows where it is."

I told him there had been another complaint about that same problem some fifteen years ago, "As a matter of fact she was in the pasture then. Counting back I would place her around 16 years old and she does look a little wrinkled, but so do I"

How many people have a 16 year old pig?

I guess the point is we have had all kinds of farm animals since we moved here and who knows what the future will bring. We have learned that if given the chance most all of God's creatures are capable of affection and love. It can be costly, but our treatment of our critters is what we like in life, even though some think we are foolish. The only thing we have eaten from our collection has been a few eggs, because everything else always ended up as part of the family.

Owls have always fascinated me. I had one that would come to a favorite spot I had on Crooked Pine camp. Every time I would go to this particular spot to watch for game, it would not be long before this owl would show up and sit on a fence post right in front of me. He would move his head from side to side several times; just after getting there and then he would just stare at me. I would try to talk to him but he didn't pay any attention. I have always kicked myself for not taking a picture of him; he was only ten feet away from me; but we did not have cell phones with cameras back then. We had baby coons and plenty of snakes. Jaime, my youngest, had an Indigo; a nine footer in an aquarium in the bedroom. My mother-in-law came to visit and had a fit about the snake in the house. After she had been there about a week, we were sitting in the living room watching television, when she started to scream. Jaime's snake had escaped and was crawling down the hall. She left the next day. Good way to get rid of mother-in-laws!

We had a tame gopher land turtle in our fenced in back yard. He dug a den under concrete slab for his den. We could call him from the back door and he would come to us. He loved bananas and would eat them right out of our hand.

We kept a chipmunk in a cage in our living room that would bite the fire out of you if you tried to pick it up. One evening I was relaxing in my chair, when he started chirping at me, and wouldn't stop. I knew something must be wrong but I was almost afraid to look. I opened the cage and put my hand down, he climbed into it and looked at me; he continued chirping and throwing its head back. We discovered his two front teeth had grown so much they were penetrating the roof of his mouth. We took him to our veterinarian, Dr. Boyd, and he trimmed the teeth off and gave us a lesson about not feeding it shelled nuts. We now know to feed rodents hard nuts so their teeth don't grow. That little squirt was so thankful; he never bit anyone the rest of his life.

I once found a burnt turkey nest on a prairie. I watched it from concealment until I was sure the hen had abandoned it. I carried nine eggs to the road that evening and found a white laying chicken to set on them within hours. Only two hatched. We avoided going around the rather large cage during daylight hours so they would not be too familiar with humans. Only one survived to adult hood and we returned her to the Everglades near where I had found the nest.

The most beautiful creature we have had is a peacock, and he likes to sit in front of me when I am on the back porch typing and watch me. He roosts up the tree his MaMa peacock taught him to go. He is here for breakfast in the morning and returns for supper in the evening. Living in the country, we can let him roam freely. One neighbor named him "Fred." Our family has surely been blessed with the closeness and love of all kinds of critters God put on this earth. It is hard for some to understand the double side of my psychic that I can hunt and still love animals. I guess it is the primeval instincts that are in most men.

Bigfoot or Skunk Ape?

What is your guess?

Of all the years that I have roamed the outdoors and heard tales of an ape-like creature existing there, this photo below, of a track in the Everglades, is the only thing I ever saw that I could not explain. It was a single track, rather large, as shown by the beer can, and the lack of claw marks, lead me to believe it was not a bear. The mud was pleanty soft enough to have shown claw marks. We had a multitude of bears on our Crooked Pine lease, so I was very familiar with bear tracks and this track is not like any of them.

You be the judge!

Unknown Track?

Wildcat?

Enlargement of Body Pattern

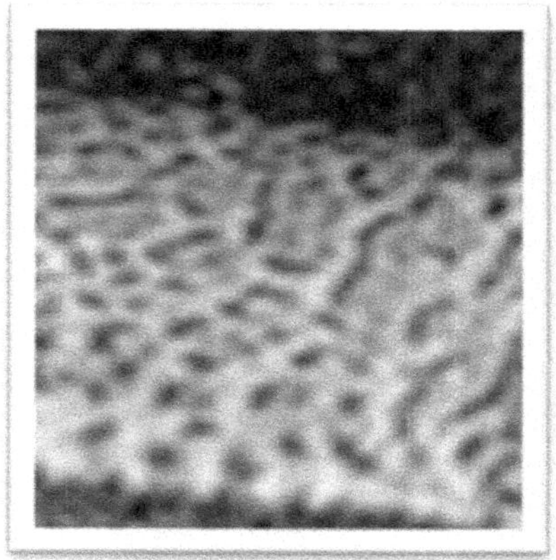

These photos were taken 12/25/09 by the FWC somewhere in Gulf Hammock with a camera set up to catch poachers.

A wildlife biologist was taken to the site and estimated the weight of the animal to be in the 140/160 pound range, from the size of the tracks and depth in the mud.

I have seen skinned and mounted multiple wildcats, hunted them for years with dogs, and I have never ever seen any cats close to looking like this. The largest wildcat I ever saw weighed 38 pounds.

I do know that the Gulf Hammock area used to have a cat that was described as being between a wildcat and a panther in size. The last sighting I could find was reported in a local newspaper in 1919.

Strange things: One

I don't know if it's because I look up a lot or I am just lucky. I know that I have spent a lot of time in areas where there is not a lot of reflective light. I consider myself to have an open mind. I try to reason through things and have been pretty successful with everyday changes and challenges.

A divorce liked to have killed me; but I survived and

as they say, "In the end things do work out for the better."

Some of the things I have witnessed are unexplainable and can't be figured out with the knowledge man has today. Some of you may label me a kook, but I witnessed these things, and I have gotten old enough to not give a hoot what people think. I am not looking for anyone to approve or disapprove my writings; I just would like to record them before they are forgotten.

I guess being outdoors at night, (returning from some stand or camping out in faraway places), gave me the opportunity to observe things that were happening around me. The hunting camp we called "Fools Paradise" was about sixty or seventy miles west of Miami. There were no developments in the other directions. The other camp which we called, "Crooked Pine," was even farther away from civilization. It was an eighty mile drive from Miami to the place where we left our cars and then it was over a one hour drive in our swamp buggies to where we had our camp; so both of these places were desolate. I spent about 35 years of my time, on weekends and holidays, either hunting or relaxing with my family in these two camps.

Contrary to common belief, the Everglades are beautiful. The nights are hard to describe; a clear sky at night is lost to most people because of the pollution and reflection of civilization. One really forgets how a clear starlit night looks anymore because of the reflections of the city light against the sky. Oh, you can't take away from the beauty of the moon as it comes up over Miami, but I have been in the glades (on clear nights) when you didn't need a light to walk through the woods. Adding the full moon just makes it even brighter.

My first observation of something strange was around the time when the U.S. was trying to get a man in space, and they were firing the Atlas rockets off at Canaveral.

My friend (Tom Knowles), and I, both got off work around 4:00 in the afternoon. We knew where several deer were bedding up on the outskirts of Miami. It was a mile walk in the shallow water, from the road to where there was a hardwood island of about 2 acres. I would bring a couple of my beagles along. One of us would get about a hundred yards away from the island on the west side and the other the same distance on the east side. I turned the dogs loose, after we were both set at our spots, and they would start working the island.

This particular day, the dogs jumped something; but they ran whatever it was back toward where we had parked the car. After we heard the dogs voices fade out of hearing we both knew by instinct that the hunt was over. I started toward the car, and gave a whistle to Tom, to come on; we might as well go back to the car. I got back on the trail and went about half way back to the car before I stopped. I could see and hear Tom walking through the water about one hundred yards behind me.

I was standing there waiting for him to catch up, when I saw this object in the air, about a hundred feet up and over the spot where I had been standing waiting for the dogs to strike. It was the time of day when you would have just turned on your head lights, so there was still plenty of visibility left. I called out to Tom, pointed, and said, “Look at that!”

Tom turned around and an object was over the hardwood island and gaining a little speed. When I first saw it, it was just there, not moving. It was only traveling about the speed of a blimp. As we looked, it went in a straight line toward the east; for maybe for another couple of hundred yards. Then it made a sharp turn up, put on a burst of speed, and went out of sight straight up. This whole process took about two minutes from the time I spotted it until it was out of sight. My guess is its size was about 60 or 70 feet long. It was about 10 feet thick at the center point and very sharp on both ends. It had small squares on the side that appeared to be windows, but there was absolutely no light reflecting from it anywhere. If you were to make a cross section drawing, (end to end), it would resemble a cross section of a blade on a double edge knife. There were no lights, the only thing I saw was a flash just before it disappeared out of sight. When it was close to us, there didn’t seem to be any color to it. It was gray, like the dusk sky. Thinking about it later, I guess it was when it got out of the earth’s curvature that we saw the sunlight flash against it. You know, how you can see the tops of thunderheads on some days, well after the sun has gone below the horizon. We went on back to the road to wait for the dogs and I tried to analyze what we had just seen. Tom had flown saber jets and he said he had never seen anything like what we had just seen.

As we were standing there, I was facing the north, and I said to him again, "Look at that!"

There was a real bright light going across the sky from the north toward the southeast and out in front of it was a half-halo or crescent looking light. It moved on across the sky and went on to the southeast until it disappeared. I told Tom I was going to call the Miami Herald to see if anyone else had seen the things. As soon as I called and started to explain, the woman interrupted me and told me it was an Atlas Rocket from Canaveral and the halo was normal.

When she finished and I said, "OK that explains that one. What was the other thing?"

I never got an answer.

Strange Things: Two

I will try to keep my stories chronological, as well as I can recall. Hunting at the "Fools Paradise" camp was a little different than the other camps I had hunted in and around South Florida. The area we hunted was limited in size and we knew we had to return to the cabin instead of the road. It didn't take us too many trips until we were very familiar with our area.

Until the time I decided to establish a camp, I would try a different spot every time I hunted. I was impatient and did a lot of walking. My first cousin (Ron) and I had been east of the camp and were trying to roost some turkeys we had seen earlier in the day. Neither of us had a light but we were confident we could find our way back without one, as it had been real clear the night before. We were actually successful in hearing turkeys fly up. We were so close we had to wait until pitch dark to keep from spooking them, as we slipped out of there. It was a long way back to our camp and we had to circle ponds and skirt thick spots to make it back. There was no one back at the camp to hang a light out for us, to home in on; so it was a little tricky to get back. We missed our direction a little, but we began to see familiar areas. We knew we were a little south of where we wanted to be. Ahead was a hardwood head that ran east and west and was about three hundred yards long. We knew that if we went about a hundred yards to the north of that head we would find the path that we used and it would lead us right back to the camp.

When we got about half the length of the hardwood head, both of us stopped dead in our tracks. Somebody had shot a green flare up in the air from the other side of the hardwood head. It appeared to be the kind of flare that I keep on my boat for emergencies.

My mind clicked, *"Wait a minute that flare is moving too slow!"*

As I was thinking this, it made an abrupt turn to the right and went off at a different angle; then it accelerated as it dropped below the tree line and disappeared. My cousin and I stood there for a few moments dumbfounded before either of us spoke.

I was kidding but I said to him, "Let's go see what that is?"

He told me. "If you go see what that is, you're going by yourself."

We talked about the possibilities of what it could be, but as is with all strange occurrences, who knows? What made it strange was we were over two miles from the road, and we had never seen anyone so far away from the road. The area is called, "Inside the loop." The actual Loop Road branches away from highway 41 and makes a 35 mile loop; then it returns back to Highway 41 about 25 miles farther on. For someone to come to that spot, from the other direction, would be a 7 or 8 mile walk through some of the roughest country in the Everglades.

This is not the only time a strange green light was seen by people in my family. After I moved on to another camp, my nephew and his friends continued using that spot to camp. Both he and his son have seen an unusual light over the years. **Five sightings over twenty five years!**

Over the years, the other thing that all of us have seen is a much smaller green light that is low to the ground. It dances around in the cypress and is always seen 15 or 20 feet off the ground in the thicker trees. Every time I saw this light, it looked like it was the size of a golf ball that glowed. In 2008, and I had just had dinner with my nephew's son, (Chris) and he said he had seen those lights as recently as a month ago.

He told me, "I was about ten the first time I saw the lights. I was with my dad and truthfully, it really scared me. Even though no one knows what they are, my friends and I have seen them many times as I have been growing up. It doesn't bother me anymore. I still wonder what causes it, but I don't let it scare me."

Strange Things: Three

When I changed hunting camps and moved to the one off Alligator alley, odd things started happening and lasted over the 22 years that I belonged to the camp. Not all the experiences were mine, but I will try to relate them the best that I can. The camp land area was 5,600 acres. To put a little perspective on the size, we had to put a fence around the camp and bring in a few scrub cows, so we would qualify for taxes under an agriculture standing. That fence ended up being 13 miles long. In the past, the area was split up into 160 acre homesteads by the government, crude roads were built, and some were still visible. Those roads were strictly horse and buggy, and where there was swamp, the homesteaders must have waded the horses through the swamp. Baron Collier (the man the Collier County is named after), bought the land (as homesteaders failed in their farming attempts), until he amassed millions of acres.

I don't want to mislead you when I say, "roads," for a standard jeep could not make it into the camp during most of the year. Most of the buggies in our camp were equipped with large tractor tires or aircraft tires that had some sort of cleat or chains. The road from the Alligator alley was a crude country road that no one maintained any more. The locals called it Jones Grade Road and apparently at one time, it had a trading post on it. North of our lease, the Seminole Indians had a locked gate where the road passed through their properties. We were able to travel this road with our pickups, to a point parallel to our property; then we had to leave our cars and transfer everything to our swamp buggies. (These vehicles were a motley looking bunch of equipment, for everyone's personality reflected in their creation. Mine was the strangest!) From here we had to go 2 miles west to get on our property. Then we had another 3 miles (about an hour in travel time, depending on the water depth) to reach the camp area.

Over the years, three plywood cabins 16' x 16', a cook house 16 x 24, a generator shack, and a bathroom, (complete with all the amenities) had been constructed. If someone arrived at camp before you, it was really a strange sight for any newcomer to see. There was a central switch that turned on all the lights at once, so the whole place was lit up. I always told people if you were to establish the center point away from all civilization that would be our lease. Our membership averaged from 10 to 15 people. We have had as many as 25, with guests, and we still were not crowded. I have been there in the summer with my family, when we were the only ones there.

It was during one of these slow weekends that I had an encounter that I will never forget. My swamp buggy only carried four passengers, but I usually carried a small, boxed in, high wheeled trailer for my dogs. This trip I was bringing my dogs and the trailer doubled for three more passengers. By the time we arrived at the buggy and had packed away all our gear for the weekend, it was approaching 10:00 P.M. We were in no hurry and we were all having a good time. My buddy Bruce, my son Jaime, Art, a Viet Nam vet and two of his friends were all aboard and on our way into the camp. We were on our property and at a place where we had another half hour travel to the camp. I had left the old bumpy homestead road, and was circling around a small cypress pond that had flat, even ground all around it. It was a short cut that made for a lot more comfortable ride. On the back side of the pond, (about 100 feet from the first trees) the land raised up, palmettos were there, and the land carried on level from there. This whole area in daytime would be clear vision, even with the sparse trees in the pond, because they had no leaves. The pond was probably 50 yards across and we were 30 yards from the pond. At this point we were not over 100 yards from the palmettos, and if anything I have over exaggerated the distance.

Dave the Viet Nam vet, hollered out, "Look at that chopper on fire."

What we were witnessing wasn't a helicopter, as Dave first thought, but we had no idea what it was, nor to this day do I know. Whatever it was, it chose that time to come off the ground, from where it was parked behind that cypress head, in that small space between the palmettos and the cypress head. I really didn't witness it coming off the ground; it could have been there at that height all along, where it chose then to light up. Let me describe it as well as I can: What I saw was an object that had a light in the center and it was bright! I could not see any discernible shape or outline of any craft. Sparks were rotating out from this light to a diameter of about 50 or 60 feet. It was stationary off the ground at about 30 feet high, and it just hovered and pulsated. It was lower than the tops of the tallest trees on that pond, because I could see a couple of bare tops between me and the sparks. The light would dim and the sparks would increase in intensity. When the light would get bright, the sparks would decrease again. The best way to describe the sparks was like a pinwheel that you see at some Fourth of July celebrations. It was spinning at just about the same speed, only this pinwheel was horizontal instead of upright. The time between these pulses was about 30 seconds. We were all there staring in amazement as this phenomenon taking place in front of us. The really weird thing to me was there was not a sound coming from it. We were whispering stupid remarks back and forth between us, but other than that, it was eerie quiet. I didn't time it; but it continued this pulsating for three or four minutes before it moved. At first it moved slowly and went up at an angle of about 20 degrees away from us. It never went fast in this stage of travel, and it looked like it went up to a height of about a mile. It stopped at that point and hovered again for a full five minutes. All seven of us watched this whole procedure as it unfolded. When it moved next, it went south in a hurry, and in a few seconds it disappeared. I don't know if it disappeared from speed or if it turned out its lights.

I remember Dave saying, "Well it convinced me. I never believed in UFO's, I always thought the people who had seen them had a screw loose or something"

He paused for a minute and said, "One thing for sure I ain't going to be telling anyone."

We finally cranked the buggy up and headed on

into camp, chattering about the event. We drove up on the high ground and saw the welcome sight of the lights of the camp. We knew that Bill and Jessie had come in ahead of us, because their buggy was not at their parking place and one of their cars was parked in place of it.

We pulled into the yard and I released the dogs as we unloaded the gear. Jessie and Bill were nowhere to be found. Their jeep was parked in the yard, but we couldn't find either of them. We all were worried, when my son started to screaming something at the cook shack; I got scared. I ran over to where he was and he was pointing to blood on the steps of the cook building.

He was sobbing, "They got them" he repeated over and over.

Luckily just at that moment Bill and Jessie came across the yard, with a couple of cottontails, wanting to know what all the excitement was about. We discovered that one of the dogs had cut her foot in the trash pile and was the donator of the blood. Both of them had seen the lights from the pinwheel as it was climbing, and had watched it as it was hovering; they also watched its rapid departure.

Strange Things: Four

This one I have to repeat from what I was told.

One of the members of the cabin I was in was rather eccentric and at that time I thought he was old. (65) He had a big home on the bay in Miami and a young, beautiful wife. He was very well off and had to have every trinket that came along in life. He and Jessie were about the same age and spent more time at the camp than anyone else. They couldn't ride in together because Norman's jeep had so much hunting gear stowed away in it that there wasn't any place for anyone to ride but Norman. He even had a four thousand dollar BB gun, isn't that impressive? Jessie on the other hand was a retired auto mechanic whose wife had left him after 45 years. They were an odd pair to be spending so much time together in the middle of nowhere. Jessie supplemented his income by raising red wigglers in his yard in Miami and making deliveries to bait shops once a week. Both of them were nice guys but totally different. One evening they were sitting under the shed on the picnic table beside the cook shack, telling lies to each other, (as was common with the whole group); when Jessie saw the reflection of headlights on the trees (about a quarter of a mile back down the dirt road that we had come in on). He made the remark to Norman that it looked like someone was on their way in. Well they kept sitting there and no one came.

After a while, thirty minutes or so, Jessie got up and said, "They must be broke down, I'm going to get my tool box and go down there to see if I can help."

Norman said, "I'll ride with you."

They got in Jessie's jeep and rode to where they could see the drop off from the ridge the camp was on. Jessie stopped and told Norman to look. Norman didn't see anything at first, other than there was no vehicle where they thought it should be. Jessie said Norman's face slowly turned white as he realized the area, for about fifty yards in a circle, was lit up like daylight but there was no source for the light. There were no head lights, spotlights, or anything that could cause the light; yet it was as lit up as if you were in a stadium. Jessie said nothing as he just backed up several hundred feet back down the road, before he turned around. He told me later that he was afraid to take his eyes off the spot, because he couldn't understand what he had just seen, and frankly it scared him. They both went to their separate cabins for the night and the light went out in about an hour.

They told everyone about the lights as new people arrived, but they got the usual response; a sideways look as they said, "Yea, sure, too much Ancient Age tonight Jessie?"

Strange Things: Five

It was not very long after the sighting of the lit up area that Norman and Charlie (the oldest and charter member of the camp), went to a large hardwood island in the center of a big slough that went through the center of our property. To get there you had to traverse the deepest water on the property. This island was about ½ mile long and 50 yards wide at the widest. There were huge water oaks furnishing lots of acorns. Also there were several clumps of Sable palms in the area, with small patches of palmettos scattered under the trees. A large cypress strand completely encircled this island. I always felt as if I was in a special place there. I spent a lot of time on that island, for the game liked to use it because food was handy and it was so secluded. The road to get to it crossed the north end of the property and it was the way to cross from one side to the other on the property.

Charlie and Norman went out to the camp during the week and had the whole 5600 acres to their selves. They had spent the whole day without scoring, so they decided to go to this oak island to see if they could kill a wild hog. They had seen signs of hogs rooting where the road crossed the island. They parked the jeep late in the afternoon and discussed what the plan was for the hunt. Charlie was going to go to the far end of the island and watch for hogs to come up on that end of the island, and Norman would go in about half way and pick a spot to watch.

Charlie was the first to see anything, and that wasn't until the last light of the day. As it turned out it was a large sow. When Charlie shot in that failing light, he didn't make a killing shot. The hog went down, but she started squealing. In the confines of that island it was almost ear piercing. Charlie got up to finish her off and stop the noise. Charlie knew that Norman would arrive soon to help him drag her back to the jeep. Charlie took a better look at the hog and decided that it would be easier if they had a rope to drag her. He hollered to Norman to go back to the jeep and get the rope in the back of the Jeep. Norman heard Charlie and went back to the jeep for the rope. He decided to leave his gun in the jeep; for it was a long walk back to where Charlie had the hog. He also picked up his flashlight because by now it was pitch dark; and in this place when the sun goes down, it really gets dark. There were no bright stars to light the way under this dense canopy of trees. The only light Charlie had, was a small light that was attached to his key chain.

Just about the time Norman got to where he could see the dim light of Charlie's small light, something started splashing around in the water, just off the end of the island in the trail the hog had used. They described the noise as being just out of sight and loud. Whatever it was, it followed them in the water off the island, just out of sight, as they dragged the hog back to the jeep. The trail on the island was on the east side and it was in the dry edge. They hadn't gone very far when a creature started screaming. It got louder and louder as they neared the jeep. The screaming kept up as long as they were on that island pulling the hog. They were both scared from the encounter and neither could explain what was in the swamp. Norman was a green horn as far as hunting went, but Charlie was a different story. He had hunted the Everglades before there was a road where Highway 41 is now. He had hunted bear and wild cats and was very familiar with the noise a panther makes when it screams. In fact we all were, for there were several on the property; and most of us had seen or heard them at one time or the other.

Both changed their hunting habits. Charlie never went hunting away from that camp again without company. One of his practices before that incident, he thought nothing of going off by himself. He told me he had never heard anything like it. He didn't have any idea what it was, but he wasn't taking any more chances.

He said, "That thing, whatever it was, didn't like it that I had killed that hog and was doing what it could to tell us it didn't like it."

"I will never put myself in a position like that again."

Norman now was another story. Norman was bunking in the same cabin as mine. When my bunch came out the next weekend, I went to open my cabin door and it was locked. It wasn't locked from the outside; it was locked from the inside. Norman was asleep and he had installed several slide bolts on the inside so that he could lock himself in. I noticed that after that incident, he did not go out before daylight and he was always back before dark.

Strange Things: Six

This one is short and I don't know if this is correct. It was so clear at night that a lot of the time after supper was over and the dishes were done, we would cut off the generator for more peace and quiet. It is hard to describe how the night sky looks in a place like that. There is absolutely no pollution in the air and there is no reflection of lights from anywhere. On one trip someone brought a man as a guest that was employed at Cape Canaveral, and what he told us and pointed out was real interesting. You could always see airplanes that were cutting through the sky heading to and from places in all directions. They were easy to identify because of the blinking white, red and green lights. He was showing us the different objects in the sky that were orbiting the earth. He even knew some of the Russian stuff that was floating around up there.

We pointed out one and he looked and said, "No that's impossible."

He went on to explain that all satellites orbit the earth in a general direction from west to east. All the nations that have objects in space have to use the earth's rotation to help get into orbit.

He said, "That thing is going from east to west and I don't have any idea what it is. There are no lights, and it appears that all we are seeing is the reflection (just as the satellites). It shouldn't be going in that direction but there it is doing it."

We saw several objects after that over the years that were going backwards.

Close Calls

I can't recall having a premonition, but I have had a lot of strange things happen to me over my life time that have been close calls. I like to think that someone is watching out for me for a reason that I have yet to learn. I guess the first was when I was a child I remember breaking away from my mother's hand, running across a busy street, and causing a wreck from a driver trying to miss me.

I later almost drowned trying to help my friend that

had fallen in the water over his head. A stranger fishing on the other side of the canal heard the scuffle and ended up saving us both. What brought that stranger to that spot, on that day, I have never understood, for no one ever fished there.

I fell out of a boat at night while cleaning slime from fish off of my hands. We were underway going back to shore from fishing on the reef. I had no vest on and I am terrible at swimming any distance. All my hollering did no good, for no one heard me or missed me as they were facing forward. We were several miles from shore. I thought my goose was cooked as I watched the boat pull away from me at a high speed. I took my pants and shoes off and tied the legs of the pants with knots and raised them over my head, then I swung them over my head to collect air. The first couple of times it didn't work, but I finally was able to make a pretty good flotation device. By this time I couldn't even hear the boat in the distance and it became unbelievably quiet. It seemed like an hour but in reality, it was probably not more than a few minutes, I hear my buddies calling for me and the motor of the boat running at a slow rate. They had used their heads when they missed me. They had turned the boat 180 % and were following back in the center of the wake they had left in the water. Luckily it was a calm night and I didn't mind losing my shoes at all when I climbed back aboard that boat.

Several times when I was riding motorcycles I

avoided death while others were terribly injured or killed. Two of us were riding side by side when an apparently parked car, suddenly decided to make a u turn directly in our path. I managed to miss the car only clipping the bumper with my crash bar, but my friend plowed head on into the side injuring him with lifelong injuries. I didn't have a scratch.

Another time my girlfriend and I were on my bike and we were on the left side closest to the yellow line. My friend and his wife were on our right and we were just riding along enjoying the evening.

Suddenly someone shouted "look out!"

Just ahead the arm for a train crossing was coming down without any apparent reason. No lights were on and no train was moving. I swung to the left and missed it but my buddy ducked and tried to go under it. He was lucky but his wife didn't duck, and her life ended that instant.

I have been in several wrecks in autos and never any serious injuries. Three different times while riding with someone else driving and having an accident, I have ended up with knots on my head while shotguns were slamming around inside the vehicle. I even got where I insisted that guns be stored in the trunk.

I was driving a Volkswagen, had a wreck, and when I put my right hand down to raise up, I put my hand on the bumper of a Buick because that was all the room I had left.

I was loading clay pigeons in a low house and at station 8. A woman accidentally shot right through the house and it ripped my shirt front and only put a small scratch on my chest.

Another time I was scoring trap and a shooter fired his gun with the barrel resting on a block of wood on the concrete. Everyone on that line was injured but me.

Walking through the woods with a friend, he fired his gun while it was pointed at me, and the shot went right between my legs.

I have had a moccasin hang his fangs into my pants leg without getting me. I stepped on a coiled up rattlesnake and ended up with only a chipped tooth as I jerked my leg up and cracked myself in the chin. I even sat on a pigmy rattler early one morning when I chose a spot to call turkeys. I only realized my blunder when I felt something squirming under me.

In the Air Force I made a last minute decision to wear my parachute to do an operation that I had done many times before without one. This time it saved my life, for we experienced a freak air pocket that caused me to fall out of the back of a C-119 over Greer, South Carolina.

In Watertown, N.Y., I was switched from one plane to another because a crew member got sick and I took his place. I then stood in horror in my new plane waiting to take off as the plane I was supposed to be on, crashed on takeoff and slid behind us and took out several planes. It looked like a movie happening before me and it was horrible. I still remember the blood all over the snow.

Here in the mountains I was looking for ginseng as sort of a therapy after my bypass operation. I had packed a lunch for I would usually spend the day. I sat down on a big comfortable log, in the shade, and took my time eating and enjoying the solitude. I sat there close to an hour and finally decided to go ahead and start my afternoon search. I got up and took about three steps when a huge branch fell from overhead. It completely destroyed the old log that I had been sitting on. I had been about 2 seconds from certain death.

Laurie and I went south with a truck and trailer to purchase a tractor and our travel took us through Gainesville Ga. The weather was terrible and as we got closer to Gainesville, it started to hail and accumulate. I could hardly see so I decided to pull over and wait it out. There was no place to really be safe from traffic coming up behind us, so I figured it would be safer to get back on the road. We hadn't gone another mile when we saw a huge funnel cloud cross Hgw 129 in front of us with all the debris flying around destroying everything in sight. That momentary stop saved us from being right where it crossed. Call it luck-- I don't.

I have been through several major operations. Heart bypasses and such, and I keep waking up after each event.

I do believe in premonitions, for my mother tells of dreaming about the Hindenburg air ship crashing and burning a week before it happened. She described the dream almost as good as the reporter that was on the scene.

However, personally, other than the incident crossing the street, because this happened before I accepted Christ as my Savior, I have a deep belief that my Savior has been my protector and it's very comforting to me. It may sound strange, but when He's ready, I'm ready.

Horn Tooting

I am going to do a little horn tooting with these next two letters. The first my nephew (Harold Eugene Bell) sent me. It was unsolisited and it really pumped up my ego. The second is from my first cousin (Ron Bell) after I had fowarded my nephew's letter to him.

Original Message

Sent: Monday, September 08, 2008 11:54 AM

Subject: (no subject)

"A Tribute"

As we grow older we reflect back more often to things we learned along the way about life and those who taught us. Sometimes things are self-learned although most are taught by the important people in our lives. Sometimes we learn by others mistakes and of course, our own. Take my own father for instance. He taught me, indirectly, how by being an alcoholic and womanizer it will ruin your life, hurt your loved ones and eventually lead you into being a very lonely old man. Watching how he treated my mother by chasing anything that wore a skirt only taught me that if I was lucky enough to find the right woman to share my life with, I'd never fail because I do not want to die a lonely man, like he did. Seeing how my mother was able to raise three children alone with no child support, making $45.00 a week is almost unfathomable. We never lacked a thing, had a roof over our heads, clothes on our backs and food in our bellies. As long as I live I will always remember how she put her children above all, and to this day, she still does. We were also fortunate in that my mother rekindled a relationship with an old neighborhood and school friend of hers after she divorced my father. In the beginning I was very angry thinking he could never replace my father. As I grew older, I discovered my father could never replace Andy.

Along the way there are other people in our lives that make a lifelong impact, some good and some bad. This tribute is about someone that was all good, my mother's only sibling, her brother Sonny, James Lynn

Boyer. He saw what was going on in my young life with the inevitable future broken home, and took it upon himself to treat me as his own son in many respects. He taught me how to tie my shoes, tie a hook to a fishing line and how to secure a load of glass windows to a truck by using a simple half hitch. He taught me how hard works pays off, especially how hard working on a lobster boat can be and gave me my first real paying job with Lumidoor, a company that installed glass sliding doors. He also taught me how to make my own fishing rod and I own nothing but handmade rods I made myself. He took me with him hunting when I was as young as 8 years old. I can remember distinctly shooting a shotgun for the very first time and how he laughed at the surprised look on my face from the recoil. I also remember that acrid smell of burnt gunpowder left in the empty shell casing and to this day, I'll pick up an empty shell I had just shot intentionally to smell that powder and it immediately reminds me of that day so very long ago. He'd tell me stories about his youth growing up in Miami and how during WWII as a kid he was issued hooks sparingly by the owner of the hardware store, only selling him 1 or 2 at a time and explaining how steel was in short supply and he was only delivered a couple of hooks. But all along the man had a whole box and was teaching Sonny to not waste and be sparing. To this day I'll take the hook out of a fish's stomach if it was swallowed and save it instead of just throwing it away with the guts like most people would. I can remember like it was yesterday when he took me on my first dove shoot next to a freshly plowed field in south Dade County. I didn't have a gun of my own and he'd let me use his old "Long Tom" 12 GA. He'd hand me 5 shells and told me to make each shot count, which I did, still do and I felt bigger than life that day. When I smell freshly plowed soil today it takes me back to that very fall day almost 50 years ago. Then when I was around 10 years of age Sonny started building a cabin in the middle of the Everglades. He'd bring home used form boards (3/4" pressure treated plywood) from construction sites and then he pre-fabricated the cabin and cut the wood into 8' long by 2' wide strips so they were able to be stacked and then floated to the site for the camp. My job was to remove the nails and straighten them out to be used later instead of buying new nails. Then help float the stacks of wood to the camp site. To this day I'll straighten out a nail and use it again before buying another nail. That cabin was named "Fool's Paradise" and I made my own assessment to why it was named that. You had to be a fool to walk that far in those swamps but once you got there it was a paradise. Almost 50 years later I still hunt there and walk to where our cabin was just to reminisce such fond memories. I was also taught by him that gun safety comes first, above all. I remember walking with my cousin Ron Bell through some palmetto's hoping to jump another covey of quail. I had traded a .22 rifle that was given to me, for my first new gun, which was a Mossberg single shot 410. We were walking side by side about 15 yards apart looking to jump another covey when they flew up out to Ron's side so I couldn't shoot, although I had taken the safety off. Moments later I couldn't remember if I had returned the shotgun back to safety so instead of just looking, I put my finger on the trigger (as it was pointed safely upwards) and squeezed. The gun went off and it scared Ron and me half to death, even though the shot was sent to the sky. I told Ron to NOT say anything to Sonny, but he did. For my punishment, I had dish duty for the rest of the hunting season. And dish duty wasn't so easy. We used boiling water and had a double sink outside where the pitcher pump was and it didn't matter if the mosquitos were thick as smoke, or it was 30*, the dishes got washed. If there was the slightest bit of food particle left, they ALL were done over again. Since that day my finger never touches the safety on a firearm until I'm ready to shoot and the trigger is only touched when my target is ready. Sonny had previously ordered a sporterized M1 Carbine and I remember well him saying how he was so excited getting this rifle he couldn't sleep. As I got older, around 12, I was given an M1 Carbine and used that for my first deer rifle, although I was only allowed to place one round in the chamber at a time. May have been partially the "sparing" reason but more than likely they didn't want me shooting up the woods. One morning we were walking through the cypress and jumped two bucks, Sonny was in a position ahead of me and he shot first and dropped one of the bucks. I had to wait for the second deer to pass Sonny to where I could shoot safely. Being as I only had one round, I took my time, aimed well, leading the deer a little and squeezed off the round. The deer disappeared but with all the excitement of seeing Sonny's buck drop and him running to it, I thought I must have missed. Another hunter who heard the shooting walked to us and had a couple of hounds on a leash. He admired Sonny's deer and I told him how I shot in that direction so he took his hounds and left in that direction. Within a few minutes we heard a shot ring out. My heart dropped thinking he shot my deer. We walked, or shall I say I ran, to where the old man was and beneath his feet was a buck. I said to him in a questioning manner, that he shot the buck. He said no it's your deer, I was just letting you know where we were. It was always in question to whether I shot that deer as Sonny took some shots at that deer as well, after his deer dropped. But, I took careful aim, squeezed off my only bullet and the deer disappeared. My first buck and I'm sticking to that story! Sonny eventually left Fool's Paradise to hunt on a private lease north of Alligator Alley, called Crooked Pine Ranch. Several thousand acres in some of the most pristine property the Florida Everglades has to offer. Deer, wild hogs and turkey were everywhere. Being as it was a member lease, I could only be invited by a member and Sonny was able to take me many times. During the mid 70's Sonny put me to work with him in his window business. Then in the late 70's Sonny and his family moved to the North Georgia mountains where my mother, Andy and my sister and brother moved several years earlier. I was in my mid 20's by then and continued living here although the rest of my family moved there when I was 18. To present, I stay in touch with my hunting/fishing/working mentor as often as I can and get to visit once a year when possible. But all the things he taught me has stayed. From playing practical jokes on others for a good laugh, to being practical. Appreciating the outdoors by respecting it and realizing it's a privilege not a right. Putting family first, above all. Love of country and patriotism. Not being wasteful and use every resource available. Hard work gives back. Trust family and be skeptical of all others but try to like everyone. Fight for your rights and fight hard.

I have a great family of my own now. A beautiful wife of 29 years, and two grown kids who both have 4 year degrees from college. I tried my best to duplicate what my mother, grandmother, Andy and Sonny taught me by teaching my kids what I learned from them. I did well, I know because I had good teachers and my kids are better than I ever hoped for my daughter took on more of the practicality things, like learning to save and spend wisely. She takes nothing for granted and says what's on her mind. My son loves hunting and fishing as much as I do and he should not only be thankful that I took him and taught him, but more so to the man that took and taught me, James (Sonny) Lynn Boyer.

I sent the tribute to my first cousin, Ron Bell, a boy whose father died very young. I also tried to help him as he adjusted to life without a father. This was his reply.

WOW, I can only imagine how you must have felt when you received that. It brought back a lot of memories just for me, so I know you must have been dabbing at your eyes a little bit. Ding really put his heart into it. I had no idea he could write like that. I was surprised to see my name in there, but I remember that incident with the .410 very well. I bet even today I could take you to within about 50 feet of where that happened. When I heard the shot I turned around and Ding had this "oh shit" look on his face. I can just about see it now. If I remember correctly the gun was over his left shoulder. I don't remember telling on him, however. If I did, I hope he doesn't hold that against me. I guess I thought it was the right thing to do at the time. It could just as easily been me in his shoes. And if the end result was that he learned an important lesson without anyone getting hurt, and it made him safer around guns (which I am very confident that he is today), then maybe it's ok. Ding and I have a common thread. I figured this out about two and a half years ago when Julie and I were in Florida and he took us out in his airboat for a couple of hours. We didn't really talk about it, but the signs were all there, to me. The common thread is that we both have a deep understanding and appreciation of the outdoors, but even more, we are both confident and comfortable in the woods alone. It comes from a sense of self-reliance and self-assurance when in that environment. and while we both still share that experience with a few special people .. his son, my brother, etc., the end result is almost a preference for being in the woods alone. And that brings about an even deeper appreciation and understanding, as well as enjoyment, which is not always possible when you are with other people. I am sure that like me, he learned a lot of this on his own. But I also know that the foundation for all of this, for both of us, was established by you. And reading his tribute to you just confirms it. So, although he said it much better than I could have, I owe you my thanks for that too. Ron Bell

Biography's

My Dad
Jimmy Posey (Red) Boyer

After his father died leaving six children (age eight and under), my Dad left home when he was sixteen. He took his younger brother with him, to lessen the burden on his mother caring for his four other siblings. He left a small farm community in Georgia and went to Miami to find work. He found a job with Eli Whitt and trained to be an old fashioned fountain man called a "Soda Jerk." Later he went to work at the "Hippodrome bar," a haunt of famous and infamous people, like Jack Dempsy and Al Capone. He met and married my mother when she was a beautiful eighteen. I have one sibling, a sister, Doris Joan, born after me on my birthday three years to the day. When we moved to our new house I was seven and my sister four.

My dad tried everthing to make a living. I remember he had a laundry route, a plant nursery, a lawn service and the one all the kids in the neighborhood loved, was a "Toms Toasted Peanut Man." Our neighborhood was sparse of houses and right on the edge of Miami. He bought a sundrie store close to the Orange bowl and both he and my mom worked there. During the war years he trained to be a machinest and helped construct military bases in both Cuba and Trinidad. He discovered he was a good salesman and finish out his life selling windows and later real estate.

He worked hard but when he was off, he enjoyed fishing, once catching a eighty five pound tarpon in the

Tamiami Canal. I didn't realize it but fishing was a way to put food on the table in hard times. He made our life fun without having to spend a lot of money doing it. I didn't realize while on one of the fun trips with him that they would come to an end so quickly. He died suddenly in his early fifties of a massive stroke.

---BATE---
My Mom-

Myrtis Virginia (Bell) Boyer

There is only one way to describe my mom and that is that she was "a True Lady." She didn't let us run wild, but she had the wisdom to let us explore our world. Unlike today's children, (where they have to be bribed to read something), we were eager to read and she incouraged it. I have even been punished for reading under the covers with a flashlight, running down the batteries.

I knew there were rules and she meant what she said when she set them. If I broke one, it was a long time before she would relent and extend any limits she had set. When my dad died, at fiftythree, she was left with no job and a whole lot of bills. She went to work at the University of Miami doing seceratial work and retired along with the last mechanical typewriter on the whole campus. I never could imagine how someone could type a full page without making mistakes, but she could. She was the most frugal person I ever met and there were very few people on this earth that she did not like.

She busted my butt plenty, but believe me, when she did, I was deserving of it. She was adventursome her whole life and was eager to go anywhere, anytime.

When she was in her sixties, as she was slideing down a hill in 20 degree weather on a single snow sled, she over-steared and ended up in a creek.

Just to see my hunting camp, I was talking so much about, she walked two and a half miles through water.

She even went on my swamp buggie to my other camp and spent the weekend with us. This was all after she had retired in her late sixties and seventies.

Late in life after a mild heart attack she was asked who her doctor was? She replied, "I never needed one before now."

At the age of eighty nine, she made the decision to undergo open heart surgery and a fourway bypass. Thanks to my sister's loving care, she lived on to be ninety-eight. She always had a sense of humor as illustrated by this photograph with my son in her final days. I admired her more than any woman I have ever known. Pretending to arm wrestel with my son just before she died.

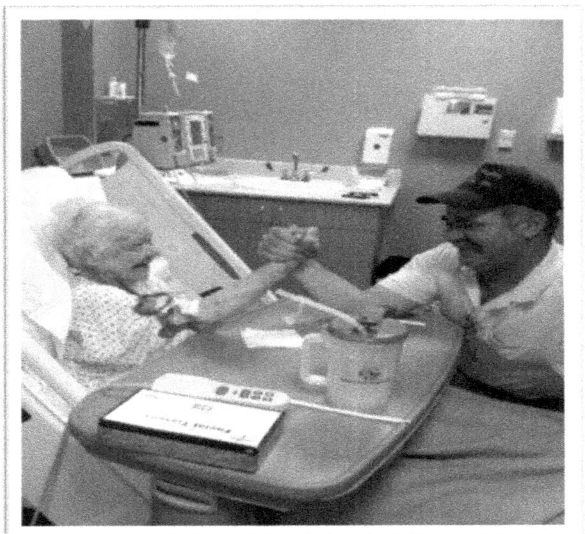

My Wife
Sandra Laurie (Arnold) Boyer

Tommy Knowles and his wife Bobbi brought this little lady along with them after calling and asking me to go target shooting. I had no idea she would be along and sure wasn't dressed to meet my future wife. Neither of us was impressed with the other. Probably the only thing we had in common was we both smoked Lucky Strike cigarettes. I went along with the plan, even though I was dressed in ragged dungarees and needed a shave. (common by today's standards) Although she had never shot a pistol, she quickly showed that she could be an excellent shot. I was still in the recovery stage of an emotional divorce and truthfully was not an admirer of the lifestyle of most stewardess's. She likewise was not very impressed with me.

As I sit here writing this we have been married fifty four years and "so far" it's going pretty good. Laurie, as I call her, is very understanding about my love of the outdoors. Although she is not a hunter, she enjoyed the excursions with our boys as much as I did.

She had completed two years of junior college in St. Petersburg, Florida, and after Jaime was born, I encouraged her to go ahead and complete her final two years at the University of Miami. She wanted to be a teacher and she chose physical education as her major, compleating and graduating in 1970. Ironically she found a job at Kinloch Park Jr. High School, the school I had attended as a boy. She taught junior high science until we moved to the Georiga mountains in 1977. She returned to school at North Georgia College and obtained her biology degree and taught in Fulton County until she retired.

My life with her has truly been an adventure. She, like my oldest son, has a love of animals, and there are not many species that we have not had as pets. We literally live in the woods on twenty two acres and our house hangs over a pond. When she retired, she was elected Chairmen of the Union County Republican Party. Currently she organizes the Branan Lodge Bridge group. We both have acquired old age diseases, but we still manage as long as our Lord will permit.

Stephen Lynn Boyer

My First Born

Steve, the healer in the family, has a special way with animals. I have always noticed that even wild animals will let him treat them. The incident that comes to mind is about a large owl. We were returning to the camp and there was a group of hunters in a buggy going in just ahead of us. We heard a shot as one of the men shot at a large owl; and it fell out of a tree. They proceeded on to camp but Steve insisted I stop and help it. The bird was obviously badly hurt because he couldn't fly. He gently picked it up and carried it to camp, where we found two milk crates that we fashioned into a cage by placing one on top of the other. He was big so he didn't have much clearance. At home we had a 20 foot long wire cage that we used for an animal pen and it made a good hospital. Steve found canned dog food was the best food to feed the owl and was eventually able to hand feed that bird. I would watch him talk to it, as he offered a small portion on the end of his finger.

The owl would grab the end of Steve's finger and pinch it, while looking deep into his eyes as if to say "You better be careful, I could cut this finger off if I wanted to."

In a few days and he was flying from one end of the cage to the other to greet him when it was feeding time. After Steve decided he was well enough to return to the woods, we loaded him back in those two milk crates and took him back to the spot where he had been shot.

He flew up in a pine tree and just sat there staring down at Steve.

He is a gentle man with animals and I think the trust they show him is an admiral gift. He is always doctoring some critter, the latest being an injured baby possum he stitched up and released. He loves the woods but is not one to kill for the fun of it.

He spent six years in the United States Air Force and missed many of our hunting adventures. He served like a paramedic for a small town in Spain. He even got a commendation from that town for providing the only medical attention they had, substituting for the lack of a doctor. You see he was a fireman and also an EMT on base.

During the time when we were allowed to shoot a doe, I saw a couple run right by him and asked, "Why didn't you shoot?"

He said, "Daddy I want my first deer to be a buck."

He stuck to that and the first one he shot was a beautiful eight point.

After Steve returned to the USA, he continued in the medical field as a medical technician with the Veterans Administration; and as I write Steve has been with them thirty five years. Many a veteran has benefited from Steve's efficient, dedicated care.

He and his wife Kay live in Ft. White, Florida on

several acres. They have had a menagerie of animals: a rescued dog named Mooch, an albino ferret that followed him across the yard and stayed 10 years, mostly birds, (parrots, guineas, turkeys all kinds of chickens). The parrots are a business, but I don't hear about them eating anything from the others except the chicken eggs.

Jaime Lorne Boyer--Second Born

As a youngster Jaime joined me on most of my trips but it was not until he came back from chefs' school in Williamsburg, Virginia that he became a serious hunter. "Lucky" is what they should have called him because of the three deer he has killed, all have big racks, (Two seven's and one twelve point). Jaime worked for the State of Georgia as a Food Service Supervisor in the Jackson, Georgia prison. When he married, his wife asked that he find a safer job after one of the other female Food Service Supervisors was killed by an inmate. He went to driving school and is now an over-the-road truck driver. Their home is on the far end of my property and I got to see my two granddaughters grow up, but they are now both away at school.

Jaime was a little too young to take into Fool's Paradise on our hunting excursions and only went during the dry times when Laurie and I would go out for a relaxing weekend. He went often to Crooked Pine Ranch, for our family found a lot of excuses to spend our spare time there. Our trips were an adventure for him and he loved the camp area and the other members. I got to where I would place him in a tree stand. One stand was two sheets of plywood and was too comfortable. Once when I approached the stand to pick him up I could see from a distance he was lying down. Underneath the stand several deer were feeding and scampered away from the noise of the buggy. On Thanksgiving Day in 1975 he fell out of a tree stand in broke his arm, but wanted to go back to the camp as soon as we left the emergency room.

Jaime was invited by the campus minister of Young Harris College to join his band of students on their tour of Europe. He worked all year, saving his earnings, and enjoyed a lifetime experience. That minister, Rev. Fred Whitley, later officiated at Jaime's wedding, baptized his baby daughters, and Steve. He has been the family pastor for the past 30 years.

Jaime's over-the-road experiences have taken him to all of the lower 48 states. He loves to pull practical jokes on his friends.

Ron Bell—First Cousin

Ron and I have enjoyed many experiences hunting together. Ron, an Eagle Scout, joined me on a lot of my excursions into all of my hunting camps and is a good outdoorsman. He graduated from William and Mary College, Virginia, worked his way from busboy to manager at the Bodega Restaurant in Miami and was general manager of Mother Tuckers' an international restaurant chain. Ron left the restaurant business and went back to school, he got married and has been in management at IBM. He and his wife, Julie train and compete retrievers and they plan on making it a full time business when he retires from IBM.

My uncle Jack, Ron's father, had taken me under his wing when I was a teen and taught me how to sail and read maps. He was fresh back from World War Two, where he had been a pilot. I jumped on any invite and loved every minute. Jack bought a two mast thirty five foot sailboat. He spent a lot of time on frequent overnight excursions and included me a lot.

Later in his life Jack and his two boys, Ron and Jeff, were very active in the Boy Scouts of America, Troop 17 in South Miami. It was only natural when my oldest son Steve turned eleven; I enrolled him in their troop and became a committeeman myself. Jack was able to attend Ron's Court of Honor when he became an Eagle Scout. Jack died young at forty seven and I could see the void in Ron's life. Ron has a love for the outdoors and has accompanied me whenever he could. Ron, like his Dad, has a devilish streak in his personality and will go to any extreme to pull a joke over on you. My wife Laurie has a tendency to be very gullible, and he has always delighted in making her believe some wild tale.

George Henry Volker III

It is hard to imagine what my life would have been without the influence of this family. My dad built a home for us on the outskirts of Miami and the Volker's moved in in their new home just down the street. Irene

Volker, his wife came from a true pioneer Coconut Grove family and George II and his parents were transplants from Cincinnati, Ohio. George was not a big man but he was as tough as nails, capturing the Golden Gloves championship, in his weight class, before he left Ohio. Their two boys were younger than me, too young for school, while I was in the third grade. George was an employee of Florida Power and Light, and was what they called a "High lineman." His skill was needed so the government kept him from going into the service. Irene was a beautiful blond lady, what anyone would describe as "feisty," and she protected her family like a Banty hen.

When I was about twelve George started taking me along with him on some of his local hunting excursions. I have often wondered why, and answered myself by reasoning that his boys were too young and he wanted company. For whatever reason, having my dad with his love of fishing and Mr. Volker acquainting me with hunting, I was fast becoming an addicted outdoorsman. Whenever he would ask, I was his companion until his boys reached the age he felt safe with them having guns. All three of us earned his confidence that we could handle guns safely, before we were allowed to shoot at game. His favorite was quail hunting and he always had several dogs in training. The small dog to his left (in the photo at the first of the book), was the best he ever owned. He favored setters over pointers but Trixie was a Brittany spaniel, not noted for Quail hunting but she turned out to be the best. I continued hunting with them on many trips after his boys started joining us.

One morning we went to pick up a fellow hunter and Mr. Volker let Trixie out of the carrier, while we went into the house to join the man for coffee. When we came back we could not find Trixie. George called and called but no Trixie. We had been there about an hour when the man said, "I know where she is." He led us behind the house and there she was, on a point, not moving a muscle, looking into a cage with quail.

After the war, the first opportunity George had to purchase a jeep, he did so. I believe it was 1946. He rigged it for quail hunting by building a hard body for it. A friend of his and I went opening day on my first big time hunting trip. My spot to ride was in the box with the dogs. A more detailed story, "*My first ever experience with a wild turkey,*" is included.

Mr. Volker resigned from Florida Power and Light and he started managing his ageing parent's apartment complexes. The Volkers sold their house and moved away from the neighborhood when I was in my teens. After his boys were out on their own, he and Irene moved to the Everglades, to a section called the "Loop Road." Originally built as the route for Tamiami Trail, it was abandoned because of politics. This location was more of a match for them and what they wanted out of life. He built and repaired air boats, made the special frog gigs for froggers, and hunted frogs at night. He became an icon in a place God made for misfits of society. It is still a redneck heaven. He and Irene always did things their own way throughout their lives and I considered him to be my mentor. Later in life they moved to Labelle, Florida to a nice little house on a creek and finally ended up moving to Ocala, Florida where they were close to their grandchildren.

Whenever I was near I always visited and tried to bring a deer or hog ham with me because I knew, as he aged, game was harder to come by. When they moved to LaBelle, I only knew the street they lived on and I was trying to locate him. I knew he loved his beer so I stopped at a 7-11 type store and asked the attendant if he knew George Volker.

He said, "Sure, I know him, in fact there he comes now"

Mr. Volker greeted me, introduced me to the attendant and purchased a six pack.

Mr. Volker told the attendant a little bit about our relationship and as a parting gesture, he pulled his top dental plate out and said, "I have to get back to the house, Irene is waiting for these teeth so she can eat lunch."

After I joined Crooked Pine Hunting camp I invited him to join me for a trip and we had a successful extended weekend. It turned out to be our last hunting experience together. I loved that old man.

Last hunting trip with Mr. Volker

Harold Eugene Bell
(Ding)

Ding, as I and the family address him, is a dye-in-the-wool outdoorsman. I suppose most of that can be blamed on me. When his mom, (my sister), and his dad split up I began to introduce him to the outdoors; much like Mr. Volker did for me. I didn't considerate it payback time because I have always enjoyed teaching young people the wonders of Mother Nature. He was my companion in both fishing and hunting and has been an excellent father to his son and daughter, teaching his son to love the outdoors as we do. It is hard to believe he is now a proud grandfather and has babysat Jonathan since he was born. As I write this Jonathan just had his fourth birthday and he is already shooting a BB gun at paper targets with accuracy.

There was a time in our lives when it became awkward for he and I to spend too much time together. My sister re-married to an old classmate of ours and I was infringing on their time together. His step father was a great dad to her three children, and I felt like I needed to give them room for a while. God has a different way of doing things and removing his biological father gave my sister and those three kids a much better life. I always hoped Ding understood. I have always enjoyed our adventures together and included him and his friends many times in my excursions.

He learned the produce business from his father-in-law and has been successful in his own produce business now for several decades.

Like me, he is outspoken about corruption anywhere he finds it. A trait I greatly admire, for I worry about the lack of involvement, or caring, most of our fellow citizens are showing.

Bruce M. DeVay

I met Bruce when I entered the seventh grade at Citrus Grove School in Miami, Florida. He and I liked each other right from the start. The only odd thing about Bruce was his name, at that time. "Beverly." As soon as he was legally able, he changed it to Bruce. All of his friends had shortened it to Bev, and eventually most everyone called him Bif. Unlike me, Bruce had an easy time with his schooling. Most weeks Bruce attended school Tuesday, Wednesday and Thursday and on Monday and Friday his elderly father let him stay home, on the pretext of helping him with his needs. He still made excellent grades.

After high school both of us joined the Air Force Reserve and were activated at the beginning of the Korean War. Our Air Force serial numbers are only one number different.

I was Bruce's best man when he married right after basic training and was miserable having to be away from his young bride.

After USAF duty, he obtained a job as a rod man on a surveying team with the City of Miami, where someone ran over his foot. They put him at a desk in the drafting department, from where he worked his way up to be the boss of the whole department. Bruce refused to continue his education and the Miami City commission, with a special resolution, created the command appointment of director; bypassing the education requirement. He really was smart.

We started fishing and camping together at about thirteen. We utilized the bus system to get us to the bay. Sometimes we would go all the way to South Beach and fish off the jetties on Government Cut. We obtained a 16 foot flat bottom boat with a two and one half horse- power inboard motor that we were fearless as to where we went with it. It was so slow it took us hours to get anywhere, but we would still go deep-sea fishing.

We even built a small shack on Fair Island by collecting driftwood. Bruce started driving his Dad's thirty-six Plymouth at fourteen and that really opened up our horizons. In several of the stories that are described in this book, we were transported there in that old Plymouth. We roamed the Keys and the edge of the Everglades and the trips were only limited only by our collection of funds and time.

After our stint in the USAF, being married put a crimp in Bruce's fishing and camping; and it was seldom we were able to enjoy the outdoors together. One thing we managed to do each year was bully netting spinney lobster. He would occasionally join me on a trip outdoors, but it wasn't until I joined the Crooked Pine Hunting Club that he decided to join also, and we were finally enjoying the woods together again.

Bruce smoked cigarette size cigars. After I moved to Georgia, he developed lung cancer and had to have one lung removed. The operation was successful, but at age fifty-nine, he had a massive heart attack on the way home from work. He was like my brother, as well as my good friend.

Thomas Davis

I met Thomas at Citrus Grove Junior High, just about the time he was quitting school. He was a big boy and one of those kids that were lost in the system. He was just biding his time until his sixteenth birthday so he could quit school. His father was a plasterer and Thomas went to work for the same company, doing a man's work and drawing a man's wages. He lived in the same neighborhood as Bruce and they were close friends before I met either one of them. Thomas, Bruce, and I joined each other on a lot of trips, while Bruce and I were still in high school. We liked to shrimp, fish on the causeways, or go dove hunting together. At that time it was legal to gig Snook and we were with Thomas one night when he gigged a forty pounder off of Venetian Causeway.

Thomas and I started seriously hunting together about the time Bruce's wife was weaning him from hunting. Tom and Art and I built and hunted in "Fool's Paradise," a camp inside the Loop Road, off Tamiami Trail or Highway 41.

Thomas was for sure the strongest man I ever knew. I saw him put a one hundred pound butane bottle, full of gas, on his back and carry it through the water and stumps all the way to our camp. Sometimes he would be stuccoing a house next to where I was doing glass work. I once saw him carry a five gallon bucket full of wet cement, in each hand, up a flight of stairs. In order to do that, you have to lift them waist high in order to clear the steps.

Thomas was an excellent craftsman, so I talked him into going to work for the glass company I was working for. We worked together several years until the company sold out. Then Tom went to work for a company that remodeled businesses at night.

After I joined the Crooked Pine Hunting Camp, it wasn't long before Tom joined and the four of us were all in the same camp hunting together again. Tom and I stayed in contact even after I moved to Georgia. I visited he and his wife several times and he came to Georgia to see my place. He succumbed to cancer in his eighties. I lost a good friend.

Art Prior

Art and I met when I started working for a new company and he was already employed there. Like me, he was an outdoorsman and we soon began planning excursions together. He was about ten years older than me and a true member of the "Greatest Generation."

He wasn't a braggart; in fact his widow gave me some of this information.

Kidding around with Art one day I asked him, "What claim to fame did you have during the war?"

Art said, "I was a champion; I was the 'scaredist' SOB over there."

The truth is, Art was in the D Day invasion of World

War II and fought in the major battles throughout Europe, all the way until the end of the war. The humbling story I heard about Art and his war experiences, I have to try and repeat.

Art was Catholic and carried his Rosary with him at all times. When he was preparing to go back to the front line, he discovered he had lost his beads. He rushed over to the Chaplin, who was in his unit, and told him of the loss. The Priest did not have a spare set but offered his personal beads, so Art would be protected while he was in battle. He told Art he could return them after he obtained more. Art was relieved and accepted the offer even though the Cross was rather large and bulky. The Priest explained they were the ones he received when he became a Priest. Art's unit got in a heavy fire fight and he took a round in the chest. He was amazed to find that the round hit dead center on the Cross and had absorbed most of the force of the bullet, causing only a minor injury. I don't know how Art felt at the time, but I call it Devine Intervention.

Art grew up fishing and hunting around Tampa bay, much like my life around Biscayne Bay, only difference, he never learned to swim. Art was one of those rare gentle people that I never heard speak ill of anyone.

Art only had one fault that bothered his fellow campers: he could talk to you on his outward breath and be snoring when he inhaled for the next breath.

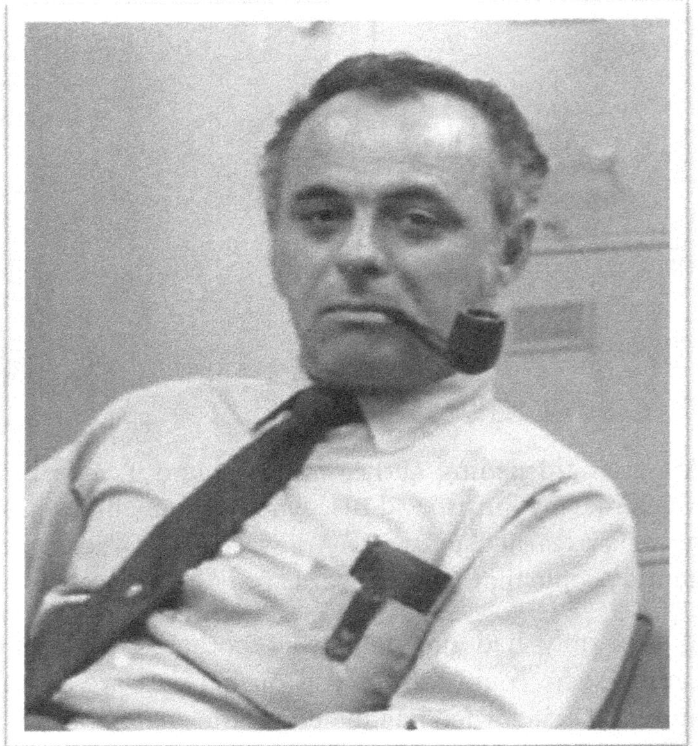

George Kaufman

George's family moved into the neighborhood when we were both entering our teens and we joined up in escapades that two young boys can get into. George attended Ponce De Leon High School in Coral Gables, while I went to Miami High, so we ran with different crowds. George dropped out of school before finishing and joined the Army, where he finished his education. We both went to work for Southern Bell on the same day, but George made it his lifelong career.

On one of our ramblings along the Tamiami Canal, that was close to our houses, my little dog uncovered a grey fox den and there were three baby foxes in there. They were so young their eyes were not even open. The dog killed one and George and I each took one home to raise. Mine turned out to be as tame as a dog, even traveling on trips with the family. We raised mine in the house and we found her to be remarkable.

George and I bought houses a block away from each other in a housing project and we joined together with the things young families do for entertainment. I was George's best man at his wedding and we have remained good friends for almost seventy years.

INDEX

Extra Information

www.ingramcontent.com/pod-product-compliance
Lightning Source LLC
Chambersburg PA
CBHW072132090426
42739CB00013B/3170
* 9 7 8 0 9 8 4 9 0 9 9 4 0 *